SPOILS OF WAR

CHRISTOPHER JOLL

For Howard,
with many thanks for your support.

SPOILS OF WAR

The Treasures, Trophies & Trivia of the British Empire

by

CHRISTOPHER JOLL

8.4.2020

NINE ELMS BOOKS

First published in 2020
by Nine Elms Publishing
Clapham North Arts Centre,
26–32 Voltaire Road,
London SW4 6DH
www.bene-factum.co.uk

Text © Christopher Joll 2020

ISBN 978-1-910533-46-8 hb

Cover and text design, typesetting and layout
by Lyn Davies www.lyndaviesdesign.com
Printed and bound in India by Imprint Press.

CONTENTS

FOREWORD

His Grace the 9th Duke of Wellington OBE DL

I AM PLEASED TO WRITE a Foreword to this most interesting book about works of art and other objects which have changed hands as a result of military battles or occupations.

The 1st Duke of Wellington in a deguerrotype (an early form of photograph) in 1844

After the Battle of Waterloo in June 1815, Arthur Wellesley, 1st Duke of Wellington was appointed by the Allies – Austria, Prussia, Russia and the United Kingdom – to command an Allied Army of occupation in France. He did his best to ensure that works of art which had been looted by the Napoleonic forces were returned to their rightful owners. For example, four important paintings by Raphael, belonging to King Ferdinand VII of Spain, were sent back to Madrid. However, before they left Paris, Wellington commissioned very high-quality copies for his own collection. Many important works of art were also returned to Italy. The Italian sculptor, Antonio Canova, was so grateful to the Duke for his assistance in recovering these items that he sent him a marble bust known as an 'ideal' head, which epitomised female beauty; Canova's gift remains at Apsley House, Wellington's London home.

After the Battle of Vitoria in northern Spain in June 1813, the entire baggage train of Joseph Bonaparte, the deposed King of Spain, was captured by the British. It contained more than two hundred paintings, which had been taken out of their frames and off their stretchers. Wellington wrote three letters to King Ferdinand, offering to return the paintings to Madrid. Eventually, a reply was received from Count Fernan Nunez, Spanish Minister in London, which said: 'His Majesty, touched by your delicacy, does not wish to deprive you of that which has come into your possession by means as just as they are honourable'. Most of these paintings are still at Apsley House or at Stratfield Saye, the Duke's house in Hampshire.

Although Wellington was strongly in favour of returning objects and works of art stolen by an occupying army, he certainly approved of the retention of that which had been captured in a military engagement, such as the hundreds of French cannons taken after various battles.

This book records the numerous events which led to so many historic and artistic objects ending up in our great museums and collections throughout the country. I commend the author for his detailed and extensive research, and for producing such an interesting and informative book.

WELLINGTON

Apsley House, *c.*1853

INTRODUCTION

From ancient times to the present day, victorious armies, navies and, more recently, air forces (and not forgetting members of the Diplomatic Corps) have seized and kept treasures, trophies and trivia belonging to their defeated enemies. Such prizes are usually described as 'the spoils of war', which the dictionary defines as: 'any profits extracted as the result of winning a war or other military activity, including the enslavement and absorption of entire defeated populations.'

So a survey of this subject could legitimately include the enforced exiles of the Israelites by the Egyptian Pharaohs and the Babylonian King Nebuchadnezzar, the Rape of the Sabine Women by Romulus and his randy Romans (albeit that they fought the war with the Sabines *after* they'd carried off and impregnated their girls), and the far more recent abduction of schoolchildren in northern Nigeria during the conflict with the jihadist militant organisation, Boko Haram. However, in the interest of propriety, brevity and focus, this book looks only at a selection of those spoils of war and other curiosities acquired by Britain's soldiers, sailors, airmen and diplomats, which are – for the most part – still available to view.

In the course of researching this book, I encountered some unease at the possibility of demands for the repatriation of certain spoils of war. The question of repatriation is currently a live issue in the museum world, fuelled by – amongst others – ongoing Greek demands for the return of the Parthenon Marbles; student activism at Cambridge University that has resulted in the promise by Jesus College to return one of the Benin bronze to Nigeria; competing Indian and

A Roman cinerary urn depicting the trophies and spoils of war in marble, in the Metropolitan Museum of Art in New York

An Abyssinian Crown at the Victoria & Albert Museum (see also page 183)

Hermann Goering: 'I intend to plunder and to do it thoroughly'

Pakistani claims to secure the Koh-i-Noor diamond; a great-grandson of the last King of Burma attempting to find and recover the great Burmese royal ruby, known as the Nga Mauk, last seen in the pocket of the colonial administrator, Colonel Sir Edward Sladen; and pressure from the Chinese government to repatriate the contents of the Old and New Summer Palaces. Both the French and the Belgian governments appear to be buckling under such pressure and have decided to return artefacts to post-colonial sub-Saharan Africa (although, given the governments concerned, whether anything will ever be returned is a moot point). In London the National Army Museum has recently returned a lock of hair taken from the dead Emperor Tewodros after the Siege of Magdala in 1868. Similarly, the Victoria & Albert Museum, which has a history of returning Imperial regalia to Ethiopia, has consented to 'loan' further items (*see* p.180); and in 1964 returned the Mandalay royal regalia, taken in 1885, to the then Burmese ruler, General Ne Win (*see* p.211). Perhaps significantly, the German Chancellor has not requested the return of Hitler's desk, nor has the French President yet demanded the return of the skeleton and hooves of Napoleon's charger, *Marengo*. In public life, a selective memory would appear to be the rule when it comes to the subject of spoils of war.

My personal view on this much-debated topic accords with the excellent academic analysis of the issue of repatriation by Tiffany Jenkins in her seminal work, *Keeping their Marbles*. This view was also held by the former Prime Minister, David Cameron who, on Indian television in 2010, said in response to an Indian journalist demanding the return of the Koh-i-Noor diamond: 'If you say yes to one, you suddenly find the British Museum would be empty… I am afraid to say, to disappoint all your viewers, it is going to have to stay put.' I do not want or need to add to this debate. However, whatever the pros and cons of repatriation, which – with the exception of the spoils of the Magdala and Burmese campaigns – are not the subject of this book, I do need to address the issue of the circumstances under which an acquisition was made and the nature of the object concerned.

The importance of 'circumstance' is highlighted by the words chosen by museums to describe the objects in question: in every case this is either 'loot', 'trophies' or 'spoils of war'. The concept of 'to the victor belongs the spoils' is as old as conflict itself, and in more recent times has even been defined and regulated by international law. But even before the age of legal regulation, the acquisition of items in the course of warfare was both self-regulated and limited to the battlefield. Although on two occasions it was state-managed on an industrial scale: Napoleon practiced wholesale

looting of European works-of-art, as did Hitler, whose Reichsminister, Hermann Goering, stated: 'I intend to plunder and to do it thoroughly', and then proceeded to steal a staggering twenty-five percent of the art heritage of occupied Europe.

Wellington at the Battle of Vitoria, 1813 (see also page 81)

By contrast, the 1st Duke of Wellington deplored looting and there are tales of it driving him into 'a great rage', as one of his Peninsular veterans noted in a letter home. The primary reason for the Duke's rage was that looting got in the way of fighting. After the Battle of Vitoria in 1813, he came close to ordering the 18th Hussars back to England for plundering King Joseph Bonaparte's baggage train instead of pursuing the French as ordered. He was also of the opinion that looting was no better than theft. As the 9th Duke points out in his Foreword to this book, Wellington organised the repatriation of much of Napoleon's European loot after the Allied victory at Waterloo in 1815 However, and it is not a contradiction, at the same time the 1st Duke supported the capture of trophies and the monetisation of spoils of war through Prize Auctions. To put it another way, he endorsed the orderly and regulated distribution and monetization of items captured under *legitimate* and regulated circumstances from an enemy, but he was opposed to the wholesale redistribution of a nation's cultural heritage.

The objects covered in this book, which are a small but reasonably representative cross-section of the tens of thousands of such items held in the United Kingdom, fall into the first three of the following four broad cate-

James Bruce, 8th Earl of Elgin
(see also page 174)

gories: battlefield souvenirs, such as a scrap of German trench wallpaper, which are of low intrinsic value; items acquired at Prize Auctions or other regulated distribution of spoils of war, some of which may have considerable value; trophies, such as Colours and Eagles, which are of low intrinsic but high emotional value; and the proceeds of formal treaties, such as the Rock of Gibraltar, the values of which are difficult to calibrate.

In the case of battlefield souvenirs, it seems to me that the circumstances surrounding their acquisition are of emotional rather than legal significance. The fact that great-great-Uncle Fred seized a Dervish spear at the point of a bayonet at the Battle of Omdurman in 1898, and it is now hanging on the wall in his descendant's sitting room is irrelevant; its original owner is unknown and its value is, even at this distance in time and without an interesting provenance, strictly limited. That the brown stain on the blade is probably blood should not alter a rational approach to it as a legitimate spoil of war.

A similar approach should be taken to the proceeds of the regulated sale of prizes, some of which may today have significant value. By the standards, *mores* and rules of the time, the purchase of such spoils was legitimate and legal. The sacking and destruction of the Old Summer Palace in Peking in 1860 was a carefully considered act of punishment by Lord Elgin and his French counterpart for the appalling atrocities deliberately inflicted on Europeans, who were treacherously imprisoned, brutally tortured, and painfully executed on the direct order of the legitimate Chinese government. That, with hindsight, it was not a proportionate response to the horrors perpetrated by the Chinese government on British and French citizens is irrelevant, and in no way invalidates the subsequent ownership of items acquired by the British and French at the time.

The treatment of trophies should be equally unequivocal. The determination to capture an enemy's symbol of national or unit *esprit de corps* – usually under bloody, violent and life-threatening circumstances – was a central part of warfare from ancient times to the First World War. Their actual capture or loss, as illustrated in the pages which follow, was almost as important as the outcome of the battle. The idea that, in happier times, these potent trophies should be returned to their original owners has been consistently rejected, and no shame or embarrassment should attach to their retention.

As to the fourth category of spoils of war – those of great value – here, I believe, the issues as well as the scale are different. The legitimate transfer of objects or territory under the terms of a peace treaty are no less valid because the treaty was signed by the victor and the defeated, in circumstances in which there must have been an element of duress. To deny the legitimacy of such treaties would be to invalidate all international agreements made at the conclusion of a war, with a resulting chaos in international relations. A nation state, or its successor in title, may choose unilaterally to give up a possession or a claim defined in a treaty, but it cannot demand a return to the *status quo ante bellum* without a wholesale renegotiation or a further war. England may no longer demand the return from the French of Calais, Normandy and the Aquitaine, but to have abandoned such claims does not legitimise Spain's demand for the return of Gibraltar. The fact that history is littered with such incidents does not make repudiation of a treaty term valid: the surrender of the Koh-I-Noor diamond by the Sikhs was a specific term of the Last Treaty of Lahore, which ended the Anglo-Sikh Wars in 1849. Its return, in a hugely altered state, cannot now be demanded on the grounds of duress.

So, the items described in this book – and the thousands more that have not been included – are the proud, legitimate and inalienable property of their present owners. In giving them greater exposure than they have enjoyed to date, I hope that one of the consequences will be increased visitor numbers, and consequent revenue growth, for the UK's hard-pressed military museums. I also hope that the book's sales will assist SSAFA The Armed Forces Charity in its mission, as I will be donating a proportion of my royalties to this worthy cause.

CHRISTOPHER JOLL
Bath, 2020

The Eagle of the French 22nd Regiment, captured at the Battle of Salamanca during in the Peninsular War, 1812 (see also page 81)

©*Lancashire Infantry Museum, Preston*

FOR
Eileen Joll
1916–2014

THE CAMPAIGNS

CHAPTER I

HUNDRED YEARS' WAR
(1337–1453)

A saintly & controversial spoil of war

Joan of Arc's Ring (Rouen, 1431)

On Wednesday 25th May 2016 a rare souvenir of the Hundred Years' War, in the form of a plain fifteenth-century silver ring, was offered for sale at the Timeline Auctions sale room in London's Bloomsbury, with a pre-sale estimate of £10–14,000. A very few minutes later, the trinket was knocked down for an eye-watering £297,600.

This extraordinarily valuable ring had been described in the auction catalogue as having 'a faceted outer face, expanding shoulders, and two rectangular and angled fields to the bezel; the hoop with incised niello-filled florid lozenges and triangles, the design giving the appearance of three crosses, the ends of the shoulders with black letter I and M (for Iesus Maria), the lateral faces with black letter IHS and MAR (an abbreviation for Jesus and Maria); a small section inserted later to the hoop, sufficient possibly to enlarge it from a band suitable for a small, feminine finger to a larger male (?) hand'. This, however, was no ordinary piece of medieval jewellery. It was, according to lore, research and documentation, a devotional ring that had been given to Joan of Arc by her parents as a first communion gift, and later stolen, looted or acquired by the English Cardinal Henry Beaufort.

opposite
Joan of Arc's Death at the Stake
by Hermann Stilke

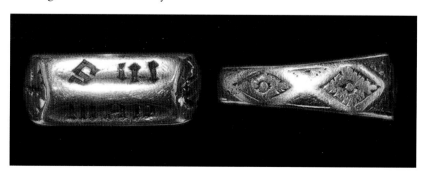

Joan of Arc's ring

Jeanne at the Coronation of Charles VII by Dominique Ingres

above right
Cardinal Beaufort interrogates Joan of Arc in prison by Paul de la Roche

After a successful but brief military career lasting almost exactly a year, on 23rd May 1430 Joan of Arc (also known as the Maid of Orléans) was captured by the Burgundians, allies of the English in their war with the Orléans family for the crown of France. Eventually, she found herself in Rouen Castle, being tried for her life. Ostensibly, the Maid's crime was not successfully waging war against the English and Burgundians, but cross-dressing, for which she was tried by an ecclesiastical court on the capital offense of heresy.

Although the heresy charge (but not the cross-dressing which was admitted) was trumped up, Joan was nonetheless found guilty and sentenced to be burnt at the stake. Not surprisingly, she was later acquitted at a posthumous hearing in 1456, beatified in 1909 by Pope Pius X and canonised in 1920 by Pope Benedict XV – but not before she had had to face an agonising death on a pile of burning faggots in Rouen's old marketplace on 30th May 1431. Interestingly, the Maid's body was not fully consumed by the fire and had to be re-burned twice before she was reduced to ashes. This gruesome fact may have been remembered by O. Henry, the American novelist, on his own deathbed. Seemingly deceased, one of Henry's relations suggested that his demise could be confirmed by feeling his feet, on the perfectly reasonable grounds that no one died with warm toes. 'Joan of Arc did,' murmured Henry, before turning up his own.

Meanwhile the ring, which had either been shamelessly looted by Cardinal Beaufort whilst Joan was being crisped to a frazzle or had been given to him by the condemned woman before her fiery execution, depending on whether the French or the English version of the story is believed, was passed down as an heirloom through the Cardinal's family, the Cavendish-Bentincks.

Sometime before the First World War, Lady Ottoline Morrell (*née* Cavendish-Bentinck), an intellectual socialite with the rather unkind but thoroughly well-deserved nickname of 'Lady Utterly Immoral', gave the celibate Maid's ring to one of her lovers, the artist and rampant philanderer, Augustus John. Thereafter it passed through various hands and auctions until it was sent for sale in Bloomsbury in 2016 by 'an Essex gentleman', later identified as Robert Hasson; in an interview with the BBC, he stated that his father, James, a French doctor who had come to England with General de Gaulle during the Second World War, had bought the ring in a Sotheby's auction in 1947 for £175.

Lady Ottoline Morrell by Adolf de Meyer

Immediately after the 2016 auction, the ring's new French owners, the Fondation Puy de Fou, took the saint's trinket back in triumph to their historical theme park near Nantes. There, to mark the ring's return to the Motherland, a lavish pageant was staged in front of a crowd of 5,000 joyous Frenchmen, women and children – and the world's media. This martial display, which was hardly calculated to enhance the *entente cordiale*, included medieval knights in armour, whose horses were caparisoned in colourful heraldic cloths, and the Cadets of the Saint Cyr Military Academy, resplendent in their Second Empire ceremonial uniforms of red trousers, blue tunics and peaked kepis topped with fluttering swans' feathers.

Although probably not an adverse reaction to the triumphalist pomp and circumstance, the ring's ceremonial arrival in France had nonetheless stirred up a hornets' nest in England. The Fondation Puy du Fou had, with a Gallic shrug, ignored the UK's rules and regulations which state that 'items of national and historical importance with a value in excess of £39,000 and which have been in the UK for more than fifty years' require an Export Licence. This was a category into which the Maid's ring undoubtedly fell. The Export Licence process normally takes a month, but it can take much longer if the export is challenged, as time is then given to allow the item to be acquired by a British institution at the hammer price. Even within the European Union, these strict rules have to be observed, and the Fondation Puy du Fou had very publicly put two fingers up to them. It was not long before the Fondation received a letter from Arts Council England, demanding that Joan of Arc's ring be returned to the UK, pending the necessary Export Licence procedures.

Monsieur Nicolas de Villiers, owner of the theme park and an accomplished showman, responded by staging a well-attended international press conference, at which he gave a de Gaulle-like statement of considerable robustness. To loud French boos, he asserted that the ring was not part of England's heritage, and to loud French cheers, that it was part of France's. Monsieur de Villiers also rather optimistically claimed that the ring was the last bone of contention between the English and the French, and that its return to France was 'an act of appeasement', a phrase with unfortunate resonances on the English side of the Channel. He ended with a challenge that has been used on more than one occasion by the British, when France has requested or demanded the return of its Napoleonic Eagles, saying: 'Ladies and gentlemen from Britain, if you want to see the ring, then come to Puy de Fou. For the rest, it is too late'. Or, to put it into the English vernacular: 'If you want it, come and get it.' At the time of going to print, Joan of Arc's ring remains in France and the Export Licence dispute continues.

CHAPTER 2

ENGLISH CIVIL WAR
(1642–1651)

The Missing Member of the Marquess of Montrose
The Right Forearm of a Royalist (Philiphaugh, 1645)

Whilst most British spoils of war have been acquired during or after conflicts with foreign nations, the English Civil War and its aftermath produced some gruesome trophies of its own, including the missing forearm of James Graham, 1st Marquess of Montrose.

Montrose was a young aristocratic Scottish Covenanter-turned-ardent-royalist, who had chalked up a successful career as an army commander in Scotland, with successive victories over the English Parliamentarians' Scottish allies, the Covenanters, at the Battles of Tippermuir and Aberdeen in 1644, and Inverlochy, Auldearn, Alford and Kilsyth in 1645. However, he met his Waterloo in the autumn of that year at the battle of Philiphaugh. After failing to raise a new army he followed up his defeat with six months of guerrilla warfare in the Highlands, but he was ordered to lay down his arms by the imprisoned King Charles I and went into exile in 1646, where he joined the Prince of Wales in The Hague. Following the execution of King Charles I in 1649, Montrose spent much of his time trying to persuade the new, but as yet un-crowned King Charles II, that the fastest way to recover his English and Scottish thrones was via an invasion of Scotland led by himself. The future Merry Monarch was initially not convinced, believing that a better route was via Catholic Ireland, but this route was effectively closed by Cromwell. Eventually, Montrose's advice found favour with Charles, and on 4th March 1649 the exiled King appointed the bellicose Highlander as Lieutenant Governor of Scotland and Captain General of his (non-existent) Scottish Army.

However, before Montrose could set sail for Scotland in his new roles, he had to raise money and men. So, for the next seven months, he trailed around the states of northern Europe with his glossy new commissions and a begging bowl. By September he had amassed an Army comprising

James Graham, 1st Marquess of Montrose by William Dobson

Cromwell at Dunbar by Andrew Carrick Gow

eighty officers and a hundred Danish soldiers. These he dispatched to the Orkneys as an advance party under the command of George Hay, 3rd Earl of Kinnoull, with orders to raise more troops locally, whilst he continued to try and drum-up further men and equipment on the continent. Eventually, in March 1650, the gallant Montrose arrived at Kirkwall, Orkney, from where he launched his invasion of the mainland with an army that comprised, in total, 500 European mercenaries, 700 Orcadian crofters, and a cavalry unit of forty men and horses. This was not quite as crazy a venture as it sounds, for Montrose had reason to believe that many of the Highland clans would rally to his standard. In the event, they did not. Nonetheless, Montrose pressed on in a southerly direction towards Edinburgh and the seat of Scottish power.

On 27th April, at Carbisdale in Ross-shire, the Covenanters, under Colonel Archibald Strachan, were waiting for him, with a small but well-trained force of infantry and cavalry. Rather than a battle, Carbisdale was a slaughter from which Montrose barely escaped, wounded and friendless. For several days, disguised as a shepherd, he managed to evade capture, eventually seeking shelter at Ardvreck Castle, the home of a former comrade-in-arms, the MacLeod of Assynt. Unfortunately for Montrose, the MacLeod was not at home, but his wife Christian [sic] was – and she was the daughter of the Munro of Lemlair, who had been one of Montrose's opponents a few days before. Displaying the finest of female virtues, she betrayed him to the Covenanters who carted the royalist off to Edinburgh where he was summarily hanged on 21st May 1650.

Although Montrose was spared the horror of a traitor's death – hanging, drawing and quartering – he was not granted a quick and clean end by the axe. Instead, after being slowly strangled at the end of a noose for three hours, his dead body was dismembered, and his head and four severed limbs were sent for public display in Edinburgh, Glasgow, Perth, Aberdeen and Stirling. Usually, under such circumstances, his body parts would have been displayed until picked clean by carrion crows, and then reassembled and interred. Not so in Montrose's case. Although, following the Restoration of the monarchy in 1660, three of his limbs and his head were re-united with his previously buried torso (see post script below), and given a State Funeral on 11th May 1661 in Edinburgh, his right forearm was missing.

The Execution of the Marquess of Montrose in Edinburgh

Jacobite historians have established beyond reasonable doubt that Montrose's missing mummified right hand and forearm, which showed clear signs of having been nailed up as a display, had been acquired by a certain Captain John Pickering, a Cromwellian officer, who removed the grisly spoil of war to his estate in Yorkshire, where it was treasured as a family heirloom. There it remained until it was sold in July 1891, along with Montrose's sword, to a Mr J W Morkill, who had it photographed to accompany a monograph on the subject for the Society of Antiquaries of Scotland.

The fate and location of the arm after 1891 remains a mystery to the present day. One theory, that it had at some point after the date of the monograph been reunited with the rest of Montrose's body, can be

All that remains of the Marquess of Montrose

discounted, as his coffin in St Giles' Cathedral was swept away in 1829 during the installation of a coal cellar in the crypt. His interred remains were at that point lost, and the elaborate monument to Montrose erected on the prompting of Queen Victoria in 1888 is just that – a monument not a tomb. However, while researching his monograph on the forearm, J W Morkill had contacted Francis, 10th Lord Napier, a diplomat and former Viceroy of India, who was descended from Montrose's close relatives. Napier's reply stated clearly that he felt such a relic should be afforded a decent burial. As it has never been seen since, it seems likely that Morkill arranged for this to happen quietly, perhaps near or below the elaborate nineteenth-century monument in St Giles' Cathedral.

Postscript Although not a spoil of war, it seems appropriate in the context of his arm to relate the saga of Montrose's heart. Following his execution and the dispersal of his head and limbs, the gallant Marquess's torso was buried on the 'burgh muir [moor] of Edinburgh'. But it was not to lie there undisturbed. That night, on the orders of Elizabeth, Lady Napier, the wife of Montrose's nephew, the torso was disinterred and the heart removed, before the remains were re-buried. The heart was then embalmed, placed in a casket, and sent to the 2nd Marquess, then in exile in the Netherlands. He returned the precious organ to his father's body in time for the State Funeral in 1661. The casket subsequently passed out of the Montrose family, was taken to India by sea, stolen by an Indian Prince, recovered and returned to Europe by land, and then disappeared during the French Revolution.

CHAPTER 3

WAR OF THE AUSTRIAN SUCCESSION (1740–1748)

The Beat of the Drums

Two Pairs of French Kettledrums (Dettingen, 1743)

The village of Dettingen in north-west Bavaria, now known as Karlstein-am-Main, was the site of a strategically important battle in the War of the Austrian Succession (1740–1748). This conflict, the origins of which lay ostensibly in the legitimacy of a woman ruling the Habsburgs' European empire, was in reality both a dispute between France and Austria over continental supremacy, and an opportunity for a Prussian land grab. It was also the last clash of arms in which a reigning English sovereign, King George II, commanded an Army in battle.

Fortunately for the reputation of the British monarchy, the battle against the French was won by the combined armies of Britain, Hanover and Austria on 27th June 1743. The Allied victors were known as the Pragmatic Army, because they were in the field to impose the Pragmatic Sanction of 1713, an international treaty that recognised Empress Maria Theresa as the legitimate Habsburg sovereign. During the battle, King George, perhaps

The Battle of Dettingen 1743

because his horse at one point bolted with him, displayed an admirable degree of pragmatism himself, by relying on the tactical advice of the senior professional soldiers on his Staff, notably Field Marshal John Dalrymple, 2nd Earl of Stair, who had originally been appointed Commander-in-Chief (before he was pushed aside by the King), Field Marshal Leopold Philippe, 4th Duke of Arenberg, and Field Marshal Count Wilhelm von Neipperg.

The defeat of the French, under the combined and unfortunately (for them) contradictory command of the Dukes de Noailles and de Gramont, was strategically important, because the French had been attempting a knock-out blow that would deliver a quick end to the war, followed by the dismemberment of the Habsburg Empire. The Battle of Dettingen was therefore an important setback to the land-hungry, male-chauvinist rulers outside the Habsburg domains, and a significant advance for the eighteenth-century feminist cause within it.

In addition to its strategic significance, the battle produced the order by Lieutenant Colonel Sir Andrew Agnew of Lochnaw to his Royal Scots Fusiliers not to fire 'until you see the whites of their eyes', an Army maxim that survives to the present day. George II's victory also resulted in a rich musical legacy in the shape of the *Dettingen Te Deum* and the *Dettingen Anthem*, both composed by the King's pragmatically sycophantic composer, George Frideric Handel, and in the capture of two pairs of French kettledrums.

Although captured arms, armour and other weapons, both large and small, are the most obvious trophies to emerge from warfare – either in their original state or adapted into some other form – there are other notable examples of spoils of war that are of a strictly non-military nature, including musical instruments.

In almost every land (and some sea) conflict since time began the presence of music on the battlefield, to raise the human spirit, blot out the sound of gunfire and to convey orders, has been part of the experience of war. Up until the end of the nineteenth century, the presence of military bands on the field of glory was a given, and since then lone pipers, trumpeters, buglers and drummers have featured right up to the present day, including a very select group of military instrumentalists who have won the Victoria Cross whilst musically engaged in battle.[1] However, although in the eighteenth century virtually every cavalry Regiment possessed a mounted band – and a select number of units including Britain's Household Cavalry, France's Guarde Républicaine and the Sultan of Oman's Royal Omani Police still do – the presence on the battlefield of bandsmen on horses was, with the exception of trumpeters, rare.

Quite why the mounted bands of King Louis XV's Army became embroiled in the fight against the Pragmatic Army has never been properly explained. It is possible that they got caught up in the ultimately disastrous charge against the British front line led by the Maison du Roi (the French equivalent of Britain's Household Cavalry), which was ordered by the Duke de Gramont without the permission of the Duke de Noailles; or

1. These include awards of the Victoria Cross to Trumpeter Samuel Parkes VC (1815–1864) of 4th Queen's Own Light Dragoons during the Charge of the Light Brigade (1854); Drummer Thomas Flynn VC (1842–1892) of the 64th Regiment of Foot, Trumpeter (later Corporal) Charles Anderson VC (1827–1899) and Trumpeter Thomas Monaghan VC (1833–1895) both of the 2nd Queen's Dragoon Guards, and Bugler William Sutton VC (1830–1888) of the 60th Rifles during the Indian Mutiny (1857–1858); Drummer (later Corporal) Michael Magner VC (1840–1897) of the Duke of Wellington's Regiment during the assault on Magdala (1868); Piper (later Sergeant) George Findlater VC (1872–1942) of the Gordon Highlanders during the Tirah Campaign (1897–1898); and, during the First World War, to Piper Daniel Laidlaw VC (1875–1950) of The King's Own Scottish Borderers, Drummer Joe Spencer Bent VC MM (1891–1977) of The East Lancashire Regiment, Drummer William Kenny VC (1880–1936) of the Gordon Highlanders, Piper Jimmy Richardson VC (1895–1916) of 72nd Seaforth Highlanders of Canada, Piper Walter Ritchie VC (1892–1965) of The Seaforth Highlanders, and Bandsman Thomas Rendle VC (1884–1946) of The Duke of Cornwall's Light Infantry

French kettledrums captured
by Ligonier's Horse

they were overwhelmed when the British cavalry counter-charged. For whatever reason, in addition to losing a great many men and horses, the French cavalry also lost not one but two pairs of kettledrums, which puts one in mind of Lady Bracknell's memorable remark on the subject of multiple loss, misfortune and carelessness.

The first pair of kettledrums was captured by Ligonier's Horse, otherwise known as the Black Horse.[2] When de Gramont launched his cavalry against the British, the Black Horse at first had a very bad time of it, being completely surrounded by the Maison du Roi and nearly losing their Colonel's Standard. By the end of the battle, however, the Standard (which still exists) was secure, albeit that the Standard-bearer, Cornet Henry Richardson, had received thirty-seven wounds in its defence. The Regiment had lost one officer, one Warrant Officer and twenty-one men killed and a further thirty men wounded; but it had gained a fine pair of plain copper kettledrums, which are now on permanent display in the Museum of the Royal Dragoon Guards in York. These kettledrums were, despite the regimental claim that they belonged to the Maison du Roi, almost certainly the property of a French cavalry Regiment of the Line, possibly the Gendarmes (not to be confused with modern-day French police), who were closely engaged with the Black Horse in support of the Maison du Roi. This hypothesis is supported by silver plaques attached to the drums, which state only that they were captured from 'French Cavalry'.

The second pair of Kettledrums
Made in silver, these unquestionably belonged to the Maison du Roi. They were acquired by The King's Own Regiment of Dragoons,[3] who

2. Later the 7th Dragoon Guards and now the Royal Dragoon Guards

3. Now The Queen's Royal Hussars (The Queen's Own & Royal Irish)

Silver kettledrums captured from the Maison du Roi at Dettingen

successfully counter-charged the numerically superior French cavalry. After the battle, King George commanded that these silver kettledrums should be borne by a drum horse ridden by a regimental Sergeant Kettledrummer, one of whose early appointees was the black Jamaican, Henry McGilchrist (b.1754, who served as a musician for thirty-seven years, being discharged in 1810). It is worth noting that the King, who may have taken an elitist view on the subject, issued no such command in the case of the less prestigious copper kettledrums captured by Ligonier's Horse, perhaps because they had belonged to a mere Regiment of the Line.

Unfortunately, the Hussars' original Maison du Roi kettledrums were destroyed in a fire in 1847, but replicas were made and are still carried at the head of The Queen's Royal Hussars on ceremonial parades. Uniquely amongst British cavalry Regiments, these kettledrums are never covered by drum banners, the battle honours being embossed directly onto the sides of the drums. There is, however, an uncomfortable coda to this story: in 1772, when the Hon Charles FitzRoy, a descendant (on the wrong side of the blanket) of King Charles II, commanded the Regiment, his wife rather cruelly presented a large silver collar – also embellished with the regimental battle honours and not unlike the spiked collars worn by mastiffs at the time but without the spikes – to be worn by the Sergeant Kettledrummer when in Full Dress. To the chagrin of many subsequent Sergeant Kettledrummers, the collar is still worn today.

CHAPTER 4

SEVEN YEARS' WAR
(1756–1763)

A Twice-Looted Indian Bottle
The Nawab of Bengal's jade flask & other fabulous spoils of war
(Murshidabad, 1757)

On 27th April 2004, Christie's in London offered for sale a small selection of items from the collection of treasures and spoils of war acquired in India by Major General Robert Clive, 1st Baron Clive of Plassey, better known today as Clive of India, the son of a worthy but impoverished Shropshire squire.

The most valuable of these items, a jewelled jade flask that had belonged to Clive's defeated enemy, Siraj ud-Daulah, the last independent Nawab of Bengal, had a pre-sale estimate of £1 million, and in the event sold to Sheikh Saud Al Thani of Qatar for a sum just short of £3 million.

Of Indo-Mughal origin, the 10-inch-high jade flask is extravagantly decorated with gold-set bands of emeralds and studded with ruby flowers. It had originally been part of an immense collection of jewels and jewelled

Clive of India, engraving after a portrait by Thomas Gainsborough

The Battle of Plassey, 23rd June 1757

Newab of Bengal's jade flask

items which were looted from Muhammad Shah's Delhi treasury in 1739 by Nadir Shah, the invading Persian monarch, who with some justification compared himself to Genghis Khan. Having overthrown the twelfth Mughal Emperor and captured his priceless treasures, Nadir Shah, in a gesture of his military prowess that cannot have been misunderstood by the recipients, sent a large number of these spoils of war to the Imperial Court in St Petersburg and the Sublime Porte in Constantinople. Other parts of Nadir Shah's booty were dispersed, doubtless for diplomatic and military reasons, to various rulers (including the Nawab of Bengal) along his return route to Persia.

Other items from Clive's Mughal collection bought in the sale at Christie's by Sheikh Al Thani, included a carved dagger dating to the reign of the great fifth Mughal Emperor, Shah Jahan, sold for £733,250 against a pre-sale estimate of £35–50,000, and a flywhisk dating from the reign of the sixth Mughal Emperor, made from banded agate and inset with rubies, estimated at £5,000–8,000 but sold for £901,250. The story as to how all these items came to be in a London saleroom is part of the history of the British Empire.

Britain's serious interest in India started in the first year of the seventeenth century, with the creation of the British East India Company, a joint-stock company established to exploit the growing trade with the Far East and the highly lucrative spice trade in particular, for which India was an important market. Initially, Britain's military involvement in the sub-continent was limited to the defence of its coastal trading stations at Calcutta, Madras and Bombay. However, by the middle of the eighteenth century the Company's troops, whose sole duty until then had been guarding Company property, became embroiled in the minor wars that were perpetually breaking out between the various Indian kingdoms and princely states. Many of these conflicts were proxies for the Anglo-French struggle for control of India, itself just one of the power tussles that made up the Seven Years' War then being waged by and between virtually every European power in their own back yards, as well as in North America, West Africa and India.

The Anglo-French confrontation in India peaked at the Battle of Plassey on 23rd June 1757. After a bloody struggle, the East India Company's troops under the command of Clive, who had arrived in India in 1744 as a humble clerk, defeated the forces of the Francophile Nawab of Bengal, Siraj ud-Daulah, who fled the battlefield on a camel but was soon captured. A short while later, he was brutally dispatched on the orders of his successor, the

newly installed Anglophile Nawab, Mir Jafar, who (with a British-imposed three-year interval from 1760 to 1763) ruled Bengal as the British East India Company's compliant puppet until 1765.

Immediately after Clive's victory, the new Nawab threw open the Bengal treasury and invited Clive to take what he wanted. Within its stone walls the victor of Plassey found gold, jewels and other treasure worth £1.5 million (2020: £264.5 million). Showing considerable restraint, Clive took for himself a mere £150,000 (2020: £26.4 million) in cash and various items, including the Mughal jade flask which became the centrepiece of the Shropshire lad's valuable collection of spoils of war. It is worth noting, in light of what followed, that Clive took a further £500,000 (2020: £88 million), which he distributed around all the East India Company officers, soldiers, sailors and clerks, plus wisely £24,000 (£4.2 million) for *each*

Robert Clive & Mir Jafar after the Battle of Plassey, 1757, by Francis Hayman (detail)

member of the Company's management committee. There was not much left in the Bengal treasury by the time Clive had finished this early exercise in wealth redistribution.

When he left India in 1760, Clive had amassed a personal fortune, including his Bengali loot, which he himself estimated at £401,102 (2020: £79.5 million). He had been able to amass this fortune because the acquisition of money and objects by colonial administrators, both in war and in peace, was common practice at the time. However, his fortune-building was later thought by jealous contemporaries to have been excessive, and led to a Parliamentary enquiry in 1772–3 into whether he had gained his riches through questionable means. At this enquiry, Clive exclaimed: 'By God, Mr Chairman, at this moment I stand astonished at my own moderation.' Sadly, although acquitted of the charges, the enquiry added to Clive's bouts of depression and he killed himself the year after it closed.

Meanwhile, some 230 years later, although not the most valuable spoils of war to have been sold at auction, the items acquired by Sheikh Al Thani from Clive's collection amounted to a princely haul by anyone's standards. But, as with Joan of Arc's ring, all these items required an Export Licence. However, Sheikh Al Thani elected to keep the treasures in England. Following his sudden death in 2014, The Al Thani Collection Foundation have generously loaned them to exhibitions at the Victoria & Albert Museum in London and at other museums around the world.

CHAPTER 5

AMERICAN WAR OF INDEPENDENCE (1775–1783)

The Bunker Hill Cannon Ball

The Honourable Artillery Company's American trophy (Bunker Hill, 1775)
The Honourable Artillery Company (HAC) is Britain's oldest Regiment, having been established by King Henry VIII's Royal Charter in 1537. In the Drum Room at Armoury House, the London home of the Regiment, is a cannon ball perched atop a dark stone plinth, on which is a plaque which states: 'The Battle of Bunker Hill, 17th June 1775'. Most casual observers would assume that this round shot is a piece of American ordnance, acquired by a member of the HAC at the close of the engagement as a souvenir of the battle. The truth is otherwise.

The Battle of Bunker Hill was one of the opening battles of the American War of Independence (1775–1783). It was fought to secure the hills on a

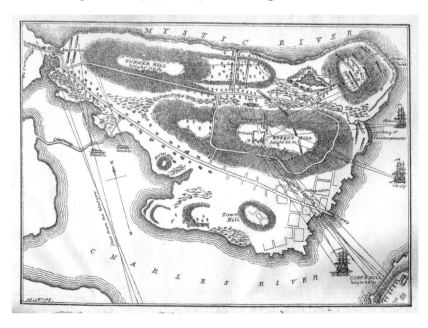

A map of the battle ground around Bunker Hill

33

The Battle of Bunker Hill, 17th
June 1775

peninsular overlooking British-held Boston, possession of which would give the occupying force command of the entrance to the strategically important Boston Harbour. In a pre-emptive night-time move, 1,200 revolutionary soldiers under the command of Colonel William Prescott marched from their base at Cambridge, Massachusetts, across the Charleston Neck, and occupied both Bunker Hill and the adjacent Breed's Hill, constructing overnight a strong redoubt on the latter feature.

Significantly underestimating the strength of the revolutionaries' fortified positions and the military skills of the Americans, the British determined on a longboat-borne beach landing, followed by a frontal assault against the Breed's Hill position, which they were confident would be easily taken by their professional troops. The British were also slow to assemble their forces, and it was ten hours from the time they had first detected the Americans on the hills before the first assault was launched at three pm. This interval not only allowed the Americans to bring up reinforcements from Cambridge, but also gave them time to consolidate the flanks of their fortifications.

The arrogance and tardiness of the British Generals – William, 5th Viscount Howe and Thomas Gage – cost them dear. The first two British assaults on Breed's Hill, supported by cannon fire from the Boston fortress across the Charles River and from the Royal Navy, were repulsed at a high cost, with eighty-one officers and nearly a thousand soldiers killed or wounded. By the time the third assault cleared the Americans from the Breed's Hill redoubt, the British had, at best, achieved a Pyrrhic victory.

Although the war would drag on for several more years, the performance of the 'amateur' revolutionary forces against the might of the British Army and Royal Navy in the battle now known as Bunker Hill was a significant morale booster for the Americans, proving at an early stage that they were more than capable of winning.

Given that during the battle, round shot was flying in both directions, the battlefield on and around Breed's Hill must have been littered, not only with the dead and dying, but also with significant amounts of spent ordnance. It would be a reasonable assumption, therefore, that the small calibre cannon ball now in the Drum Room at Armoury House is revolutionary in origin. For three reasons, however, no such assumption can be made.

The HAC's cannon ball

First, at this early stage in the war, the weapons and ammunition used by both sides came from a common source, so it is virtually impossible to assert its origin; second, the Honourable Artillery Company was not present at the battle; and third, the HAC's cannon ball was actually presented to them by the Ancient & Honorable Artillery Company of Massachusetts (AHAC), an American military unit founded in 1638, which did fight at Bunker Hill – on the side of the revolutionaries.

Unfortunately, there is no paperwork in the HAC's archives that casts any light on this gift, beyond the fact that it was given to the HAC by the AHAC. If the cannon ball was fired by the British at the Americans, then its return disqualifies it as a British spoil of war and it should not be in this book. If, however, the reverse is the truth, then the trophy is not only fully qualified for inclusion, but also acquires a uniquely ironic quality. The truth will never be known.

Colonel Tarleton's American Standard And Colours
Standard of the 2nd Regiment of Continental Light Dragoons (Pound Ridge, 1779)
Most armies around the globe have elaborately embroidered flags – variously known as Colours (Infantry), Standards (Heavy Cavalry) and Guidons (Light Cavalry) – which incorporate a unit's battle honours,

Lieutenant Colonel Banastre
Tarleton (1754–1833)
by Sir Joshua Reynolds, 1782

badges, and national and/or royal symbols. They are usually consecrated and are invariably treated with considerable deference by everyone, whether military or civilian, from the Head of State down to the ordinary citizen.

In the British Army, at the end of their in-service use, these potent symbols of a unit's *esprit de corps* are laid up with great ceremony and reverence. It is not surprising, therefore, that whilst in use Colours are closely protected and heavily guarded, whether on the battlefield or on the parade ground. The loss of a Colour brings disgrace and the capture of an enemy's Colour brings considerable glory, both to the individual who lost or captured it and to his unit.

Consequently, Colours (and their equivalent Standards and Guidons), although of a relatively low intrinsic value, are highly prized by the units themselves, so much so that thousands of men have died fighting to protect or capture them. Former enemies and later collectors also covet them. Indeed, on 14th June 2006, an anonymous collector paid the staggering sum of US$17.4 million at Sotheby's, New York, to buy a British-captured Standard and three Colours that had originally belonged to units of the American Revolutionary forces. These extraordinarily expensive spoils of the American War of Independence, sold by a descendant of the brother of Lieutenant Colonel Banastre Tarleton, are believed to be the earliest surviving American military flags and the last of the period in private ownership, hence their value.

In the summer of 1778, the third year of the revolution by the American colonists, the British began reorganizing their cavalry under the leadership of Brigadier General Sir William Erskine, who was also Quartermaster General. As part of this reorganization, a loyalist Regiment known as the British Legion, Cathcart's Legion, or often simply the Legion, was formed under the formal command of William, 10th Baron (later 1st Earl) Cathcart. It consisted of both Companies of light infantry and Troops of light dragoons, which had been separately raised over the course of the preceding year by loyalist American commanders from Pennsylvania, New York, and New Jersey. Direct oversight of the light dragoons was entrusted to the newly promoted Lieutenant Colonel Banastre Tarleton, Erskine's Brigade Major. The infantry companies were commanded by Major Charles Cochrane.

Brigadier General Sir William Erskine, later engraving after a portrait by Richard Cosway

Tarleton himself only occasionally rode with the Legion at this point, as much of his time was taken up with his duties as Brigade Major. However, on 1st July 1779, shortly before his twenty-fifth birthday, Tarleton was given his first independent command, with orders to intercept Colonel Elisha Sheldon near the town of Pound Ridge, New York. The town also

Regimental Standard of 2nd
Regiment of Continental Light
Dragoons

1. Disbanded 1763

housed an American militia commander, Major Ebenezer Lockwood, a leading revolutionary on whose head was a forty guineas reward (2020: £7,200).

Tarleton's force comprised about two hundred men, including units from the cavalry and infantry of the Legion, the 17th Light Dragoons[1], the Queen's Rangers and some Hessian Jaegers. After a night march in a terrible storm, they reached North Castle on the morning of 2nd July, from where they pushed on to Pound Ridge. Delayed by faulty information from a guide, Tarleton's advance-to-contact was not, however, the surprise which he had planned. Nonetheless, and despite being outnumbered three-to-two by the revolutionary forces, Tarleton immediately engaged them. Following some minor skirmishing, the Americans withdrew, leaving behind their baggage wagons, in which Tarleton found the Standard of the American 2nd Regiment of Continental Light Dragoons, otherwise known as Sheldon's Light Dragoons.

This Standard measures 35 × 39 inches and is made up of thirteen red and white silk stripes, with a silver-winged black thundercloud at its centre, from which dart ten gold and orange thunderbolts. This is a mythological image which refers to the awesome power of Zeus, god of lightening, thunder, law, order and justice. It was a symbol frequently used on French cavalry Standards of the (French) pre-Revolution period, which is probably why it was adopted by the American cavalry unit. Below the thundercloud is the motto: *Pat: A Concita Fulm: Nt Nati* (When their country calls, her sons answer in tones of thunder).

By the late autumn of 1779, and with France now on the side of the revolutionaries, the British government decided it would be more profitable for their war effort to hold on to New York and attempt no major campaigns in the north. Instead they would attack the southern port of Charleston, South Carolina, which would place British forces closer to the West Indies, where many believed the Anglo-French fighting would take place. In addition, the British were convinced, wrongly as it turned out, that there were large numbers of loyalists in the south, who would rise up and fight against the rebels at the appearance of a British Army. The plan was to move north from Savannah, which had been captured a year earlier, and gradually isolate the more rebellious northern colonies.

Accordingly, a force under General Sir Henry Clinton sailed out of New York harbour on 26th December 1779, bound for Savannah. Due to extremely bad weather at sea, the British troops arrived there in dribs-and-drabs, and it was not until 1st April 1780 that the siege of Charleston began.

Charleston eventually capitulated to the British on 12th May, and although a large number of American revolutionary troops were captured in the town when it fell, there were still a few units at large in the State. One of the largest of these, the 400-strong 3rd Virginia Regiment, under the command of Colonel Abraham Buford, had been on its way to Charleston when the city fell, at which point Buford had turned back to Camden.

Learning of Buford's force and fearing that it might become the focal point of renewed resistance, Clinton ordered Lieutenant General Earl Cornwallis to go after the Americans and stop them at any cost. However, before he could reach Camden, Cornwallis realized that his men were moving too slowly to catch Buford. So, he detached Lieutenant Colonel Tarleton, with 170 cavalrymen from the Legion and the 17th Light Dragoons, and 100 mounted Legion infantry, to locate, engage and destroy Buford's troops.

Tarleton arrived at Camden late in the afternoon of 28th May. He allowed his men and horses a few hours rest, then set off again around midnight, pushing his command at such great speed that before they could catch up with Buford, they became strung-out for miles along the road. By the time Tarleton closed with Buford at Waxhaws, he had only about 150 of his 270 cavalrymen with him.

In a bid to delay the Americans and to allow time for his own men to catch up, Tarleton decided on a massive bluff. He sent a surrender demand to Buford, offering him the same terms as had been agreed at Charleston, and informing the American that he was at the head of a force of 700 men. Buford declined, and to Tarleton's consternation continued moving. Tarleton had to do something to make Buford pause, allowing his own force to regroup, so he began deploying his cavalrymen into a battle formation, with Major Charles Cochrane on the right with about sixty men, Captain Erasmus Corbett of the 17th Light Dragoons in the centre with a similar number, and himself at the head of around thirty on the left. The tactic worked; Buford stopped and prepared for battle.

Despite being outnumbered by nearly three-to-one, Tarleton ordered his small troop to charge the enemy's right flank, after which Cochrane was to attack their left. Buford claimed later that at this point he offered to surrender. However, at the time of Tarleton's charge, Buford's officers were giving firing instructions to their men, which Tarleton could hear. The later accounts of Buford's attempts to surrender are complicated by

Colonel (later General Sir) Henry Clinton, attributed to Andrea Soldi, c. 1762–65

Regimental Colour of 3rd
Virginians

the fact that they are mutually contradictory. In any event, Buford may not have had anyone to surrender to, as Corbett, the officer in the centre of the British force, was a Captain and not in a position to accept such an offer. To make matters worse, Tarleton's horse was one of the first to go down in the opening volley. By the time he had mounted another and his men realized that he had not been killed, the slaughter of retribution had begun. Tarleton and his officers tried to stop it, but as he himself said years later, the men were acting with 'a vindictive asperity not easily restrained'. By the time Tarleton had brought his soldiers back under control, 113 Americans were dead, while the British had lost only five; the numbers of wounded were similarly disproportionate.

As the officer-in-command, Tarleton was responsible for the discipline, or lack of it, of the troops under his command. However, no one at the time ever accused him of ordering or acquiescing to the slaughter, which was neither planned nor intentional; in that sense, it was not a massacre. It did, however, provide the revolutionaries with a valuable propaganda weapon; and whatever the truth of the matter, 'Tarleton's Quarter' became a synonym for 'No Prisoners'. The Colonel acquired the nickname of 'Butcher Tarleton', along with the 3rd Virginians' three Colours, which as was customary had been closely guarded at the centre of Buford's line; precisely how they were captured is not recorded.

Yellow Grand Division Colour
of 3rd Virginians

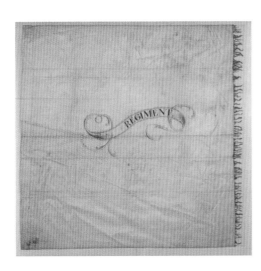

Colours of the 3rd Virginia Infantry Regiment (Waxhaws, 1780)
The first of these is the regimental Colour of the 3rd Virginians, from which several inches are missing on the right-hand side. It measures 50 × 46 inches, is made of yellow silk, painted on both sides with the device of a beaver felling a palmetto over the motto: PERSEVERANDO. Inset on the upper left corner is a blue silk panel, containing a triangle of three stars within a circle of eight stars, with two further stars at the upper left and right corners.

The 3rd's Grand Division Colour is 44 inches square, and although also of yellow silk, is rather plainer, featuring only a painted scrolling white ribbon highlighted with green, containing the word 'Regiment'.

Lastly, the 3rd's Blue Grand Division Colour is similar to the Yellow but slightly smaller, and also has a painted scrolling white ribbon, highighted in pink, containing the word 'Regiment'.

Tarleton's spoils, unlike the ten further American Colours (including a naval Ensign) seized in 1812 and 1815 (*see* p.111), were carefully conserved by his brother, and passed down through the Tarleton family until they were sold in 2006. They survive to the present day in remarkably good condition, which – along with rarity and history – may account for their great value.[1]

1. I am deeply grateful to Ms Joni Davidson of San Francisco for her invaluable research on this subject which has been passed to me by the last British owner of the Standards & Colours.

The Sword of Surrender

The sword of Lieutenant General Charles Cornwallis, 2nd Earl Cornwallis (Yorktown 1781)

In the days when combat was carried out by gentlemen, the conventions surrounding the formalities of victory and defeat were well-established and strictly adhered to. These rules covered the precise manner in which a formal surrender was conducted, and included such niceties as the 'honours of war' and the 'act of surrender', the latter being the requirement under which the defeated General presented his sword to his opposite number on the winning side. The symbolism of these acts, which continued to be observed – at least in part – until as recently as the end of the Second World War, was enormous and spoke far louder than the terms of any subsequent peace treaty.

At the conclusion of the siege of Yorktown on 19th October 1781, the surrender by Lord Cornwallis of his sword was (and remains) for Americans the single most significant moment in the evolution of the United States of America to full independent statehood. That it was not the end of the fighting, nor indeed the start of the USA's autonomous sovereignty, was largely immaterial. When Lord Cornwallis placed his sword in the hands of George Washington, the United States of America was born.

Except that it never happened. The true story of the Yorktown surrender is rather more convoluted, and is uniquely characterised by the way in which both sides deliberately used the conventions of war to trade insults and maintain face.

Whilst it is historically correct that the British forces, under Lord

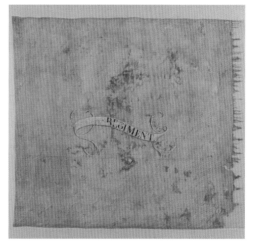

Blue Grand Division Colour of 3rd Virginians

Charles Cornwallis,
1st Marquess Cornwallis
(1738–1805)

Cornwallis's command, surrendered to the combined forces of the American revolutionaries and their French allies, under General George Washington and Lieutenant General Jean-Baptiste, Comte de Rochambeau, Lord Cornwallis did not attend the formal act of surrender and so never personally handed over his sword as tradition demanded.

The probable reason for this was that, under the negotiated terms of the surrender, Washington had refused to grant Cornwallis the 'honours of war', which would have allowed the British forces to march out of Yorktown with their heads held high, 'Colours flying, bayonets fixed, and the band playing an American or French tune as a tribute to the victors'. This was a deliberate humiliation of the British by Washington, and undoubtedly a finely calculated tit-for-tat revenge for the same honour having been denied to the Americans by Cornwallis at Charleston the previous year. Instead, the British troops were obliged to march out of Yorktown with Colours furled (but significantly not surrendered), and with muskets shouldered, whilst the bands played appropriately a popular British marching tune, *The World Turn'd Upside Down*.

But what of Cornwallis's sword?

From contemporary accounts, it appears that Cornwallis, who feigned illness in order to avoid any further humiliation, gave his service sword to his Second-in-Command, Brigadier General Charles O'Hara, who deputed for him at the surrender ceremony. Furthermore, the British were not prepared to accept further humiliation. In a deliberate move designed to keep the American revolutionaries firmly in their proper place, O'Hara presented the sword to the French commander. Rochambeau, who fully understood the significance of the gesture, was having none of that, shook his head, and pointed to George Washington. Rochambeau's unspoken meaning in doing this was also absolutely clear: it was the revolutionaries who had beaten their colonial rulers, so it was they who should receive the sword.

Gritting his teeth, O'Hara then offered the sword to Washington, but he too refused to accept it. In yet another calculated and symbolic move, he indicated that it should be given to his Second-in-Command, Major General Benjamin Lincoln, who had been humiliated by the British at Charleston, when Cornwallis had denied the Americans the 'honours of war'.

In an afternoon that already reeked of symbolic gestures of the 'V' sign variety, there was one final act of humiliation for the British. Instead of keeping it as a spoil of war, Lincoln gave Cornwallis's sword back to O'Hara. This was the grandest of grand gestures, designed to underline

the superiority of the victorious Americans; it was also the fastest-ever repatriation of a spoil of war. Significantly, it was to take almost exactly 226 years for the Americans to recover the Colours they had lost to Colonel Tarleton in the same war.

Not surprisingly, Cornwallis's disgraced sword, which despite popular belief was never put on display in the White House, then disappeared from view – unlike its owner. He was made a Knight Commander of the Order of the Garter and appointed Governor General of India in 1786, and later became Master General of the Ordnance and Lord Lieutenant of Ireland. The sword, which was appropriately engraved by its owner to establish its provenance, remained in a cupboard and has been passed down through succeeding generations of the Cornwallis family until emerging briefly in 2016 on the BBC's *Antiques Roadshow*.

The surrender of the British after the Seige of Yorktown by Charles Édouard Armand-Dumaresq. Brigadier General O'Hara is handing Cornwallis's sword to the Comte de Rochambeau, who is standing next to General Washington

CHAPTER 6

ANGLO-FRENCH WAR (1778–1783)

The Belvoir Castle Cannons & the Light Infantry's Bell

The upper-deck guns of the French warship Protée *(Atlantic, 1780)*

In the fifteen years that followed the Seven Years' War, France pursued a foreign policy of encouraging and supporting the American revolutionaries in their quest for independence from Britain. On 4th December 1777, word reached Versailles that Philadelphia had fallen, and that General Burgoyne had surrendered. Two days later, King Louis XVI assented to negotiations for a Franco-American alliance. The treaty was signed on 6th February 1778, and France declared war on Britain one month later, with hostilities beginning with naval skirmishes off Ushant in June.

In March 1780, news reached London that Captain Lord Robert Manners RN had captured the French 84-gun warship *Protée*, in a naval action off Madeira. Manners was the third son of Lieutenant General John Manners, Marquess of Granby, and grandson of the 3rd Duke of Rutland. The *Protée* was the first French ship to be seized by the Royal Navy since war had been declared two years earlier. The prizes from this engagement included silver and coin valued at £60,000 (2020: £10.5 million) and seven of the *Protée*'s upper-deck guns. In due course, these cannons were installed on the terrace of Manners' family home, Belvoir Castle in Rutland, and are fired on the current Duke's birthday and to mark other celebrations.

The responsibility for firing the guns has recently fallen to Robert Osborn, a former Welsh Guardsman. Osborn lost his left leg after being injured during the battle for Mount Tumbledown in the Falklands War in 1982, exactly 200 years after Lord Robert Manners had lost his during the Battle of the Saintes in 1782. Severely wounded by a cannon ball, which broke both his legs, and simultaneously struck by a splinter of wood that pierced his breast and tore into his right arm, Manners had continued to give orders for several moments, until his strength failed.

Death of Lord Robert Manners, showing the moment he was motally wounded

After being carried below, his left leg was amputated; but he died eleven days later of tetanus and septicaemia.

The Battle of the Saintes, 12th April 1782

The ship's chapel bell of the French ship Ville de Paris *(West Indies, 1782)*
What is a large chapel bell of a French warship, captured by the Royal Navy in 1782, doing in the Shropshire Regimental Museum in Shrewsbury Castle? The museum houses various regimental collections, including that of the King's Shropshire Light Infantry, a unit which has never in spite of its distinguished history fought as Marines. The answer is both extraordinary and tragic.

The origin of the 85th Light Infantry dates back to 1759, when Colonel John Crawford raised the Royal Volontiers [*sic*]. This was the first British Regiment of light infantry, and it was raised with the specific role of fighting in the densely wooded colonies of North America.

In spite of distinguished service in the Seven Years' War in Brittany and Portugal, the 85th never reached the American colonies. At the conclusion of the war in 1763, the British government was keen to reduce its defence costs and the 85th was disbanded, only to be re-formed as the Westminster Volunteers in 1779 for service in the American War of Independence.[1]

1. In 1783 the Westminster Volunteers were disbanded, only to be raised again in 1793 as the 85th or Bucks Volunteers. This was its third, but by no means last incarnation. Eventually, they did serve in the United States, capturing two American Colours at the Battle of Bladensburg on 24th August 1814. In 1881 the 85th became the 2nd Battalion King's Shropshire Light Infantry, and is now part of The Rifles

45

The *Ville de Paris*

However, in spite of its original specialist role, the Regiment was still not sent to the woods of Pennsylvania, but was deployed instead to the West Indies. There it was plagued by disease, which resulted in the reduction of the Regiment's strength to just seventy-one men by 1781.

In 1782 the remnants of what was described as 'one of the finest corps that ever left the shores of England' embarked in Jamaica to sail for home on the *Ville de Paris*, a large three-decker French ship of the line. Originally laid down in 1757 as the 90-gun *Impétueux*, her construction was funded by the City of Paris, and in recognition of this beneficence she was renamed *Ville de Paris* in 1762. Completed in 1764, too late to serve in the Seven Years' War, the *Ville de Paris* first saw active service in 1778, when the French sided with the American colonists in their War of Independence.

After the indecisive Battle of Ushant between the French and the British on 27th July 1778, the *Ville de Paris* was up-gunned to 104 cannons. In March 1781 she sailed for the West Indies as the flagship of Admiral François Joseph Paul, Comte de Grasse. Under his command, she fought at the Battle of Fort Royal on 29th April 1781, the Battle of the Chesapeake on 5th September 1781 and the Battle of St. Kitts on 25th-26th January 1782. Finally, at the Battle of the Saintes on 12th April 1782, the *Ville de Paris* was captured by the British fleet under Admiral Sir George Rodney and taken into British service.

The first task assigned to the *Ville de Paris* under the Red Ensign was to transport units of the British Army back to England, including the remnants of the 85th. Tragically, the troop convoy, with the *Ville de Paris*, was struck by a powerful hurricane off the coast of Newfoundland. In accordance with the motto of her namesake city, *Fluctuat nec Mergitur* (Tossed by the waves she does not sink), she turned turtle on 17th September 1782, faring better than the other French prizes, *Glorieux* and *Hector*, the Royal Navy's HMS *Centaur* and HMS *Ramillies*, and most of the merchant fleet, all of which sank below the waves. Altogether around 3,500 lives were lost, including the entire ship's company of the *Ville de Paris*, bar a solitary soldier of the 85th. Legend has it that this man, in spite of the bell's weight, had the presence of mind, the religious zeal or the mindless stupidity to save it from the ship's chapel. The truth is a little less heroic. The bell, which had been damaged, had actually been left in Newfoundland for repair, before the killer hurricane struck. It was later sent on to the Regiment unrepaired.

46

CHAPTER 7

FRENCH REVOLUTIONARY
WARS (1792–1802)

The Spoils of Egypt

A section of the main mast of the French flagship L'Orient (Aboukir Bay, 1798)
The year was 1798. The worst excesses of the French Revolution were over, but the governance of France was still in flux, a situation in which the upwardly-mobile Bonaparte brothers were playing an increasing role. General Napoleon Bonaparte, fresh from his victories in Italy and with ambitions that already stretched well beyond the borders of his nation, had become the leading power broker in the French Republic. Bonaparte, recognising rightly that England posed a serious and long-term threat to his geo-political strategy, persuaded the President of the French Directory, Paul François Jean Nicolas, Vicomte de Barras, that the conquest of Egypt (a province of the degenerate Ottoman Empire) would be an effective first stage in the seizure of Britain's interests in India. The latter would be achieved with the help of Tipu Sultan of Mysore and other Indian Princes. Barras agreed, and on 19th May 1798 Bonaparte, at the head of an Army of 40,000 men, embarked on the French fleet at Toulon for Alexandria.

Rear Admiral Sir Horatio Nelson
by L. F. Abbott

En route, for the loss of only three men, Bonaparte ended the 268-year rule of the Knights Hospitaller (or the Knights of St John) on Malta, seized the strategically valuable harbour of Valetta, and then loaded millions of francs from the Maltese treasury and many treasures from the island's churches onto his flagship, *L'Orient.* Some of Napoleon's Maltese spoils made it back to Paris, where they can be seen today. These include the ceremonial sword and dagger of the sixteenth-century Grand Master of the Knights Hospitaller, Jean de la Valette. Following this looting, Bonaparte managed to evade the Royal Navy and landed unopposed in Egypt on 1st July. By the end of the month he had defeated the ruling Mamelukes at the Battle of the Pyramids on 20th July, and was master of Egypt. Meanwhile, Nelson and the British fleet were scurrying around the Mediterranean in search of the French.

The Destruction of the French ship, *L'Orient*

Finally, on 1st August, Nelson discovered the French fleet was at anchor in Aboukir Bay. By midnight on that day he had destroyed it, and unfortunately almost all the Maltese treasure, which was blown to pieces along with most of the ship's company, when *L'Orient*'s gun-powder magazine spectacularly exploded. After the burning hull sank, all that remained above the briny were seventy survivors, the body parts of the rest of the 1,000-strong crew, and a large section of the ship's main mast, which had landed on the deck of HMS *Swiftsure*.

At the outset of the Battle of the Nile, the morbidly fatalistic Nelson had told his Captains that, depending on the outcome, he would either

garner a peerage or a place in Westminster Abbey. It is probable that Captain Ben Hallowell, one of Nelson's 'Band of Brothers' and Captain of HMS *Swiftsure*, which was closely engaged with *L'Orient* during the battle and played a major role in her destruction, remembered this remark. In any event, he had his ship's carpenter make a coffin from part of the timber of *L'Orient*'s mast, and sent it to the Admiral with a somewhat tongue-in-cheek letter that read:

The Battle of the Nile, 1st–2nd August 1798

> Sir,
> I have taken the liberty of presenting you a coffin made from the main mast of *L'Orient*, that when you have finished your military career in this world you may be buried in one of your trophies. But that that period may be far distant is the earnest wish of your sincere friend,
> Benjamin Hallowell

The newly ennobled Baron Nelson of the Nile was so pleased with the funerary spoil of war that he propped it against the wall of his cabin, behind the chair in which he customarily had dinner. It was indicative of Nelson's sense of humour, so famously displayed at the Battle of Copenhagen three years later, when he ignored a signal to discontinue action by putting his telescope to his blind eye. It is known that he took the coffin to his next command, and that from 1801 it was put on display at Nelson's country house, Merton Place. It later reappeared, following Nelson's death in 1805, together with the French musket ball (*see* p.69) that propelled him into it.

As a *post script* to this tale, the 4-foot-long mast head of the mast in which Nelson rests, complete with an iron sheave to take the signal halyard and a brass lightening conductor, was recovered from the sea and presented to Nelson. At some point following his death, it passed into the ownership of the Lords Commissioners of the Admiralty, who lent it to the Royal United Services Institution Museum. It is now on display at the National Maritime Museum, Greenwich.

The Rosetta Stone (Rosetta, 1799 & Alexandria, 1801)

In an armoured-glass display case in the British Museum in London is a large chunk of granodiorite, an igneous rock similar to granite. Incised with script in three languages and a now barely visible painted inscription, 'Captured in Egypt by the British Army in 1801', the Rosetta Stone is a spoil of war originally unearthed from the sands of Egypt in 1799, during the French occupation. Described as 'the most famous piece of rock in the world', this fragment of an ancient Egyptian *stele* was the key that unlocked the meaning of hieroglyphs, the written language of the Pharaohs.

General Napoleon Bonaparte's presence in Egypt was initially successful. Having landed his Army of the East and a vast team of French scientists in Alexandria, established a secure base, and defeated the governing Mamelukes, thereafter he imposed French control on the Nile delta. Although any hope he may have had of withdrawing his army from Egypt at some point in the future was dashed, once Nelson had destroyed the French fleet.

Almost exactly a year later, French soldiers under the command of Colonel d'Hautpoul were strengthening the defences of Fort Julien, two miles north-east of the Egyptian port city of Rosetta, when Lieutenant Pierre-François Bouchard unearthed a slab with inscriptions on one side. It was a *stele* dating from 196 BC in the reign of Ptolemy V. Bouchard was an engineer, an academic and a member of the Commission of Arts & Sciences. He immediately showed the stone to Michel-Ange Lancret, a member of Bonaparte's Institut d'Égypte, and the chief engineer-scientist assigned to the Rosetta region. When both of them translated the final Greek sentence of the

The Rosetta Stone

inscription, which stated that the other scripts were native words with the same meaning, they realised that the stone was important. Lancret wrote immediately to the Institut's headquarters in Cairo, and Bouchard was given the task of transporting the stone to the Egyptian capital for examination by the French scholars. They correctly determined that the three inscriptions – the upper text in Ancient Egyptian hieroglyphs, the middle portion in Demotic script, and the lowest in Ancient Greek – were indeed versions of the same text, and would therefore provide the first key to the translation of Egyptian hieroglyphs. News of the discovery and its implications spread quickly throughout Europe, and excited considerable scientific and popular interest.

Meanwhile, military and naval matters had not been going entirely General Bonaparte's way. His mirage of linking up with Tipu Sultan and driving the British out of India was rapidly evaporating in the Egyptian desert, thanks to a major revolt in Cairo in October 1798. Then in 1799, after commencing work on the Canal of the Pharaohs (later known as the Suez Canal), Bonaparte led an ultimately unsuccessful campaign in Syria against Ottoman forces, culminating in a virulent outbreak of plague amongst his troops. Back in Egypt, all was not well either and it took the land Battle of Aboukir on 25th July 1799 for General Bonaparte to defeat the Ottomans and reassert French control there.

In the meantime, the political and military situation in France was also deteriorating. At the urging of his brother Lucien, Bonaparte slipped out of Alexandria on 23rd August, leaving the French Army of the East under the command of General Jean-Baptiste Kléber. The future Emperor reached Paris in October, and by 9th November he was First Consul and the effective dictator of France. Although he had taken Ottoman flags captured at Aboukir with him, Bonaparte had left his Army of the East and the Rosetta Stone in Egypt.

In January 1800 Kléber, by then cut off from France and under armed threat from the British and the Ottomans, negotiated a peace treaty with his enemies, which set the terms for a French withdrawal from Egypt. In delight, the French scientists packed their bags and the Rosetta Stone, and set off for Alexandria. Delayed by another outbreak of plague, which left them stranded for a month on an island in the middle of the Nile, they eventually embarked on a ship for France, only to be told that the terms of the peace treaty had been overturned. The disgruntled, home-sick *savants* returned to Cairo in April, leaving the Rosetta Stone in storage in Alexandria. In March 1801, British and Ottoman forces landed in Egypt.

General Napoleon Bonaparte in Egypt, by Jean-Léon Gérôme

The Assassination of General
Jean-Baptiste Kléber

By April they had seized the Nile Delta, and by August the French occupation of Egypt was at an end. It was, however, just the beginning of a dispute over the possession of the key to the hieroglyphs.

Back in June 1800 General Kléber had been assassinated by an Arab Syrian in Cairo. His successor, General Jacques-François Menou, drafted a surrender agreement in August 1801, which stipulated in Article 16 that the departing French scientists could take with them 'all the monuments of art and antiquity collected by them in Egypt'. This did not specifically name, but clearly included, the Rosetta Stone. The British commander, Lieutenant General Sir John Hely-Hutchinson, rejected Article 16, stating that whilst the French could remove whatever they had brought with them to Egypt, the items that had been collected 'by the French Republic shall be considered as public property, and subject to the disposal of the Generals of the combined Army' of British and Ottoman forces. An increasingly vitriolic correspondence between the two military leaders then commenced, in which Menou claimed that everything except two sarcophagi had been collected at private expense and therefore belonged to the individuals concerned, and that the Rosetta Stone belonged to him personally.

Hely-Hutchinson was having none of this and curtly informed Menou in writing on 5th September that, 'In all the countries where the French have waged war, they have seized everything that seemed to them suitable to take. Since the fate of arms has decided against you … I demand all these objects and you may be sure that I shall not let a single part of them leave for France.'

In further correspondence, which became progressively more acrimonious, Menou continued to claim that as he had found it, which of course he had not, the Rosetta Stone was his personal property, not that of the French Republic. He also threatened that he would inform the whole of Europe that his property had in effect been stolen from him 'at the command of Monsieur the English General'. When Hely-Hutchinson repeated his demands, two of the increasingly hysterical French scientists threatened to destroy everything in their possession and thereby brand the English General not only as a thief, but also as a cultural vandal.

Eventually, after a further series of threatening tantrums by the French and a steely determination by the British not to give in to these Gallic histrionics, a compromise was reached. The French scholars were permitted to relocate to France (aboard a British ship), along with their scientific notes and botanical samples, but *not* with any antiquities. To

General Jacques-François
Menou

make sure of this, Hely-Hutchinson ordered Colonel Turner of the 3rd (later Scots) Guards, with the support of a detachment of artillerymen, to remove the Rosetta Stone from General Menou's residence in Alexandria and to take personal charge of it. This Turner did, conveying it under guard back to London some three months later, where he presented it to King George III, who had the *stele* lodged with the Society of Antiquaries and later promoted Turner to General officer rank. It was only at the end of 1802 that the King officially presented the Rosetta Stone to the British Museum 'as a gift', where despite occasional harrumphing from the French, it remains to the present day.

General John Hely-Hutchinson, 2nd Earl of Donoughmore

Colours of the French 2nd & 3rd Battalions of the 19th Demi-Brigade of Infantry of the Line (Egypt 1801)

Because Colours are made of silk, cotton, canvas and gold wire, they are eminently perishable, which is why despite their military significance so few have survived. These losses include the Colours of the French 19th Demi-Brigade, allegedly captured by the British in Egypt in 1801. Given the importance of captured Colours, it is surprising that, in the days before conservation became the watch-word, these iconic trophies of victory were usually displayed in damp, moth-infested buildings, where no attempt was made to preserve them. Up until the early-nineteenth century, the British national depositories for captured Colours were St Paul's Cathedral and the Chapel Royal at St James's Palace. As the Reverend Sydney Smith, a wit, writer and a Canon of St Paul's Cathedral, noted:

> As Damp destroys Cloth, and Religion has little to do with War, the worst depository for Flags of Triumph is a Church. Accordingly, the Trophies of the Duke of Marlborough were (in the great repairs of St Paul's in 1820) found to be utterly perished – not a rag remained.

His colleague, the Reverend George Robert Gleig, a former soldier and Chaplain of the Royal Hospital Chelsea from 1834 to 1846, added: '… the staffs [of these captured Colours] were used by the vergers as poles wherewith to hunt the rats and other vermin out of the vestry-rooms'.

This deplorable situation was improved in 1829, when King George IV presented twelve Colours to the Royal Hospital Chelsea. These trophies

Chapel at the Royal Hospital
Chelsea

had been taken from 'the Americans, Algerines [*sic*], Genoese and French during the last [Napoleonic] war'. They were hung on the side walls of the Chapel, a building at the heart of the hospital founded by King Charles II in 1682 for old and disabled soldiers. In July 1835, King William IV commanded that the captured Colours held at St Paul's Cathedral and East India House also be removed to the Royal Hospital, together with '13 Eagles and 22 Colours captured from different nations', which came from the Chapel Royal at St James's Palace. During Queen Victoria's reign, this national collection was further enhanced with trophies taken from the Russians, Chinese and Soudanese, bringing the total to 126.

Writing in 1837, the Reverend Gleig described the collection in the Royal Hospital's Chapel:

> I allude to the profusion of banners, richer, more varied, and grouped with even purer taste, than those which ornament the walls of the dining-hall. In the chapel are deposited the standards of Tippoo Saib [*sic*], the whole of the eagles, thirteen in number, that were wrested from Napoleon's legions, flags from the Americans, from the French, from the Prussians, from the Spaniards, from the Rajah of Bhurtpore, from the king of Ava, from every power in short, with which, in every quarter of the world, during the last half-century, England has been at war. I cannot pretend to describe the effect produced by the display of these banners, as they wave over the heads of the very men whose personal exertions contributed to acquire them; nor account for the half triumphant, half mournful glance, which from time to time the veterans turn towards them.

In 1947, fourteen of the Colours were returned to the Regiments that had captured them. Of the remainder, after ninety years of hanging unprotected from the ravages of light, very few of the 126 captured Colours at the Royal Hospital were still identifiable. Were it not for the work of Captain John Ford, a Captain of Invalids at the hospital from 1840 to 1856, the Royal Hospital's former collection would now be unknown. Fortunately, Captain Ford, a talented draughtsman and a retired officer, took it upon himself to record the designs of all the captured Colours hanging in the Great Hall and the Chapel. As he did not have the benefit of scaffolding, the Captain used a 'spyglass' to discern the designs high above his head.

In 1860, many years after Ford had completed his labour of love, Prince Edward of Saxe-Weimar, a naturalised English soldier who eventually rose to the rank of Field Marshal, was carrying out research into two

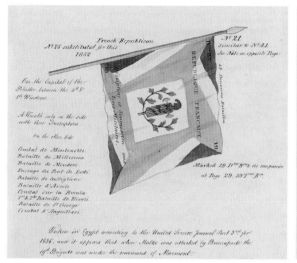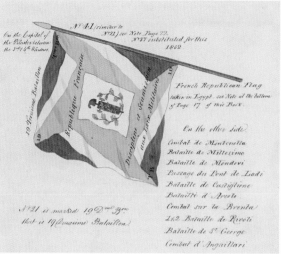

French Colours of 2nd & 3rd Battallions of the 19th Demi-Brigade © *Royal Hospital Chelsea*

Hessian Colours held at the Royal Hospital, and was pointed in the direction of the home of Captain Ford, who although he had retired in 1856, still lived on the premises. Prince Edward recorded that he found the Captain, 'in bed and almost speechless. I apologised for my intrusion, but the old man assured me that it was one of the happiest days of his life, inasmuch as the labour of many years in compiling the manuscript Flagbook [*sic*] was not in vain.'

Prince Edward mentioned this meeting to Prince Albert, Queen Victoria's consort, who said that he would endeavour to procure the manuscript after the death of the old officer. He didn't have to wait long, as Captain Ford faded away only a few weeks later. However, before he could acquire the book, Prince Albert himself died. Notwithstanding the tragic loss of her husband, Queen Victoria bought Captain Ford's *Flag Book* for the Library at Windsor Castle, but had the forethought to present the Royal Hospital with an autographed copy.

Among the Colours lodged in the Chapel of the Royal Hospital from the late-1820s were two captured from the French Revolutionary Army. The illustrations of these in Captain Ford's *Flag Book* – No 21 (2nd Battalion) and 41 (3rd Battalion) – also list the ten battle honours of the 19th Demi-Brigade, which were identical on both Colours. These comprised all the most important victories of the Italian Campaign of 1796–97, including the iconic engagement at Pont de Lodi, which confirmed Bonaparte's belief in his military infallibility. In addition to listing the Battalion's battle honours, Captain Ford annotated his drawings with the comment that the 19th Demi-Brigade was commanded by General August de Marmont. A personal friend of Bonaparte, Marmont had accompanied him to Egypt, was promoted to *General de Brigade* whilst there,[1] and left Egypt with Bonaparte on 23rd August 1799.

Captain Ford asserted in his *Flag Book* that these two Colours had been captured from the French 'in Egypt'. Sadly, for Ford's otherwise unblemished reputation for accuracy, the British did not land in Egypt until March 1801, eighteen months after General de Marmont had left to return to France. Furthermore, French military records show that the 1st and 2nd Battalions of the 19th Demi-Brigade were never in Egypt. In fact, they were left in Malta as part of the garrison, following the French capture of the island in 1798, a duty possibly designated by Bonaparte and de Marmont to give the units the break from battle they so richly deserved after the Italian campaign.

The 1st and 2nd Battalions remained in Malta until September 1800, when the French garrison capitulated to the British. The surrender came at the end of a two-year siege and naval blockade, during which the gallant 19th Demi-Brigade and their colleagues had been forced by starvation to eat all the horses, mules, dogs, cats and rats in Valletta. The terms of the surrender were absolute, with the island, all its military supplies, and a number of French warships being handed to the British, although they magnanimously granted the French commander, General Henri-Claude Belgrand de Vaubois, the 'honours of war', which would have included the rights of the 1st and 2nd Battalions to retain their Colours. In any event, General Belgrand de Vaubois, and those of his men who had not succumbed to starvation, were swiftly repatriated to Marseilles.

So, it would seem impossible, from the known whereabouts of the 2nd Battalion, that their Colour could have been captured in Egypt, as Captain Ford recorded. The mystery behind Colour 41 of the 3rd Battalion is even more intriguing. If this was captured by the British, it must have been acquired either during the siege of Fort Julien near Rosetta in March-April 1801, or at the siege of Cairo, which surrendered in July 1801, or at the final capitulation of the French at Alexandria in August 1801. If it could ever be proved that either or both of these French Colours were captured at Fort Julien, it would give the preceding account on the acquisition of the Rosetta Stone an incredibly neat symmetry, particularly as the commander of the engineers at the fort was the newly-promoted Captain Pierre François Bouchard, now returned to command on the site of his famous discovery (*see* p.50).

1. *General de Brigade* is the French equivalent of Brigadier or Brigadier General in the British Army; the rank of *Brigadier* in the French Army equates to Corporal in the British Army. General Officer ranks in the British Army seem to be illogical in terms of ascending seniority. This is because the ranks no longer conform to their logical original form (shown in square brackets) which were, in ascending order: [Corporal] General, [Sergeant] Major General, Lieutenant General and [Captain] General

The Turkish Gun (Siege of Alexandria, 1801)

Whilst questions remain concerning the capture of the Colours of the 19th Demi-Brigade, no such doubts exist about the ornate cannon that sits proudly to one side of the entrance to the Headquarters of the Household Division at Horse Guards. This fearsome and ancient weapon, with its abnormally long barrel, was a well-travelled piece of ordnance even before it came to rest on Horse Guards Parade in London in 1802.

In addition to extensive oriental decorations and embellishments, a Turkish inscription is cast into the barrel, which reads:

> The Solomon of the age the Great Sultan Commander of the dragon guns. When they breathe roaring like thunder May the enemy's forts be razed to the ground. Year of Hegira 931

A plaque establishes that the fifty-two-pound gun was made in 1524 by Murad, son of Abdullah the Chief Gunner, for the Ottoman Sultan Suleiman I, better known as Suleiman the Magnificent. There is some speculation that it may have been deployed at the Battle of Mohács in 1526, given its size and importance. During this action, the Ottoman forces annihilated a force of Hungarians and Serbians, who were the last military barricade protecting the approach to the gates of Vienna and the Habsburg Empire.

Turkish Gun

Turkish Gun (detail)

However, by 1797 the gun was certainly part of the Ottoman defences at Alexandria in Egypt, and a year later was seized there by the French when they occupied the port. Unsurprisingly, given the ongoing threat from the Royal Navy, the French left Murad's masterpiece on its wooden gun-carriage on the fortifications. There it remained until September 1801, when General Menou, commander of Bonaparte's Army of the East, conceded defeat to an Anglo-Ottoman force. The British units included the 3rd Guards, the Regiment whose Colonel later removed the Rosetta Stone from General Menou (*see* p.52); and it was Turner's men who removed Murad's cannon, minus its carriage, from the fortifications.

By 1802 the gun barrel was back in England and installed on Horse Guards Parade, mounted on a magnificent new cast-iron gun-carriage made somewhat prosaically, given the barrel's origins, by Messrs J & E Hall of Dartford in Kent [2]. There is nothing prosaic, however, about the design of the gun-carriage on which Murad's barrel lies. Supported on cast-iron wheels decorated in the Imperial Roman-style then popular, with massive lions' head hub caps, the gun carriage includes a breach support of a large sphynx; this was the same motif that was added to the 3rd Guards' regimental Colour with the battle honour 'Egypt' in 1801. The cheeks below the trunnions on either side are embellished with the Royal Coat of Arms, the figure of Britannia ruling the waves with a lion at her feet, a gaping crocodile and a 'trophy' of arms. Significantly, lest there be any doubt as to the cannon's capture by the tartan army, this fact is emphatically confirmed by the additional presence on the gun carriage of two large Stars of the Order of the Thistle, the regimental badge of the 3rd (later Scots) Guards.

2. J & E Hall, established in Dartford in 1785, was one of the most important industrial companies in England, specialising in heavy foundry-based engineering

FOURTH ANGLO-MYSORE WAR (1798–1799)

Riches from the Tiger's Lair

Despite Clive of India's depredations in the middle of the eighteenth century (*see* p.29), the East India Company contrived to be one of the most successful acquirers of spoils of war in the years up to 1800. Their ongoing conflicts with the native rulers of India and their French allies, now known as the Anglo-Mysore Wars, broke out repeatedly during the last thirty years of the eighteenth century. They finally culminated in the defeat of Tipu Sultan, a committed Francophile and the ruler of the large southern Indian state of Mysore.

Tipu Sultan was the eldest son of Hyder Ali, an illiterate Muslim soldier, who by 1761 had clawed his way onto the previously Hindu throne of Mysore. Determined to give his son a start in life that would fit him to rule Mysore, Tipu was afforded the best possible education, and from the age of seventeen he was entrusted by his father with important diplomatic

Tipu Sultan

The Surrender of Tipu Sultan's Sons by Robert Home

59

and military missions. Following Ali's sudden death from cancer in 1782, the twenty-two-year-old Tipu pounced on the throne of Mysore, from where he launched a new programme of aggressive military campaigning. His father had already fought against the East India Company and several neighbouring rulers who were allied with the British. In the Second (1780–1784), Third (1790–1792) and Fourth (1798–1799) Anglo-Mysore Wars, his son continued this campaign, by fighting the forces of Britain's East India Company with his French-trained Army.

Needless to say, the British were not pleased by their early setbacks, whilst Tipu, a rather dumpy little man who was always smothered in jewels, was hailed by his subjects and allies as the 'Tiger of Mysore'. The reason for this soubriquet, and Tipu's obsession with tiger imagery, may owe something to a probably-apocryphal story that he had killed a man-eating tiger with a knife when the animal leapt on him, while he was sauntering through a Mysorian forest with a French friend. True or not, Tipu famously declared that 'in this world I would rather live two days like a tiger, than two hundred years like a sheep'.

Death of Tipu Sultan

To underline this statement, he installed six of the beasts in a pit at his Seringapatam palace, where it was widely believed that they were fed on his captured enemies. Tipu also adopted the tiger as his badge and had it featured prominently on all his regalia, in his palaces and on his weaponry; he also kept a 'Dream Book', in which he detailed his preoccupation with tigers and his association of the cult animal with the extermination of non-Muslims. In short, Tipu saw himself as a royal tiger, created by God to devour his enemies, and particularly the British. In order to hammer home the point, he had the walls of the houses in Seringapatam painted with scenes of tigers mauling Europeans.

Cannons & a mortar (Seringapatam, 1799)

Tiger cannons outside the Officers Mess at RMA Sandhurst

Tipu was finally defeated and killed on 4th May 1799 at the siege of Seringapatam. The assault against him was planned by the Governor General of India, Richard Wellesley, 2nd Earl of Mornington (shortly to become Marquess Wellesley). He was assisted by the Governor of Madras, Edward Clive, 2nd Baron Clive (eldest son of 'Clive of India'). When the Nizam of Hyderabad, an ally of the British, sent a contingent of infantry, cavalry, and thirty-six guns, Colonel Hon Arthur Wellesley (Mornington's younger brother and the future Duke of Wellington) was appointed as his senior adviser.

Following the battle, Tipu's palace was found to contain innumerable tiger-embellished or tiger-themed treasures, many of exquisite workmanship, mounted with gold or silver, and beautifully inlaid and embellished with tigers' heads and stripes. Inevitably, quite a few of these treasures and trinkets found their way into British knapsacks. Less easily transportable were the 927 cannon which the British captured, all of which were stylised as tigers or were tiger-themed.

A number of these tiger cannon found their way back to England. Two flank the doorway to the Officers Mess at the Royal Military Academy Sandhurst (a building designed by the author's great-grandfather, Harry Bell Measures CBE LVO). Until the Royal Artillery Museum closed a few years ago, an extraordinarily grotesque four-pound mortar, fashioned as a seated tiger, could be seen there.[1] At Powis Castle, Lord Clive's country seat in Wales, there are two cannons with tiger-head muzzles which joined the Indian loot acquired by his father.

Tipu's Ring (Seringapatam, 1799)

Unlike some rulers, Tipu believed in leading from the front. During the Siege of Seringapatam he took his place in the firing line, where assisted by a team of loaders he blazed away with the best of his troops. However, as the British stormed the ramparts, Tipu was wounded. His men tried to get him back to the palace in a litter, but they were not fast enough. The stricken Tiger was overtaken by British soldiers, who killed him and pocketed all the jewellery he was wearing. Later in the day, Tipu's corpse was found by Arthur Wellesley, under a pile of bodies next to a gateway. The state of the body was described by an eyewitness, Major Allan:

> His dress consisted of a jacket of fine white linen, loose drawers of flowered chintz, with a crimson cloth of silk and cotton round his waist; a handsome pouch with a red and green silk belt hung across his shoulder; his head was uncovered, his turban being lost in the confusion of his fall; he had an amulet on his arm, but no ornament whatever.

Like Tipu, Colonel Arthur Wellesley had publicly expressed his distaste for looting, which he considered to be little better than theft. When put in command at Seringapatam the day after the siege, he ordered four soldiers to be hanged and others flogged for plundering, raping, and indiscriminately killing the fort's inhabitants. Nevertheless, he himself acquired a heavy gold ring with the name of the Hindu God Rama in raised Devenagri script. Perhaps because it was Wellesley who

1. The Royal Artillery Museum closed in 2016 and all its exhibits are currently in store, with no public access. The author is grateful to the Chairman of the Friends of the Royal Artillery Collection for allowing access to the stored items, in order that this extraordinary spoil of war could be photographed for this book by Paul Cattermole

Tipu's tiger mortar. Image courtesy of © *Paul Cattermole on behalf of the Friends of the Royal Artillery Collections & with the permission of the Trustees of the Royal Artillery Historical Trust*

Tiger cannon, Powis Castle

Lord Fitzroy Somerset (later 1st Baron Raglan) by William Haines 46

found Tipu's body and checked his pulse for life, this ring was thought to have been taken from the late ruler's bloody corpse, but given the eyewitness account above and the fact that Tipu was a Muslim, this has since been discounted. It seems more likely that the ring was taken from Tipu's collections in the palace.

Wellesley, whose views on spoils of war were to be comprehensively displayed, thirteen years later, following the Battle of Vitoria (*see* p.98), gave the ring to his niece, Emily Wellesley-Pole, who in turn gave it to her husband, Lord FitzRoy Somerset, whose name was later engraved on the inside of the ring. Somerset was Wellington's ADC at Waterloo and was later to gain immortality as the 1st Baron Raglan, the inept commander of the British Army in the Crimea. Later still, in 1895, Tipu's ring was loaned to the Royal United Service Institution by the 3rd Baron Raglan until it was removed in 1952 by the 4th Baron. Eventually, after a disputed then aborted sale of Raglan family property in 2012, Tipu's ring was offered for sale in 2014 at Christie's, where it sold to an un-named buyer (later revealed to be the Indian industrialist, Vijay Mallya) for £140,500, against a pre-sale estimate of £10–15,000.

Tipu's Bedroom Sword (Seringapatam, 1799)

Not for the first time, such were the wars of the eighteenth and nineteenth centuries, the original acquirer of Tipu's bedroom sword had a direct connection with other spoils of war covered in this book. Major General David Baird led the storming party over the walls of Seringapatam and commanded the Anglo-Indian forces at the Siege of Alexandria in 1801.

Baird was later described by the then Duke of Wellington as a 'gallant, hard-headed, lion-hearted officer'. His detractors thought otherwise and described him as a 'bloody old bad-tempered Scotchman'. The latter verdict may be due to the fact that Baird had been taken prisoner by Tipu's father in 1780, during the Second Anglo-Mysore War, and remained in captivity, bound in chains, for four years. Mysorian dungeons were probably not conducive to good humour, and to make matters worse Baird had a bullet lodged in him which wasn't removed until his release. In support of his critics, Baird's mother, on hearing that her son and other prisoners were in fetters, is said to have remarked: 'God help the *chiel* [chap or bloke] chained to our Davie'.

The sword, one of the six known to have belonged to Tipu, is forty-two inches in length. The straight blade has a double-edged point and is inlaid in gold with the orb and parasol mark of a Mughal-era swordsmith; the hilt has Arabic inscriptions in praise of Allah; the back of the blade bears the Perso-Arabic inscription: 'Sword of the Ruler'; and the scabbard is of green velvet-covered wood, embellished with silver-gilt mounts part-decorated with tiger stripes. Thanks to a later inscription on the blade, the provenance of this sword is not in any doubt. It reads:

> The Sword of Tippoo Sultan found in the bed chamber after Seringapatam was taken by storm on 4th May 1799 and presented by the army to General Baird through their commander Major General Harris as a token of their high opinion and his courage and conduct in the assault which he commanded and in which Tippoo Sultan was slain.

Tipu's bedroom sword and a number of other Baird treasures were for many years on display at the National War Museum of Scotland in Edinburgh, before being sold in 2003 by the dour Scotchman's descendants, who doubtless subscribed to the North British proverb that 'mony a mickle maks a muckle'. It was bought by Vijay Mallya for £175,000. By 2012, press reports quoted him as saying that he had 'given away' Tipu's sword, because his family said it was bringing him bad luck. However, in April 2015, he sold the sword at Sotheby's for £505,250. Its present whereabouts are unknown.

Tipu's Tiger (Seringapatam, 1799)

Arthur's brother, Richard, Lord Mornington, also acquired and gave away a souvenir from Tipu's palace. His was an eighteenth-century semi-automaton, in the form of a carved and painted wooden model of a tiger in the act of savaging a near life-size English soldier. Said to be the Anglophobic Tipu's favourite toy, the clockwork mechanism inside the casing moves the victim's hand, whilst he emits wails of despair and the tiger grunts with satisfaction. In addition, and somewhat curiously, a flap on the side of the tiger folds down to reveal the keyboard of a small pipe organ with eighteen notes, presumably so that Handel's *Dead March* from *Saul* could be played as the hated Englishman succumbed to the ravening beast.

Tipu's mechanical Tiger

The Victoria & Albert Museum's scholars believe that Tipu's tiger toy may have been made in the wake of a tragedy in 1792, when the eldest son of General Sir Hector Munro, who had inflicted a crushing defeat on

Tipu and his father in the Second Mysore War, was out hunting on an island near Calcutta. According to newspaper reports, the young man was carried off by 'an immense royal tiger ... 4.5 feet high and nine long', sustaining injuries from which he did not recover. In England the 'Death of Munro' was memorialised in clay by the Staffordshire potteries. In Mysore, Tipu may have celebrated it by commissioning the oversized toy.

Six years later, and faced with six of the real things in a pit in the palace grounds, Lord Mornington ordered the enemy-fed tigers to be shot, but sent the toy tiger to London, with the intention that it be exhibited at the Tower of London. It never got there. Instead, it was kept by the Governors of the East India Company and from 1808 it was put on display in their museum at East India House in Leadenhall Street. There it became one of the museum's most popular exhibits, confirming the view that the British public has a pronounced taste for the macabre. The Indian Museum, as it became known, moved several times before parts of the collection, including Tipu's Tiger, were transferred to the South Kensington Museum, later renamed the Victoria & Albert Museum, where it can be seen to the present day.

Tipu's Throne (Seringapatam, 1799)

Napoleon, in one of his more republican moods, famously declared that a throne was nothing but a wooden bench covered in velvet. He had obviously never seen Tipu Sultan's, which was the most magnificent of all the spoils seized by the British following the fall of Seringapatam. A confection of gold, silver and precious stones, and covered in the inevitable tiger symbology, Tipu's throne was in fact a large elevated and canopied platform, upon which the Tiger never actually sat. This was because he had been waiting for the most auspicious day on which to ascend his new throne, and – in emulation of the great Mughal Emperor Akbar – he wanted to be accompanied by a new royal bride. Unfortunately for Tipu, the British rudely intervened before the omens were right or a suitable Princess was available for the great occasion.

Tipu Sultan's Throne

After the fall of Seringapatam, the throne was seized by the customary Prize Committee, and to the dismay of later scholars, collectors and dealers in Indian art, it was broken up. Fortunately, before this happened, it was sketched by Thomas Marriot, ADC to the Commander-in-Chief. Allowing for certain artistic inaccuracies of scale and proportion, his drawing and a contemporary eyewitness account, published in the *Asiatic Annual Register* of 1800, vividly describes the throne before it was dismantled:

The support was a wooden tiger as life, covered with gold in the attitude of standing; his head [and] forelegs appeared [at] the front and under the throne, which was placed across his back. It was composed of an octagonal frame, eight feet by five, surrounded by a low railing on which were ten small tiger heads made of gold, beautifully inlaid with precious stones; the ascent to the throne was by small silver steps on each side. From the centre of the back part, opposite the large tiger's head, a gilded iron pillar rose, seven feet high, surrounded by a canopy superbly decorated with a fringe of pearls. The whole was made of wood, and covered with [a] thin sheet of purest gold, richly illuminated with tiger stripes and Arabic verses. The huma [bird] was placed on the top of the canopy, and fluttered over the Sultan's head.

Tiger head from Tipu's throne.
Royal Collection Trust © Her Majesty Queen Elizabeth II 2018

Following the break-up of this extraordinary artefact, its components were either sold off by the Prize Committee to defray the expenses of the war or held by the East India Company. Initially, the latter were put on display at East India House, where they inspired the following cautionary verse published in the *Scots Magazine*:

Sic transit gloria mundi
(Stanzas on viewing the ornaments of Tippoo Sultaun's
Throne in the Treasury at India House)

Ah! What avails the golden ore?
The ruby's or the di'mond's flame
When Heav'n's high hand protects no more
And grandeur is an empty name?

The Huma bird from the top of the canopy was acquired by the Marquess Wellesley for the East India Company, who presented it to King George III in 1800. The large tiger's head, complete with rock-crystal fangs and an articulated tongue, was presented to King William IV by the East India Company in 1831, at the prompting of the Duke of Wellington. Both are now on public display at Windsor Castle.

Bird finial from Tipu's throne.
Royal Collection Trust ©Her Majesty Queen Elizabeth II 2018

For the rest, the existence of only four – or possibly five – of the three-inch-high, gem-encrusted tiger head finials can be confirmed. The first finial was acquired by Surgeon Major Pulteney Mein of the 74th (Highland) Regiment of Foot, either by allocation or at the Prize Auction. Mein had witnessed the demolition, writing later: 'This gorgeous throne was barbarously knocked to pieces with a sledgehammer'. His tiger's head was sold at Sotheby's in 1973 and then offered for sale by a London antique dealer in 1974, but has since disappeared from view and its current whereabouts are unknown.

The second tiger head, known as the Hope-Wallace finial, lay for years in Featherstone Castle, Northumberland, the seat of Thomas Wallace, 1st Baron Wallace of Knaresdale, an MP who never went to India but was on the Board of Control of the East India Company from 1807. It was presumably in this role that he acquired the finial. Sometime later, the tiger's head was placed in a bank vault, until it was discovered by Bonham's Islamic Department on a routine valuation. It was bought at the auction house in 2009 by the Qatari Al Thani Collection for £389,600.

The third known finial was also sold at Bonham's, eighteen months later, by an anonymous Canadian owner, whose forebear was Lieutenant General Sir Thomas Bowser, a long-serving officer in the East India Company's army. Bowser, like General Baird, was held for four years by Tipu's father; he may even have been chained next to the disagreeable General. In any event, he died in 1833 as a direct result of the effects of being manacled for all that time, but not before he had had his revenge on Tipu at Seringapatam. This third finial sold for £434,400.

The fourth finial was given to Lady Henrietta (*née* Herbert), wife of the 2nd Baron Clive, by Lord Mornington, and is on display at Powis Castle. The possible fifth tiger head is reputedly held in an anonymous private Cornish collection. The missing five (or possibly six) finials may also still exist, probably – given the number of Scotsmen at the fall of Seringapatam – in attics north of the border.

Tipu's throne detail – Tiger's head

Tipu's Tent (Seringapatam, 1799)

Finally, and by no means the least of Tipu's treasures from Seringapatam, is his printed cotton chintz tent. Acquired by the 2nd Baron Clive, it is also on view at Powis Castle.

Based on contemporary images and records, scholars believe that this tent may actually be the one in which Lord Cornwallis, then Governor General of India, and his entourage were formally received by Tipu's sons on 26th February 1792, following the Treaty of Seringapatam which ended the Third Anglo-Mysore War. This treaty stipulated that Tipu was required to surrender large tracts of his territory to the British East India Company, and that two of his eleven boys were to be held as hostages until Tipu had paid a significant war indemnity to the British to cover the costs of the war against him.

The Surrender of Tipu's sons
by Henry Singleton

The young Princes were subsequently treated well, in marked contrast to their grandfather's treatment of Generals Baird and Bowser. The affecting scene of their handover to the British was painted by several artists of the day, including Johann Zoffany, although only a watercolour by Thomas Marriott illustrates the transfer taking place outside a *cannaut* or canvas awning, with a distinctive patterned border. However, in support of the view that this is the same tent, a military observer at the time, Major Dirom, noted that it was scalloped at the top, with richly ornamented borders, and referred to it as 'the green cannaut or tent used by the Sultaun [*sic*] in the field, of which we had so often traced the marks during the war.' Dirom also described the scene of the handover:

> Lord Cornwallis, attended by his staff, and some of the principal officers of the army, met the Princes at the door of his large tent as they dismounted from the elephants; and, after embracing them, led them in, one in each hand, to the tent; the eldest, Abdul Kalick, was about ten, the youngest, Mooza-ud-Deen, about eight years of age. When they were seated on each side of Lord Cornwallis, Gullam Ally, the head vakeel, addressed his Lordship as follows: 'These children were this morning the sons of the Sultan my master; their situation is now changed, and they must look up to your Lordship as their father'.
>
> Lord Cornwallis, who had received the boys as if they had been his own sons, anxiously assured the vakeel and the young Princes themselves, that every attention possible would be shewn to them, and the greatest care taken

of their persons. Their little faces brightened up; the scene became highly interesting; and not only their attendants, but all the spectators were delighted to see that any fears they might have harboured were removed, and that they would soon be reconciled to their change of situation, and to their new friends. The Princes were dressed in long white muslin gowns, and red turbans. They had several rows of large pearls round their necks, from which was suspended an ornament consisting of a ruby and an emerald of considerable size, surrounded by large brilliants; and in their turbans, each had a sprig of rich pearls. Bred up from their infancy with infinite care, and instructed in their manners to imitate the reserve and politeness of age, it astonished all present to see the correctness and propriety of their conduct.

That must have been very reassuring to Lord Cornwallis, given the brutality of their grandfather and the relentless Anglophobia of their father. Good manners were not, however, enough to ensure their elder brother's succession to the throne on the death of Tipu Sultan in 1799. Instead, the British installed the four-year-old Maharaja Krishnaraja Wadiyar III, the infant grandson of the Hindu ruler of Mysore dethroned by Hyder Ali Khan back in 1761. In the meantime, Tipu's family was sent to permanent exile in Calcutta, where the two boys taken hostage by the British were reunited with their relatives.

Noor Inayat Khan GC

No descendants of Hyder Ali were ever again to grace the throne of Mysore, but one in particular was to give exemplary and gallant service to the British Crown, 145 years after Tipu's death. Noor Inayat Khan GC, a descendant of one of Tipu's uncles, was a British Special Operations Executive agent in France during the Second World War. Betrayed in 1943, this gentle and unworldly woman 'fought like a tiger' when the Germans tried to capture her. Interrogated but apparently not tortured, Noor Inayat Khan twice attempted to escape and was then imprisoned at Pforzheim in Germany, in solitary confinement and shackled at her hands and feet. After ten months, she was sent by the Germans to Dachau concentration camp, a hell-hole that made the dungeons of Seringapatam look like the Ritz Hotel. There she was shot in the back of the neck on 13th September 1944. Hyder Ali Khan and Tipu Sultan, both of whom revered courage, would have been proud of her.

CHAPTER 9

WAR OF THE THIRD COALITION (1805)

Nelson's Nemesis

A French musket ball (off Cape Trafalgar, 1805)

Sir Winston Churchill's favourite film was *That Hamilton Woman*, starring Laurence Olivier as Nelson and Vivien Leigh as Emma, Lady Hamilton; Churchill claimed to have viewed it more than eighty times. Made in Hollywood in 1941 by Alexander Korda, the film was blatant wartime propaganda. Churchill wrote two of the main speeches spelling out that dictators, in this case Napoleon doubling for Hitler, had to be challenged and defeated. The film was not without controversy in the USA. Prudish American censors demanded that Nelson and Emma be depicted, quite incorrectly, as suffering agonies of guilt for their marital infidelities. Korda was also summoned to appear in front of the US Senate Committee on Interstate & Foreign Commerce, on suspicion of creating pro-war propaganda. He was, in fact, in the pay of the British Secret Intelligence Service (SIS), with specific instructions from the Prime Minister, Winston Churchill, to make morale-boosting films, in support of the war against Hitler's Germany. His appearance before the American Committee was cancelled when the United States joined the war, following the bombing of Pearl Harbour by the Japanese in December 1941.

Nelson & Lady Hamilton

Besides being a sentimental romp and historical-action-propaganda film – the depiction of the hoisting of the famous signal 'England expects that every man will do his duty' must stir even the least patriotic heart – the movie also perpetuated the myth that as the British and French fleets approached each other off Cape Trafalgar on 21st October 1805, Captain Thomas Hardy (the Captain of HMS *Victory* and one of Nelson's 'Band of Brothers') urged the fatalistic Vice Admiral to remove the Stars of various Orders of Chivalry on his Undress uniform, lest he be an easy target for French sharpshooters. This story is so embedded in Britain's popular culture that it has the force of absolute fact, as does Olivier/Nelson's

69

The Battle of Trafalgar, 21st October 1805 by Clarkson Stansfield

reply: 'I won them in battle, didn't I? Then I shall wear them in battle.' Alternative versions are: 'In honour I gained them, in honour I will die with them' or that it was 'too late to be shifting a coat', Nelson adding that the Stars were military Orders and he did not fear showing them to the enemy.

The report in *The Times*, the day after the news of the victory at Trafalgar and Nelson's death reached London, to the effect that the bullet which killed Nelson had actually entered his body through one of these Stars, is as fanciful as the Hardy story related above. The four Stars were worn on the left breast of Nelson's Undress uniform coat, but the bullet that fatally wounded him entered through the top of his left shoulder; and anyway, Nelson could not have removed them as they were embroidered copies, as opposed to being the original metal versions, sewn onto his tunic. Yet another version of the Hardy story is that he begged Nelson to cover his Stars, but the *Victory*'s surgeon, Dr William Beatty, pointed out, as early as 1807, that: 'it has been reported, but erroneously, that His Lordship was actually requested by his Officers to change his dress, or to cover his Stars'.

Nonetheless, there can be no doubt that Nelson's decorations would have made him a target for the French sharpshooters manning the rigging of the 74-gun *Redoutable*, assuming they could see that far through the smoke of battle. However, it is doubtful they had any idea who they were shooting at, beyond the fact that senior officers of all

Vice Admiral Viscount Nelson in all his glory

navies wore more gold braid and decorations than junior ones, so making anyone thus dressed and pacing the quarterdeck a more desirable target than a sweaty tar manning a cannon.

Whether or not the French Marine in the mizzen-top of the *Redoubtable* recognised Nelson will never be known, as the sharpshooter also perished during the battle. What is known is that, at a quarter-past-one, Hardy realised that Nelson was no longer pacing the quarterdeck with him. He turned to see Nelson kneeling on the deck, supporting himself with his one remaining hand, before falling onto his side. Hardy rushed to him, at which point Nelson said: 'They have done for me at last, Hardy … my backbone is shot through.'

The French Marine's bullet had indeed penetrated Nelson's left shoulder, severed his spine at the sixth and seventh vertebrae, cut through the left lobe of the lungs, severed part of the pulmonary artery, and lodged in the muscles of his chest. Death was to come as his lungs slowly filled with blood over the next three hours. Nelson's fate had been sealed by the French marksman. Nonetheless, the Admiral was carried below by Sergeant Major Secker of the Royal Marines and two of *Victory*'s sailors. As he was being carried down, Nelson draped a handkerchief over his face to avoid causing alarm amongst the crew. He was taken to the ship's cockpit where he told the surgeon: 'Ah, Mr Beatty! You can do nothing for me. I have but a short time to live: my back is shot through'.

Under the circumstances, it was a remarkably accurate self-diagnosis. In the heat of the below-decks cockpit, Surgeon Beatty made him comfortable and had the dying Admiral fanned. Later, after he complained of feeling hot and thirsty, the surgeon brought lemonade and watered wine for Nelson to drink. Several times Nelson asked to see his Flag Captain, Hardy. Eventually, at about two-thirty, Hardy came below and informed Nelson that twelve or fourteen enemy ships had surrendered. When Nelson asked 'I hope none of *our* ships have struck, Hardy?' the Captain replied, 'No my Lord, there is no fear of that'. The Admiral then told Hardy that he knew he was dying, and begged him to pass his hair and all his possessions to Emma, Lady Hamilton.

At about twenty-minutes-past-three, Hardy returned to the cockpit to see Nelson again; and, while holding his hand, congratulated him on a brilliant victory, which he said 'was complete'. Nelson, after reiterating his certainty that he was close to death, added in a low tone, 'Don't throw me overboard, Hardy'. He then continued, 'take care of my dear Lady Hamilton' and famously said, 'Kiss me, Hardy'. Beatty recorded that

Nelson lying mortally wounded on HMS *Victory*'s quarterdeck

Nelson's last moments in HMS *Victory's* cockpit

The musket ball which killed Nelson

Hardy knelt and kissed Nelson on the cheek, at which point the Admiral murmured, 'Thank God, I have done my duty'. After standing for a few minutes in silence, Hardy knelt again and kissed Nelson's forehead. 'Who is that?' asked the Admiral, and when the Captain replied, 'It is I, Hardy', Nelson cried, 'God bless you, Hardy!'

Nelson died at half-past four. In accordance with his instructions, and in the absence of any lead to make an inner coffin, his body was stripped, apart from his shirt, and his hair was removed, before the corpse was placed in a barrel of brandy. Nelson's second-in-command, Lord Collingwood, decided to return the body to England on a fast frigate, but the crew of the badly damaged flagship protested and their cause was upheld. The brandy barrel was strapped to the ship's mainmast and placed under a twenty-four-hour guard.

Almost everything connected with the death of Nelson was treated as a relic. The one exception was the brandy in which the Admiral was transported from Trafalgar to Gibraltar, where the barrel was drained and refilled with fresh 'spirits of wine', and the original brandy was reputedly drunk by the crew of HMS *Victory*. It was therefore inevitable that the bullet which killed Nelson would be preserved. On Saturday 4th December, two months after his death and as HMS *Victory* was being towed up the Thames estuary, Doctor Beatty and his assistants performed an autopsy on Nelson's remarkably well-preserved body. When the autopsy was complete, Beatty had the body embalmed in cotton bandages and placed in a lead casket, which was filled with a solution of brandy, camphor and myrrh, and then sealed. Once Nelson's body was landed at Greenwich, it was removed from the lead casket, viewed by some of his friends including Hardy, dressed by sailors in a shirt, stockings, uniform 'small clothes' (or underwear), waistcoat, neckcloth and a night cap, and placed in the wooden coffin made from the main mast of *L'Orient* (*see* p.48).

During the autopsy, the musket ball was retrieved. It was duly mounted for Beatty, beneath glass in a hinged silver locket with a gilt-metal rope-work border and suspension loop. Beatty is said to have worn the locket for the rest of his life, and left it in his Will to King William IV. In the event, the King predeceased him. Following Beatty's own death in 1842, his family presented the locket and its contents to Queen Victoria. The grisly French musket ball, still fused to lace from the epaulette of Nelson's Undress uniform jacket, a bizarre spoil of war if ever there was one, can be viewed at Windsor Castle.

Nelson's State Funeral Carriage

By Christmas Eve 1805, Nelson's mortal remains had been ceremonially transported by boat to the Royal Hospital for Seamen at Greenwich, and from Monday 5th to Wednesday 7th January 1806 lay in State in the Painted Hall there.

This Lying-in-State, with the casket surrounded by captured French Colours, was followed on the Wednesday afternoon by a grand procession up river, which reached Whitehall Steps at three o'clock, accompanied by artillery salutes from the Tower of London. An hour-and-a-half later the casket was placed on a bier in the Admiralty.

At eleven o'clock on Thursday, 9th January 1806, the brandy-pickled body of The Most Noble Lord, Horatio Nelson, 1st Viscount Nelson of the Nile & of Burnham Thorpe in the County of Norfolk, 1st Baron Nelson of the Nile and of Hillborough in the County of Norfolk, Knight of the Most Honourable Order of the Bath, Vice Admiral of the White Squadron of the Fleet, Commander-in-Chief of His Majesty's Ships & Vessels in the Mediterranean, 1st Duke of Brontë in the Kingdom of Sicily, Knight Grand Cross of the Sicilian Order of St Ferdinand & of Merit, Member of the Ottoman Order of the Crescent, Knight Grand Commander of the Order of St Joachim, Colonel of the Royal Marines, Doctor of Civil Law (Oxon), Freeman of Bath, Salisbury, Exeter, Plymouth, Monmouth, Sandwich, Oxford, Hereford & Worcester, and hero of the Battles of the Nile, Copenhagen & Trafalgar, was loaded onto a nautically-themed funeral carriage. A vast funeral cortege then escorted this carriage to the St Paul's Cathedral, accompanied by thirty-one Admirals, a hundred Captains and 10,000 sailors.

Based on a four-wheeled carriage chassis, designed to be drawn by six horses, the platform and wheels of Nelson's funeral car were draped with swagged and tasselled black velvet, on which were applied, over the wheels, crossed green palm leaves for a victor, and between the wheels the word 'TRAFALGAR' in gold lettering. Resting on the platform was a black-painted and gilded rectangular wooden bier, constructed to resemble a first-rate ship-of-the-line, the centre section of which was emblazoned with Nelson's overlapping coats-of-arms of an English Viscount and a Neapolitan Duke, separated by the names of his adversaries' sunken ships including *L'Orient*. Fore and aft were scaled-down copies of a ship's gilded prow, complete with the bare-breasted and winged figurehead of 'Victory' bearing more palm leaves and a crown of laurels, and the gilded and fenestrated stern from which flew at half-

The Grand Funeral car used at Nelson's State Funeral

Nelson's funeral car at
Greenwich Hospital

mast HMS *Victory*'s White Ensign. On this nautical-looking catafalque rested Nelson's coffin, now contained within an elaborate ormolu-embellished, black leather-covered casket.

To shield the late Admiral's remains from the elements, the funeral car had a domed canopy supported on four columns, which had been carved and painted to resemble palm trees. The canopy itself was covered, swagged and tasselled in black velvet, and surrounded by a four-sided, neo-classical, gilded pediment, on which was painted Nelson's personal motto: *Palmam Qui Meruit Ferat* (Let him wear the palm who has deserved it). Six plumes of black ostrich feathers and a large wooden carved-and-painted Viscount's coronet topped off the extravagant vehicle.

After the burial service under the dome of the Cathedral, the surrounding arches of which were draped with spoils of war in the form of several battle-scarred French and Spanish naval flags, the casket was lowered into the crypt, while Nelson's styles and titles were read out by the Earl Marshal. Once within the burial chamber, the casket was transferred into a black marble, sixteenth-century sarcophagus originally intended for Cardinal Wolsley, and the pall bearers' wands of office were broken and deposited in the tomb. Meanwhile, the jolly jack tars who had followed the coffin shredded the *Victory*'s two Union flags and the White or St George's Ensign, flown from the stern of the funeral carriage, into souvenir strips. This was despite the fact that these flags were supposed to have been interred with the late Admiral. When scraps of these flags come up for sale, as they do from time to time, they sell for tens of thousands of pounds.

After the State Funeral, Nelson's funeral car was taken to Greenwich, where it was put on display in the Painted Hall. There it remained for twenty years. Unfortunately for posterity, conservation was clearly not the watchword of the naval pensioners at the Royal Hospital, and by 1826 the car was in such a serious state of decay that it had to be dismantled. Other than coloured engravings made at the time, all that now remains of Nelson's State Funeral car are the busty figurehead, somewhat redolent of Lady Hamilton (who was barred from the funeral and later died in poverty in France), and a scrap of the black velvet, both held at the National Maritime Museum at Greenwich. Fortunately, HMS *Victory*, complete with a brass plaque marking the spot where Nelson fell and the cockpit on the orlop deck in which he died, can still be visited at Portsmouth.

Figurehead from Nelson's funeral car ©*National Maritime Museum, Greenwich, London*

Scrap of black velvet from the pall used on Nelson's funeral car ©*National Maritime Museum, Greenwich, London*

CHAPTER 10

WEST INDIES CAMPAIGN (1804–1810)

The Flight of Eagles from Martinique & Guadeloupe

On 18th May 1804 the First Consul of France, Napoleon Bonaparte, was elected Emperor of the French by ninety-nine percent of the nearly four million enfranchised citizens of his adopted country. This result set a splendid example for future dictators seeking democratic legitimacy through electoral fraud.

Just over six months later, on 2nd December, Napoleon crowned himself Emperor at Notre Dame Cathedral in Paris. The extraordinarily lavish ceremony had a heavy Imperial Roman theme. This act was then rather reluctantly blessed by Pope Pius VII, whom Napoleon had effectively ordered to attend.

The Coronation of Emperor Napoleon I at Notre Dame Cathedral

The use of Imperial Roman symbology, not only at the Coronation but across most aspects of Napoleon's reign, was no accident. It was in fact a deliberate reference to the glories of Ancient Rome, and more importantly a reminder of the fact that Rome, which like France had thrown out its Kings, was a republic which was nonetheless headed by an Emperor from 27 BC. This Imperial Roman cross-referencing had actually started with the creation of the Consulate in 1799, but it was to take full flight with the establishment of the First French Empire.

Eagle finial of the Colours of the 45th Regiment

Up until Napoleon's self-Coronation, the Regiments of the French Revolutionary Army had carried Colours, which from time-to-time they lost. However, soon after the great event of 1804, the Regiments of what was shortly to become the *Grande Armée* were presented with an *Aigle de Drapeau* (Flag Eagle) on 5th December. These were shamelessly based on the Eagles of Imperial Rome, and Napoleon made it clear to his troops that these new Eagles bore the same significance as their former Colours. In other words, to lose an Eagle would bring shame to the Regiment concerned; Eagles had to be defended to the death.

The original design for these new symbols of Imperial muscle was sculpted by Antoine-Denis Chaudet, with copies then cast in the workshop of Pierre-Philippe Thomire, the greatest French bronzier of the nineteenth century. The Eagles were in the form of the eponymous bird with an open beak, one claw resting on a thunderbolt, on a plinth embossed with the Regiment's number. In the case of the Guards, the numbers were replaced with the words: '*Garde Impériale*'. Weighing about four pounds, the gilded-bronze Eagles were mounted on top of blue staffs, from which flew new Colours made of silk and embroidered with gold wire. Up to 1812, when the new, expanded *Grande Armée* was created, these Colours resembled those of the Revolutionary Army, specifically those of the Demi-Brigade of Infantry, with a white diamond in the centre and the corners filled in (from clockwise top left) red-blue-red-blue. The names of the 156 Infantry Regiments of the Line before 1812 were written in gold on the obverse, and the words 'Valeur et Discipline', together with the Battalion number, on the reverse. As with the Demi-Brigades, the number of Battalions in each Regiment was usually three, depending on recruitment, and each of them had its own Colour, topped by an Eagle bearing the regimental number. Hence, the 82nd Regiment of Infantry of the Line, which had three Battalions, in consequence had three Eagles (Nos 10, 14 & 22 in the Royal Hospital's *Flag Book*), all of which were captured by the British at the Siege of

above, left to right
Three Eagles of 82nd Regiment
© *Royal Hospital Chelsea*

above, far right
Eagle of 26th Regiment
© *Royal Hospital Chelsea*

Martinique on 24th February 1809, along with a single Eagle of the 26th Regiment (No 50 in the *Flag Book*).

The French possessions in the West Indies, Martinique and Guadeloupe, were a secure base from which privateers and French Navy warships could raid British shipping. In consequence, they were a major threat to Britain's trade with its own sugar-producing islands. In Martinique and Guadeloupe, slavery was still in force, while the British had abolished the slave trade within its own empire in 1807. The islands also provided a concentration point for larger-scale French operations in the region. Accordingly in the autumn of 1808, the British government ordered the Admiralty to send a mixed naval and military force to take out the French threat and end slavery in the region, starting with Martinique.

Eagles of the French 82nd & 26th Regiments (Martinique, 1809)
Ten thousand soldiers, under the command of Lieutenant General George Beckwith, and including the men of the 23rd Regiment of Foot and the 7th Regiment of Foot,[1] were loaded onto a Royal Navy Squadron of twenty-nine ships under the command of Rear Admiral Sir Alexander Cochrane. In a nineteenth-century version of D-Day, this amphibious force made simultaneous landings on both the southern and northern coasts of the island. By 10th February, Martinique was in British hands, except for Fort Desaix, a well-sited and armed position intended to protect the capital, Fort-de-France, which had been bypassed during the British advance. In a siege lasting fourteen days, the French suffered two hundred casualties before finally surrendering.

Details of how the Eagles from the Martinique campaign were actually captured are thin on the ground. In 2009, the then curator of the

1. Later the Royal Welsh Fusiliers and the Royal Fusiliers.

Fusiliers Museum at the Tower of London asserted, in a highly inaccurate article on the Martinique campaign, that the 7th Regiment of Foot's trophy was acquired at the fall of Fort Bourbon. On a notice in the display cabinet holding their Eagle, the Royal Welch Fusiliers Museum at Caernarvon Castle states that it was surrendered on 24th February. This would seem to indicate that all the Martinique Eagles were captured at the fall of Fort Desaix.

By 1947, when one of the three Eagles of the 82nd Regiment was given by the Royal Hospital Chelsea to the Royal Welch Fusiliers, and again in 1957, when the second Eagle of the 82nd was presented to the Royal Fusiliers, only the Eagles on their staffs remained. However, Captain Ford's *Flag Book* (*see* p.54) records that in 1841 curiously none of the Martinique Eagles had their thunderbolts, one Eagle of the 82nd still had an intact Colour, and the Eagle of the 26th had about half the Colour remaining. Unfortunately, Captain Ford only painted the obverse, so the battalion numbers are not known. The other Eagles, including the Eagles of the 82nd and the 26th still held at the Royal Hospital, were either missing their Colours or only had scraps of fabric with no identifying marks.

The Unclaimed Eagle of the French 66th Regiment (Guadeloupe, 1810)
With Martinique safely in British hands, General Beckwith and Admiral Cochrane turned their attention to the island of Guadeloupe, and with a slightly smaller force than the one used to capture Martinique, set sail for the island on 27th January 1810. Neither the 7th nor the 23rd Regiments of Foot were included in this force, but the 1st, 15th, 19th, 25th, 63rd and 90th Regiments of Foot were.[2]

The British arrived off Le Gosier later that evening, and immediately landed the greater part of the force at the village of Sainte-Marie. This force then split, with one half marching south towards Basse-Terre and the other north. Neither met serious opposition, the French militia forces deserting in large numbers and abandoning their fortifications as the British approached. On 30th January, the French commander, General Jean Augustin Ernouf, took up a position with his remaining garrison on the Beaupère-St. Louis Ridge, which guarded the approach to Basse-Terre. Later that day, Beckwith's remaining troops came ashore to the north of Basse-Terre, outflanking the strong French position at Trois-Rivières and forcing their withdrawal to Basse-Terre itself.

With his capital coming under bombardment from gun batteries set up by the Royal Navy, on 3rd February General Ernouf marched his men

Handover of the Eagle of 82nd Regiment to the Royal Welsh Fusiliers, 17th December 1957

2. Later the Royal Scots, the East Yorkshire Regiment, the Princess of Wales' Royal Regiment, the King's Own Scottish Borderers, the Manchester Regiment and the Cameronians, respectively

Eagle of 66th Regiment
© *Royal Hospital Chelsea*

out of Basse-Terre to meet the British on the plain at Matabar. He immediately attacked the British and initially drove them back, but was outflanked by a British force attacking from the north. While the French were retreating, Cochrane seized the opportunity to attack the undefended town of Basse-Terre, landing a force of Royal Marines which captured the town, cutting off the French forces' line of escape. On 5th February, the French surrendered.

In the aftermath of the elimination of French power in the West Indies, all the expedition's officers and men were voted the thanks of both Houses of Parliament, and ten years later the Regiments that participated were awarded the battle honour 'GUADALOUPE 1810'. Interestingly, although the written histories of these Regiments mention their presence at Guadeloupe, none of them lay claim to the capture of the Eagle of the 66th Regiment of Infantry; nor is General Beckwith's Dispatch any help, merely stating that: 'Captain W H Wilby, one of my Aides de Camp, has the honour to be the bearer of this Dispatch and of the Eagle of the 66th Regiment'. It therefore seems likely that, most unusually for an Eagle, it was not captured, but was an *objet trouvé*, which may account for why it still remains regimentally unclaimed at the Royal Hospital Chelsea.

During his tenure as Governor of the Royal Hospital, General Sir Jeremy Mackenzie received a request from the French Army for the 'loan' of one of the Eagles in the Royal Hospital's collection. In Sir Jeremy's words: 'The modern successor Regiment were celebrating the anniversary of the raising of the original Regiment. We said yes, but if they did not return the Eagle, we would invade again to get it back! They borrowed it – and returned it.'

PENINSULAR WAR
(1807–1814)

A Convocation of Imperial Eagles

By way of contrast to the paucity of precise information surrounding the British acquisition of Eagles in the West Indies, there is generally no shortage of anecdotes, fanciful or otherwise, concerning those captured during the Peninsular War.

The Peninsular War was fought between Napoleon and Bourbon Spain, the latter assisted by its allies, the United Kingdom and Portugal. The aim of the combatants was control of the Iberian Peninsula. It began in 1807, when the French and Spanish invaded Portugal, and escalated in 1808, when France turned against Spain. Meanwhile, in Richard Brinsley Sheridan's words, the British were 'doing no more than filching sugar islands', and – as he might have added – collecting French Imperial Eagles in the Caribbean.

General Marquess Wellington at the Battle of Vitoria, 21st June 1813

The recently abdicated Spanish
King Ferdinand VII

At the start of the nineteenth century, Spain was in a state of political turmoil. Napoleon exploited this situation by occupying the country and dragging his elder brother, Joseph, off the formerly-Bourbon thrones of Naples & Sicily, where he had ruled precariously since 1806, and installing him on the equally shaky Spanish throne in 1808.

With the recently abdicated Spanish King Ferdinand VII held under guard in a French chateau, the legitimist government of Spain appealed to the British government for help. In August 1808, a British Army duly landed in Portugal under the command of Lieutenant General Sir Arthur Wellesley. Last seen in this book in India at the Siege of Seringapatam in 1799 (*see* p.60), Wellesley had since defeated another native ruler in the Second Anglo-Maratha War (1803–1805), returned to England where he was elected a Member of Parliament, served as Chief Secretary for Ireland, and then returning to military duties defeated the Danes at the Battle of Køge in 1807, when they failed to surrender their fleet to Britain, leaving it at risk of falling into French hands.

At first, the British armed intervention in the Peninsular did not go so well for the General. Following the highly controversial Convention of Cintra, which allowed General Junot's defeated French forces a free pass out of Portugal after the Battle of Vimiero in August 1808, Wellesley and his superiors were recalled to London to face a Board of Enquiry.

On the north terrace of Alnwick Castle, the seat of the Dukes of Northumberland, there are five eighteenth-century cannons, that are illustrated and described in the current Duke's book, *Lions of the North* (Scala, 2019), as 'captured at the Battle of Vimiero' and taken back to the castle by Captain (later Admiral) Hon Josceline Percy. This raised a query, as the Royal Navy was not involved in the battle. Christopher Hunwick, the Alnwick archivist, was duly consulted on the apparent anomaly. He replied that the cannons, which are of Portuguese not French manufacture, 'were [allegedly] brought to England by Captain (later Admiral) Hon Josceline Percy commanding HMS *Hotspur*, who was charged with the duty of conveying Marshal Junot and his Army to France, after the Convention of Cintra. A newspaper report from August 1862 records that [the] five six-pounders [on the ramparts of the castle] were Peninsular spoils presented by the Duke of Wellington to the late Duke of Northumberland; the 3rd Duke was well acquainted with Wellington, who visited Alnwick Castle in 1827. However, although it is true that Josceline Percy did convey Marshal Junot back to France, it was not on HMS *Hotspur*, but on HMS *Nymph*. Josceline's daughter

Sophie, in her memoirs, recalls the friendship formed between Junot and Percy, and writes in detail of gifts given by Junot; there is no mention of guns. Neither does she make any mention of them when describing her visits to Alnwick Castle. Another explanation could be that they were given as a gift from the exiled Portuguese Royal Family living in Rio de Janeiro; Josceline Percy was stationed there from 1813 to 1815. It is worth noting that the 2nd Duke had a long-standing relationship with the Portuguese Royal Family as an informal military advisor.'

Given the terms of the Convention of Cintra, which allowed the French to take *all* their equipment with them, the lack of any mention of the guns in correspondence, the fact that they were Portuguese and not French, and the later connections with the exiled Portuguese Royal Family, it seems likely that their provenance as spoils of war from the Battle of Vimiero may have been misattributed.

Death of Lieutenant General Sir John Moore, mortally wounded at Corunna

While Wellesley was away in London, his former comrade-in-arms in India, the irascible Major General Sir David Baird, arrived in Spain in October 1808, under the command of Lieutenant General Sir John Moore. But Baird, along with all the British forces, was forced out of the Peninsular following the Battle of Corunna on 16th January 1809, an action which cost Sir John Moore his life. Towards the end of the battle, which was a brilliantly fought rear-guard action, Moore was mortally wounded by a cannon ball. He was carried from the field in a blanket by an escort of Guards and the Black Watch, but died later that evening. Ever the practical soldier, Moore had always said that he should be buried where he fell, and so was hurriedly interred alongside his old friend and fellow casualty, Brigadier General Robert Anstruther, of the 3rd Regiment of Foot Guards, with the 1st Guards Chaplain, Rev A J. Symons, officiating. Following the capture of Corunna, the French flew a Tricolour at half-mast over the citadel, fired a salute over Moore's grave, and Marshal Soult ordered that a monument be erected to honour a much-respected opponent. It remains there to the present day, tended carefully by the citizens of Corunna, who still venerate Moore's memory.

Whilst all this was going on, there was a major Spanish insurrection against the French, which Napoleon himself ended with his veteran troops, although he did not linger in Spain having achieved his aims. Meanwhile in London, cleared of any culpability in the Cintra affair, Sir Arthur Wellesley was appointed to command a new British campaign against the French, and arrived in Lisbon on 22nd April 1809. On 12th May, Wellesley crossed the Douro River and utterly routed Marshal Soult's French troops

Cap badge of the 29th Regiment of Foot

1. Later the Worcestershire Regiment

2. Later the Gloucestershire Regiment

at the Second Battle of Porto. With Portugal secured, Wellesley advanced east into Spain to unite with the Spanish royalist forces for an assault on the French I Corps at Talavera, to be followed by the capture of Madrid, and then a swing north to clear the French out of Spain.

The lost Eagles of the French 24th & 96th Regiments (Talavera, 1809)
Wellesley reached Talavera in the late afternoon of 27th July. During this action, the honour of capturing the first French Eagles in the Peninsular War went to the 29th Regiment of Foot.[1] Praised by Sir Arthur as 'the best Regiment in the Army', the 29th had a critical role to play in the battle. Together with the 48th Regiment of Foot,[2] they were ordered after nightfall to clear the French off the tactically-important Cerro de Medellin hill, and then to hold it against a likely counter-attack the following morning. The French riposte duly materialised in the shape of two massive columns of battle-hardened troops, comprising the 24th and 96th Infantry Regiments of the Line, each of three Battalions. In a forerunner of the 'Thin Red Line' at Balaclava forty-five years later, the 29th formed two ranks, lay down behind the crest of the hill out of sight of the enemy, and then in a surprise move stood up to repulse the advancing French columns with rapid volley fire, before chasing them off the hill in a bayonet charge. At some point, when or how no one is exactly sure, they captured the Eagle of the 24th Regiment, then wheeled into the flank of the French 96th Regiment and captured their Eagle as well. What happened next is, as with some other spoils of war in this book, a mystery.

Wellesley's official dispatch stated quite clearly that three French Colours had been captured by the King's German Legion (although no trace of them exists today), and that two Eagles had been captured by the 29th. However, it was noted that one of these trophies was either missing its bird (which may have been unscrewed and removed by the French before it could be captured), or it had been destroyed in the bloody fighting to acquire it. Seeking to minimise the loss of these important totems, Marshal Jourdan played down their capture, stating:

> The pretended flags or standards that Wellesley glories in having taken or destroyed are nothing more than small flags (fanions) placed at the right and left of each Battalion to keep the ranks aligned and that are thrown away by those who carry them when they have to use their weapons.

The surviving but undesignated Eagle was presented by the 29th to Sir Arthur, who was ennobled following the battle as Viscount Wellington. He in turn returned it to the Regiment as 'a fitting trophy of their valour'. It then disappeared and has never been seen since. Perhaps, if Marshal Jourdan was right, it never existed. Who knows?

The 'Cuckoo' Eagle of the 8th Regiment (Barrosa, 1811)

Two more years were to pass before the next Eagle was captured. This time there were no doubts about how it was seized or what happened to it afterwards, at least until 1852.

The Battle of Barrosa on 5th March 1811 was part of an unsuccessful manoeuvre to break the Siege of Cádiz, which had only been invested on the land side by the French in early 1810.

The city was an important garrison-harbour for the British and had also acted as the headquarters of the Bourbon Spanish since the French invasion of Spain and the capture of Madrid in 1808. Since January 1810, Cadiz had been besieged by French troops on the land side; and a reduction in their numbers in March 1811 gave the British and Spanish an opportunity to lift the siege.

A large Allied force was shipped south from Cadiz to Tarifa and marched to engage the French siege lines from the rear. The French, under the command of Marshal Victor, were aware of the Allied movement and re-deployed to prepare a trap. Victor placed one Division on the road to Cadiz, blocking the Allied approach, while the two remaining French Divisions fell on the Allied rear guard.

3. Later the Royal Irish Fusiliers

Faced with a battle on two fronts, the British succeeded in routing the attacking French forces. During this operation the 87th Regiment of Foot,[3] yelling their fearsome war cry *'Faugh-a-Ballagh'* ('Clear the way') successfully charged the 2nd Battalion of the French 8th Regiment and captured their Eagle. The first Irishman to seize the closely guarded Eagle was a young officer, Ensign Edward Keogh. However, as his hand grasped the staff, he was shot through the heart and then bayoneted. His place was taken by Sergeant Patrick Masterson, who prised the Eagle from the Gallic grasp of the dying Frenchman, Lieutenant Gazan, and shouted: 'B'jaysus, boys, I have the cuckoo!' He held onto it with Celtic tenacity until the end of the battle.

This Eagle, embellished with a gilded bronze laurel wreath – an honour given to the 8th Regiment by Napoleon for their bravery at the

The 'Cuckoo' Eagle of the 8th Regiment ©*Royal Irish Fusiliers Museum*

Prince Regent by Cruickshank

Chapel Royal, St James's Palace

Battle of Talavera – was later incorporated into the cap badge of the 87th's successor Regiment and featured on its Colours. The Eagle itself was presented to the Prince Regent, the Regiment's Colonel. It was held in the Chapel Royal at St James's Palace until 1835, when it was sent to the Royal Hospital Chelsea. There it hung from the roof of the Chapel until noon on Friday 16th April 1852, when someone broke in through a trap door into the organ loft, removed the Eagle (complete with its Colour and staff), and made away with it. The staff, minus its avian finial and plinth, was later found in the grounds. Why this particular Eagle was stolen and by whom will never be known. One theory is that the thief wrongly believed that it was made of gold; another is that it was stolen by a Frenchman. Whatever the truth of the matter, it was never recovered.

Five months later, on 4th September 1852, Arthur Wellesley, by now the 1st Duke of Wellington, died aged eighty-two. His body was sent to the Royal Hospital Chelsea, where it lay in State for two days before his State Funeral at St Paul's Cathedral on 18th November.

The theft of the 8th Regiment's Eagle might have caused something of a problem when all the Royal Hospital's collection of Peninsular and Waterloo Eagles were arranged on the Iron Duke's funeral car. Fortunately, as Captain Ford recorded in the *Flag Book*, the Royal Hospital had ordered that a replica be cast from one of the other Eagles in their collection. It was this Eagle which was used at Wellington's State Funeral, and was later handed over to the 87th's successor Regiment, the Royal Irish Fusiliers, on 28th September 1947. It can now be seen, along with the original staff, in the Royal Irish Fusiliers Museum in Armagh. For Imperial Eagle purists, it is interesting to note that the copy made on the orders of the Royal Hospital had two errors: first, the bird as well as the wreath should have been gilded and not left as plain bronze; second, when first transferred to the Royal Hospital, the original Eagle was missing its thunderbolt. According to the Royal Irish Fusiliers Museum website, during the struggle to capture the 'Cuckoo' Eagle, a gold leaf fell off the original wreath. After the battle, it was presented to Major Hugh Gough (later Field Marshal Viscount Gough), the commanding officer of the 87th, and he had it made into a brooch, which remains in the possession of the Gough family.

This is not quite the end of the story. In contemporary correspondence which appeared in the *Belfast Newsletter* of 1811, it would appear that a second Eagle was captured by the Irishmen at Barrosa. The French 47th Regiment, intact and fresh, was seen approaching the 87th's right flank.

Major Gough, with considerable difficulty, collected the right wing from the confused hand-to-hand fighting with the French 8th, and charged the advancing 47th. Luckily for the Irishmen, the Frenchmen had been somewhat unnerved by the treatment of their cousins in the 8th, and they broke and fled, but not before they had lost their Eagle. So, what became of it? According to the correspondence in the *Belfast Newsletter*, written by an officer who was present, the soldier of the 87th who captured it was:

> … obliged to throw it away from excessive fatigue, and a wound, which you will not wonder at when I tell you that we were under arms 32 hours, and marching 16 hours before the action commenced.

It is significant that this Eagle was not mentioned in Lord Wellington's dispatch, perhaps because it was eventually recovered from the battle-field by the French.

Marshal Michel Ney

The watery Eagle of the 39th Regiment (Foz de Arouce, 1811)

Is it right to claim an enemy *objet trouvé* as a spoil of war? Lieutenant General George Beckwith clearly thought so in the case of the Eagle of the 66th Regiment acquired in Guadeloupe (*see* p.76), and so too it would seem did Viscount Wellington. The story of the Eagle of the 39th Regiment is quickly told and involves no bloody heroics. However, it is an interesting illustration of the enormous importance attached by Wellington to their possession and their status as tangible trophies of his triumphs.

The Battle of Foz de Arouce on 15th March 1811, ten days after Barrosa, was the least successful of Marshal Michel Ney's rear-guard actions during the French withdrawal from Portugal. After a night march on 14th to 15th March, most of the French Army had crossed the Ceira River at Foz de Arouce, and had camped on the heights above the village. Ney had been ordered to bring all of his rear-guard troops across the river, destroying the bridge behind him. But he disobeyed the order and kept three Brigades on the southern side of the river, including the 39th Infantry Regiment of

Wellington by Francisco Goya

the Line. This deployment risked disaster, for the river was in flood and the only possible escape route for Ney's men was across the damaged, but still intact bridge.

Wellington's pursuit of the French was held up by a combination of heavy fog and fires that the French had lit in the town of Miranda de Corvo. The first British troops eventually reached the French positions on the Ceira at four in the afternoon. Wellington himself arrived just before dusk, and decided to surprise the enemy. In this he was successful, for Ney's men were not expecting an attack that late in the day. Worse still, thinking that they heard gunfire to their rear, Ney's 39th Regiment panicked and attempted to escape across the bridge. Their route was blocked by French cavalry deployed to counter the British attack, so the cowardly French infantrymen were forced to use a ford. Unfortunately for them, the river was too high and a significant number of them were swept away, along with the Regiment's Eagle. Wellington offered a large sum to the Portuguese peasantry for its recovery, which bore fruit in mid-June. However, it is significant that he did not give the Eagle to the British Regiment which had driven the French to a watery grave.

Nonetheless, Wellington was clearly in no doubt that the shameful provenance of the Eagle of the 39th in no way disqualified it from being included in his official Dispatches, and presented – along with other more conventionally acquired trophies – to the Prince Regent as a spoil of war. Who would have the temerity to argue with that august judgement? The Eagle of the 39th Regiment eventually ended up at the Royal Hospital Chelsea, where it can still be seen today.

The Eagle of the French 62nd Regiment (Salamanca, 1812)
In February 1812, Viscount Wellington was advanced in the peerage to Earl of Wellington, his aristocratic seniority increasing as he progressed towards the Pyrenees. *En route*, he had several more battles to fight (and Eagles to capture), the next being the Battle of Salamanca, which was fought on 22nd July 1812. It was the last stop for the British and their allies before Madrid. The battle itself involved a succession of flanking attacks on the French left wing, starting with the British Heavy Cavalry Brigade and Pakenham's 3rd Division of Infantry, followed by the 4th, 5th and 6th Divisions supported by cavalry. Cumulatively, these attacks resulted in the collapse of the French left. General Bertrand Clausel, who had assumed command after Marshal Marmont and his deputy were wounded, ordered

a counter-attack on the weakened Allied centre. Initially, the move was successful, but Wellington rapidly re-enforced the weak point and the Allies won the day. Such are the bald facts about the battle.

Battle of Salamanca: the charge of Sir Edward Packenham's 3rd Division

As to the capture of French Eagles at Salamanca, there remains some confusion and doubt. For a start, who actually captured the Eagle of the 62nd? And is the Eagle now held in the Essex Regiment Museum at Chelmsford actually the one that was acquired?

The received wisdom is that the Eagle of the 62nd Regiment was taken by Lieutenant William Pearce of the 2nd Battalion of the 44th East Essex Regiment of Foot.[4] Pearce is believed to have attacked the French Ensign carrying it, while he was unscrewing the Eagle finial from its staff, in order to hide it under his tunic. Meanwhile, a fight ensued for the Colour (less its avian finial), involving on one side two Frenchman of the 62nd, and on the other three soldiers of the 44th, including Privates Findlay and Murray.

4. Later the Essex Regiment

While this was going on, Lieutenant Pearce was still in the act of prising the gilded bronze bird from the Ensign of the 62nd, when a French soldier lunged at him with a bayonet. Fortunately for Pearce, Private Findlay (or Private Murray, according to Pearce's contemporary account) shot the Frenchman in the head before he could skewer the British officer. As a result, the trophy was drenched in the French soldier's blood and brains,

89

The Prince Regent at a military Review by J S Copley

the dried remnants of which were still on it when the Eagle was presented to the Prince Regent on Horse Guards Parade the following year.

The two French Ensigns protecting the Colour itself also perished. One of them was killed by Lieutenant Pearce. But whether or not it was he who snatched the by-now-detached flag from the dead man's hands and fixed it (with the finial, according to his own account) to a Sergeant's pike is unclear. Lieutenant Pearce then either presented both the Colour and the Eagle to his Divisional General, Brigadier General Hon Sir Edward Packenham (Wellington's brother-in-law), or by his own account sent it to 'the quarter guard with the Colours of the Regiment the night of the battle, we sleeping on the field of battle'. Significantly, everyone is agreed that the staff with its identifying regimental-numbered socle was lost on the field of battle.

It was this separation of the Colour, the Eagle finial and the staff, not to mention conflicting contemporary accounts, which have caused sub-sequent confusion as to whose name should be credited with this spoil of war. Some sources, notably the *Naval & Military Gazette* of 1844, aver that the Eagle was captured by Private Findlay (presumably referring to the detached Colour), others by Lieutenant Pearce (referring to the Eagle finial). Pearce's own account was backed up by an eye witness report in *The Soldiers' Companion or Martial Recorder* of 1824, which states:

Lieutenant Pearce of the 44th Foot had the honour of capturing a French Eagle at the glorious Battle of Salamanca… he presented it in the Field of Battle to the General [Packenham] who requested him to retain it and present it to Lord Wellington the following morning.

Perhaps, under the circumstances, it's only fair that the credit for capturing an Eagle should go to *both* Pearce and Findlay, or more simply to the 44th Regiment of Foot.

The second issue in connection with the Eagle of the 62nd arises from the belief that another Eagle, also detached from its staff and possibly from the French 101st Regiment, was also presented to Packenham on the battlefield, as attested to in another entry in the *Naval & Military Gazette* of 1844. Is it possible that the Eagles were inadvertently switched whilst in Packenham's possession? The answer to this is provided by Captain Ford of the Royal Hospital Chelsea. While compiling his *Flag Book* on the martial trophies at the Hospital, Ford added a note on 20th

May 1847. This states that he had been informed that Lieutenant Pearce had scratched his name on one of the wings of the Eagle finial. In the course of researching this spoil of war, an enquiry was made to the curator of the Essex Regiment Museum and the following reply received: 'Try as I might I have never been able to spot Pearce's name on the Eagle.' It would seem, therefore, that the Eagle in the Essex Regiment Museum is not that of the 62nd and may be that of the 101st. If that is correct, then what happened to the Eagle of the 62nd? Could it still be lurking in a cobweb-covered trunk at the Packenhams' family seat, Tullynally Castle in County Westmeath?

The Eagle & Jingling Johnny of the 101st Regiment (Salamanca, 1812)

The 88th Regiment of Foot (from 1881, the Connaught Rangers) was at the centre of the Brigade that routed the French troops at the Battle of Salamanca. During the fighting, they captured an Ottoman musical instrument, known as a Turkish crescent, from the aforementioned French 101st Regiment. Once acquired, it was quickly re-named the 'Jingling Johnny'.

This extraordinary percussion instrument, which would later be adopted by some British Army bands and the Prussian Army, comprised a mechanical pole on which was an assembly of small silver bells, suspended from two upturned crescents, below which was a gilded canopy and an inverted crescent, from the ends of which hung horse-hair tails. By turning a crank handle near the base, which would have been secured in a leather sling like a Colour staff, an inner shaft moved up and down, causing the bells to make a pleasant tinkling sound.

Captured by Bonaparte's Army of the East, probably at the Battle of the Pyramids in 1798, it had been adapted for use in the band of the French 101st Regiment by the replacement of the original crescent finial with an Imperial eagle. This was not, of course, an 'Eagle' in the understood sense of the word, but it later created a misunderstanding, which was further compounded by General d'Hautpoul, late of the 101st, who stated in his memoirs that he saw the Eagle of the 101st at Westminster in 1825. He didn't. What he saw was the Jingling Johnny still with its Imperial crest.

Following the Peninsular War, the 88th's Jingling Johnny was carried on all ceremonial occasions at the head of the band by the tallest man in the Regiment. In the aftermath of the Indian Mutiny of 1857, the Regiment spent thirteen years in India, during which time the silver bells of their instrument were stolen. In November 1870, they boarded a troopship in

Jingling Johnny of 101st Regiment

Image No 38 in the *Flag Book*,
Eagle of 22nd Regiment
©Royal Hospital Chelsea

Bombay for the long journey home. Once back at their barracks in County Galway, the 88th sent their Jingling Johnny for restoration in Paris, of all places. Fortunately, Napoleon's nephew, Charles-Louis Napoleon Bonaparte, who had installed himself as the French Emperor in 1852, had recently lost the Franco-Prussian War of 1870, and was living in exile in England. So, the instrument was safely returned by the Parisian repair shop, albeit with brass rather than silver bells, and the original red and black plumes dyed a uniform black. The Jingling Johnny continued to be carried by the Connaught Rangers on ceremonial occasions until 1903, when its mechanical pole was found to be damaged through over-use. Once again, it was sent to Paris for repairs, and at the same time a replica was made to be carried on parades.

Following the creation of the Irish Free State in 1922, the Connaught Rangers were disbanded. Quite what happened next is unknown, but by 1956 the original Jingling Johnny had been deposited at the National Army Museum, where it remains to this day. The replica, without its horsehair plumes, is on loan to the Museum of Army Music.

The Eagle of the French 22nd Regiment (Salamanca, 1812)
The final quandary arising from the Battle of Salamanca relates to the Eagle of the French 22nd Infantry Regiment of the Line. One version of its capture states that it was found on the ground among a pile of dead Frenchmen, by a Portuguese infantryman of the British-officered 12th Caçadores. A second version asserts that the Eagle was acquired by Ensign John Pratt of the 30th (Cambridgeshire) Regiment of Foot,[5] who was on detachment to the 12th Caçadores. The final version, which appears only in the Royal Hospital's *Flag Book*, is a statement by Captain Barralier of the 37th Regiment of Foot, that the Eagle of the 22nd was taken by Captain Haddock of the 87th Regiment of Foot, who was serving with the 7th Caçadores.

In these conflicting claims, a number of things are certain. Both the 7th and the 12th Caçadores were in the Anglo-Portuguese Order of Battle at Salamanca, as were the 30th Regiment of Foot. The 37th and the 87th were not, but that does not mean that the officers named were not present on the battlefield. The truth may never be known, but that has not stopped British military historians referring to 'Pratt's Eagle'. More tellingly perhaps is the fact that in 1947 the Eagle of the 22nd was handed over by the Royal Hospital Chelsea to the successor Regiment of the 30th

5. In 1881 the 30th (Cambridgeshire) Regiment of Foot amalgamated with the 59th (2nd Nottinghamshire) Regiment of Foot to form the East Lancashire Regiment

of Foot, the East Lancashire Regiment. It has been proudly on display at the Lancashire Infantry Museum at Preston ever since, along with the statement on the museum's website that:

> [The Eagle of the 22nd Regiment] is the finest and most important military trophy in the possession of the Lancashire Infantry Museum and is listed by the Home Office as a British National Treasure. As such it may not be disposed of or taken out of the country, even temporarily, without Government permission.

This is an admirable statement that emphatically confirms the general policy on the repatriation of foreign items in British collections.

Eagle of 22nd Regiment
©*Lancashire Infantry Museum, Preston*

Other Peninsular War Eagles

Following the catastrophic defeat of the French at Salamanca, the Anglo-Portuguese forces turned towards Madrid, which surrendered on 14th August 1812. Two Eagles, belonging to the 13th Regiment of Dragoons and the 51st Regiment of Infantry of the Line, were found in storage; it seems that both of these French Regiments had left them behind when they were sent to supress Spanish guerrillas. As these Eagles were not won in battle, they could not be claimed by a British Regiment, so they were eventually lodged at the Royal Hospital Chelsea where they remain.

At the Battle of Arroyo dos Molinos, on 28th October 1811, there were rumours of a captured Eagle, as the Spanish General Giron wrote to his Commander-in-Chief, General Castanos: 'The enemies have also lost an Eagle, but it has not been possible up till now to find it'. There is, however, no record in any of the Dispatches of the capture of this Eagle, nor is it in the Royal Hospital Chelsea's *Flag Book*.

The Eagle of the French 28th Infantry Regiment of the Line was captured in the Maya Pass in the Pyrenees in July 1813 by the 28th (North Gloucestershire) Regiment of Foot.[6] According to Edward Fraser, writing in his book, *The War Drama of Eagles* (1912), by the time this trophy reached London in 1814, England was at peace with France and Napoleon was in exile in Elba. Accordingly, it was not paraded as a spoil of war, nor was it later put on proud display in the Regiment's museum. The reason for this, states Fraser, was that the Eagle had been lent to an artist to make a drawing and was never returned, as it had been sold to an anonymous senior officer. This story has been cast into doubt by the

6. Later the Gloucestershire Regiment

Marshal Soult by Louis-Henri de Rudder

historian, Luis Sorando Muzás, who states in his book, *The Spanish Army of Joseph Napoleon* [*sic*] *(1808–1813)*, published in 2018, that there exists an order from Marshal Soult almost a month later, in which he designates the 28th as the only French Regiment authorized to continue taking its Eagle into combat. Interestingly, neither the Soldiers of Gloucestershire Museum nor the Ministry of Defence history of the 28th (North Gloucestershire) Regiment make any reference to the Maya Eagle, so maybe it was a chimera not an Eagle at all.

Finally, on the subject of Peninsular War Eagles, when the French Army was in full flight over the Pyrenees in the winter of 1813 to 1814, Napoleon ordered that all Cavalry Regiments were to return their Eagles to their home depot and that only the Eagle of the senior Regiment would be carried by each Infantry Brigade, the rest being repatriated.

Bombs, Pictures & Potties
The Prince Regent's Bomb (Cadiz, 1812)

With the possible exception of the Wellington Monument (*see* p.146), no public memorial has generated such a mass of scatological ribaldry as The Prince Regent's Bomb (pronounced 'bum'), otherwise known as the Cadiz Memorial. That the target for the smut was the Prince Regent, heir to the British throne, was perhaps not as surprising then as it might be today, for the Prince (later King George IV) was held in considerably less public esteem than might have been expected of someone in his position. The reason for this was a combination of the Prince's financial profligacy, misplaced personal vanity, self-evident self-indulgence and a flagrant disregard for marital fidelity that shocked even his amoral contemporaries. To make matters worse, he was grossly overweight, his enormous backside making him an easy target for caricaturists. And he took no care to offset the negative effects of his life-style through public service, a fact that was constantly lampooned by his political opponents.

Prince George's acceptance of a gift from the Spanish Regency of a captured French mortar (known as a 'bomb') in the shape of a fat phallus was bad enough. To be fair, all cannons are phallic in shape; but when it was mounted on a grotesque mythological beast, the cartoonists and satirists had a field day. So how did this monumental own-goal come about?

In addition to the convocation of Eagles acquired at the Battle of Salamanca, the victory broke the two-and-a-half-year-long siege of Cadiz. As the French retreated, a large number of giant siege artillery pieces were captured by the Allies. The particular mortar which came to be presented to the Prince Regent was of recent manufacture, having been made in Seville in 1812. Designed as a weapon of terror and mass destruction, it was capable of firing mortar bombs over three miles into the centre of Cadiz. However, as a contemporary observer noted, the shells were aimed:

> much at random, some of them falling short of the town, others flying completely over into the bay near the lighthouse on the other side, and some few... falling in the city, but from which very few casualties occurred.

The Spanish initially entrusted the mortar barrel to the keeping of Rear Admiral Arthur Legge. This distinguished matelot was a confirmed bachelor, who left sizeable legacies to his butler and several young footmen, and was at this time in command of the British Squadron at Cadiz. The bomb was delivered to Legge with a request that it be taken to London and placed in one of the Royal Parks, as a memorial to the victory at Salamanca, the liberation of southern Spain from the French, and Wellington's achievements in the Peninsular War. The Prince Regent agreed to this and commanded the Earl of Mulgrave, Master General of the Ordnance, to arrange for the Royal Arsenal Woolwich to manufacture a suitable carriage for the mortar before installing it on Horse Guards Parade.

The Royal Arsenal at Woolwich duly carried out the work, creating an elaborate bronze support for the weapon, in the form of the monster Geryon (not, as most observers assume, a Chinese dragon), with twin

Prince Regent's Bomb on Horse Guards Parade

tails and a pair of wings in place of the beast's multiple heads. The barrel of the bomb was positioned on the creature's back between its wings, with the muzzle of the mortar protruding above the gaping jaws of the monster. This particular mythological creature was chosen by Mulgrave, who had been educated in the Classics at Eton, not only because Geryon was associated with the Isle of Gades, on which Cadiz stands, but also because the story of the theft of Geryon's cattle by Hercules was an allusion to Wellington himself. To ram home the point to those not so well-read, at the rear of the mortar the Royal Arsenal's engineers placed a sculpture of the twin-headed dog, Orthrus, whose job was to guard Geryon's cattle, and who was slain by Hercules in the successful accomplishment of his tenth labour.

Saluting the Regent's Bomb uncovered on his Birthday by George Cruikshank

A Representation of the Regent's Tremendous Thing erected in the Park

To complete the monument, the engineers placed the monster and its mortar on a bronze base representing a rock on which the monster has alighted, complete with two identical explanatory plaques (in English and Latin), and a large Prince of Wales 'feathers' (the Badge of the Heir Apparent). The English inscription on the plaques reads:

> To Commemorate / the raising of the siege of Cadiz in consequence of the glorious Victory gained by the / Duke of Wellington / over the French near Salamanca, on XXII of July MSCCCXII / This mortar, cast for the destruction of the great port, with powers surpassing all others / and abandoned by the Besiegers on their Retreat / was presented as a token of respect and gratitude by the Spanish nation / to His Royal Highness the Prince Regent.

The structure weighed sixteen tons. It was unveiled on Horse Guards Parade on 12th August 1816, the Prince Regent's fifty-fourth birthday.

The media immediately named it the 'Regent's Bomb' and C.F. Lawler, who wrote of its 'width, breadth and monstrous size', predicted that the Poet Laureate would 'sing the charming odour of the thing'. Whilst the satirist William Hone celebrated its unveiling with a poem that includes the verse:

> Oh, what a Bomb! Oh, Heaven defend us!
> The thought of Bombs is quite tremendous!
> What crowds will come from every shore
> To gaze on its amazing bore!
> What swarms of Statesmen, warm and loyal,
> To worship Bomb so truly royal!

He then went on to imply, in very thinly disguised references to government ministers, that they would be queueing to kiss and brown-nose the Regent's bomb. The ribald poem was published alongside an explicit cartoon by George Cruikshank, in which the Prince Regent is depicted, face at the touch-hole end, as the mortar barrel. As the busty Isabella, Marchioness of Hertford, HRH's mistress of the moment, looks on, the Prince Regent's backside pours out smoke whilst being kissed by one politician and ramrodded by another.

Not to be outdone, Fores published a cartoon entitled *A Representation of the Regent's Tremendous Thing erected in the Park*; 'thing' was a slang

97

term for penis, and lest the smutty reference be missed, the caricature depicts a portly curate saying: 'What an erection to be sure', to which a woman lasciviously replies: 'I could gaze for ever at it…'.

As the Prince Regent bomb is still *in situ* on Horse Guards Parade, tourists can continue to gaze to this day.

The King of Spain's pictures & Joseph Bonaparte's sword (Vitoria, 1813)
Apsley House, situated on a traffic island at the junction of Piccadilly and Park Lane, is the London home of the Dukes of Wellington. Known, somewhat incorrectly, as No 1 London, this fine Palladian building houses a remarkable collection of Napoleonic-era silver, porcelain, furniture and pictures, including eighty-three Old Master canvasses that were formerly in the personal collection of King Ferdinand VII of Spain. The story of how these royal pictures came to be the undisputed property of the Marquess of Wellington, as Arthur Wellesley had become by 1813, is a remarkable one that revolves around another remarkable figure, Henry Wyndham.

Henry Wyndham was one of the more colourful characters of the nineteenth century, an era by no means devoid of aristocratic rogues, scoundrels, spendthrifts, lotharios and heroes. He was born in 1790, the second illegitimate son of the 3rd Earl of Egremont, the enormously rich owner of Petworth House in Sussex and patron of the artist, JMW

Henry Wyndham by Thomas Phillips © *Lord Egremont*

7. Later the Scots Guards

Turner. Henry's greatest claim to historical fame is that at Waterloo, on 18th June 1815, he and nine officers and men of the Coldstream Guards and the 3rd Foot Guards,[7] 'shut the gate at Hougoumont'. This action kept this strategically important farm out of the hands of the French (*see* p.130).

However, two years before that historic moment, at the Battle of Vitoria on 21st June 1813, and in the uniform of the socially-exclusive Tenth Hussars, Henry was at the head of a cavalry detachment of the 14th Light Dragoons, in hot pursuit of the defeated French army of King Joseph Bonaparte.

The defeat of the French at Vitoria signalled the end of Joseph's reign in Spain. This was an eventuality for which the usurper and his Staff had prepared by filling his coach and the accompanying baggage waggon with many of the rightful King of Spain's Old Master paintings, and quite literally a King's ransom in gold, jewellery and other treasures. The extent of Joseph's booty was described by Captain James Hughes of the 18th Hussars in his journal:

> On reaching the outward gate of the town on the Pamplona road… such a scene presented itself as I never can forget… the whole of the Royal and French Generals' equipage consisting of many coaches… treasure chests, wagons, carts and numberless servants, all in Royal livery… Our appearance had the effect of striking all with panic… the Guards fled with Joseph… whilst the Spaniards [took] advantage of the general confusion and immediately set to breaking open the treasure chests, travelling carriages etc., literally strewing the ground with bags of doubloons and dollars, not to mention jewels, watches, trinkets and all sorts of plunder…

A contemporary of Hughes' noted that the haul of loot arising from the defeat of the French at Vitoria was unequalled 'since Alexander's Macedonians plundered the camp of the Persian King after the Battle of Issus'. Joseph Bonaparte's Privy Purse alone was valued at 40 million Francs, almost all of which found its way swiftly into the pockets of the Spanish peasantry.

Joseph Bonaparte, King of Spain

In the days before the train or the aeroplane took the strain, travelling coaches were the preferred method of long-distance travel for the wealthy. Usually constructed on a long wheel base and pulled by a team of at least four horses, these coaches were equipped as an all-in-one travelling bedroom, bathroom and study, providing the privileged traveller with a warm and dry hotel room on wheels, in which he could work, eat, sleep, wash and defecate. Such conveyances, the one-man Winnebagos of their day, were the last word in luxurious travel. The Bonaparte brothers all had such carriages in their coach houses, and as their fortunes turned used them to flee the scenes of their defeats. Unfortunately for Joseph Bonaparte, he left his departure from the battlefield of Vitoria too late, and was overtaken by Wyndham at the head of his Light Dragoons.

Recognising about-to-be-ex-King Joseph's coat-of-arms on the carriage's door, Henry drew his pistol and fired it through the nearest window in an attempt to kill or seize its Bonaparte occupant. But Joseph was too quick for him, jumped out through the door on the other side, ran after his pusillanimous escort, was hauled onto a spare horse, dug in his spurs and pointed the horse's nose for the Pyrenees and home. Henry must have been disappointed at this turn of events, but not for long. An examination of the contents of the carriage proved more rewarding than Wyndham, whose father was a considerable patron of the arts and had brought up his children to know a good thing when they saw it, could ever have dreamed of.

The loss of a temporary King was as nothing to the contents of a leather trunk strapped to the back of the carriage, containing love-letters, engravings, drawings, manuscripts, and two hundred rolled-up canvasses. Although most of these pictures were of a relatively small size, their sel–ection by Joseph presumably having been determined by their portability, nonetheless they represented works by some of the greatest artists of all time, including four pictures by Velázquez: *The Waterseller of Seville; Two Young Men Eating at a Humble Table; Portrait of a Man*, and a portrait of Pope Innocent X. In addition, there was a painting by Correggio, *The Agony in the Garden*, which the then President of the Royal Academy, Benjamin West said 'was worth fighting a battle for' and suggested that it should be 'framed in diamonds'. Were these not enough, the collection also included a painting by Sir Anthony van Dyck and works by Pieter Bruegel, Sir Peter Paul Rubens, Bartolomé Esteban Murillo and Girolamo Francesco Maria Mazzola (known as Parmigianino), to name but the best-

Danaë (at Apsley House) by Titian

known artists. Initially considered to be of significantly lesser value were three works attributed to the school of Tiziano Vecelli, known as Titian. However, after considerable research, these three paintings have recently been attributed to the master himself, making the pictures at Apsley House one of the most valuable collections of Old Masters in the world, outside of royal or national collections.

To Wellington's fury, the looting after the Battle of Vitoria was on such an epic scale that it seriously impeded the pursuit of the French. Writing in his dispatch to the 3rd Earl Bathurst, Secretary of State for War, he remarked: 'We have in the service the scum of the earth as common soldiers'. The total value of the loot acquired after the battle was estimated to have been worth £1 million (2020: £69.8 million). Henry Wyndham knew of Wellington's strong views on looting. Accordingly, he had the priceless canvasses rolled up again, strapped to the back of a saddle, and sent in the pouring rain back to General Headquarters. After the war, the Duke of Wellington wrote on three separate occasions to Ferdinand, the rightful King of Spain, informing him that his pictures had been recovered. Fortunately for the Wellesley family, the Spanish Minister in England replied in 1816 to say: 'His Majesty, touched by your delicacy, does not wish to deprive you of that which has come into your possession by means as just as they are honourable'.

In addition to the haul of fine art in the carriage, Wyndham also found a richly-ornamented Sword of State, part of Joseph's royal regalia from

King Joseph Bonaparte's Sword of State. *Royal Collection Trust*
© Her Majesty Queen Elizabeth II 2018

above left
Apsley House

the time when he was briefly King of Naples & Sicily (1806–1808). This too was sent to Wellington, who in turn presented it to the Prince Regent.

An Imperial Pisspot, a Silver Beaker & a Water Tumbler (Vitoria, 1813)
While Captain Henry Wyndham marvelled at the Neapolitan State Sword and the haul of Old Master pictures he had captured in the aftermath of the Battle of Vitoria, his men had discovered an item in King Joseph's carriage which probably caused them considerable amusement and Henry some distaste when it was shown to him. For inside the travelling carriage was a heavy, bulbous, single-handled, silver chamber pot, engraved with Joseph Bonaparte's coat of arms, a gift from his Imperial brother, Napoleon.

In due course this handsome piece of sanitary ware was first hammered flat by the 14th Light Dragoons, presumably for ease of transportation, and then taken back to England, where it was expertly restored to its former shape and christened 'The Emperor'. It then found its way (presumably having first been given a good scrub) into the silver collection of the Officers Mess of the 14th Light Dragoons. They in due course evolved into the 14th Hussars, then became the 14th/20th Hussars, and finally amalgamated (in an unconscious act of military-historical symmetry) with the Royal Hussars, themselves an amalgamation of Henry Wyndham's Tenth and Cardigan's 11th Hussars, to become The King's Royal Hussars.

The Officers Messes of the Regiments of the British Army have, over the past three-hundred years, accumulated a wide range of silver, traditions

King Joseph Bonaparte's silver chamber pot

and rituals. The Royal Horse Guards (now The Blues and Royals) have a massive silver centrepiece, known as the Zetland Trophy, which is so heavy that the table has to be propped underneath to take the weight. This gift was presented to the Royal Horse Guards by Lawrence Dundas, 1st Marquess of Zetland, after six years' (rather infrequent) service with them. Regimental lore has it that he told the officers to order a piece of silver and send him the bill. When this arrived in 1872, it was for £1,000 (2020: £111,000). In the Officers Mess of the Loyal Regiment (now The Duke of Lancaster's Regiment), at Dinner Nights the Silver Fox is placed in front of the junior subaltern and the silver-mounted Maida Tortoise snuff box is positioned in front of the Commanding Officer; nobody knows why. The placement of the Maida Tortoise may be because the animal was caught and cooked for the then Commanding Officer, Lieutenant Colonel (later Lieutenant General Sir) James Kempt, after the Battle of Maida in 1806. Kempt later presented the silver-mounted shell to his former Regiment. Nor is any reason recorded as to why silver cigarette boxes and lighters are placed in front of the Commanding Officer and Second-in-Command of the Royal Highland Fusiliers (now 2nd Battalion The Royal Regiment of Scotland) for their *exclusive* use. There is, however, a simple explanation as to why an officer of The Life Guards, whose breakfast cornflakes are still served out of a priceless Paul Storr silver soup tureen, on leaving the Regiment is given an elaborate dinner by his fellow officers. and then once sufficiently inebriated is invited to ride a charger around the Dining Room table. Less understandable is the tradition of the Royal Leicestershire Regiment (now part of the Royal Anglian Regiment) that the silver and crockery used at a Dinner Night is *still* bound with black crepe to commemorate the death two-and-a-half centuries ago of Major General James Wolfe at the Battle of Quebec in 1759. Rather more explicable, but rather less digestible, is the custom since 1775 of the Royal Welch Fusiliers (now the Royal Welsh) that on St David's Day the junior subaltern is obliged to stand on the dining table and eat a raw leek.

The tradition of drinking (or not drinking) the Loyal Toast at the end of a Dinner Night is also a largely inexplicable minefield for the uninitiated. Some Regiments, including the 1st Royal Dragoons (now The Blues and Royals), the 11th Hussars (now The King's Royal Hussars) and the Royal Fusiliers (now part of the Royal Regiment of Fusiliers) carry it out from a seated position; the Royal Scots Greys (now the Royal Scots Dragoon Guards) and the Royal Ulster Rifles (now the Royal Irish Regiment) drink it *every* night at the end of dinner; and others, including The Life Guards, the 17th/21st Lancers (now The Royal Lancers) and The King's Royal Rifle Corps (now part of The Rifles) don't perform it at all. The oldest Regiment in the British Army, the Honourable Artillery Company, perform the Loyal Toast with synchronised arm gestures and shouts of the word 'Zeh!', said to refer to the seventeenth-century drill associated with priming and throwing a grenade. Elsewhere, in those Messes where Jacobite tendencies might still linger and the Loyal Toast is drunk, water glasses are removed from the table prior to the toast so that the officers cannot, by passing their port over their water tumblers, reaffirm their loyalty to 'the King over the water'. Bizarrely, in the Indian Army, the officers of Skinner's Horse still raise a glass every night to the portrait of the British Colonel James Skinner, the eighteenth-century founder of their Regiment, despite the fact that India gained its independence in 1948.

Whatever the regimental traditions associated with the Loyal Toast, the ritual of drinking from a Loving Cup at the end of a Dinner Night, so beloved of City Livery Companies, is not a widely practiced tradition in the British Army. That said, the Northamptonshire Regiment (now the Royal Anglian Regiment) circulate the Talavera Cup, which holds six bottles of champagne and has to be drained by the last drinker (as usual, the poor, bloody junior subaltern), who is allowed to leave the dining room once he has achieved the feat. This precautionary exit is not required by the East Surrey Regiment (now The Princess of Wales's Royal Regiment) who circulate the Dettingen Cup; but it may be required, this time by the unfortunate senior guest, when the Barrosa Cup does the rounds at the Royal Irish Fusiliers' (now part of the Royal Irish Regiment) dining table. These silver cups are commemorative of battles fought, but are not – like Joseph Bonaparte's silver chamber pot – spoils of war.

To the dismay of some guests, however, is the appearance of 'The Emperor' at the end of a King's Royal Hussars' Dinner Night. After the Loyal Toast and the toast to the Colonel-in-Chief have been drunk, the Mess Sergeant brings the Napoleonic silver chamber pot into the dining room, filled to the brim with champagne. The Commanding Officer rises, takes the pot, and drinks to the health of 'The Emperor'. Whether the Emperor so toasted is Napoleon or the chamber pot itself is unclear. The bedroom receptacle is then passed around the table and each person in turn stands and makes the same toast. Those drinking from 'The Emperor' for the first time, whether guests or members of the Regiment, are warmly applauded for their *sang froid*. When everyone has made the toast, the Commanding Officer directs the Mess Sergeant to invite one or more of the officers present to drain the bowl and, when the last one has done so, he holds it upside down over his head to prove that it is empty. It could only happen in a British cavalry Regiment.

Whilst on the subject of drinking vessels, and by way of a complete contrast to Joseph's armorial silver potty, there exist two further domestic trophies from his carriage.

The first is a small silver beaker. This vessel, of thimble shape with a reeded rim and a gilded interior, was probably part of a larger travelling canteen. As a label stuck to it asserts, it was acquired by Captain (later Lieutenant Colonel) Arthur Kennedy of the 18th Hussars and is still held in the collection of his lineal descendant

The second, now in a display cabinet in the Le Marchant Room at the Royal Military Academy Sandhurst, could easily have been purchased yesterday as a picnic accessory. It is a plain crystal tumbler in a protective wicker cover with lid. Beside it lies the following legend:

> This plane [*sic*] glass and wicker container was taken from Bonaparte's coach by Charles Cowly, Quartermaster of the 10th Hussars, 21st June 1813.

Readers will recall that the Regiment which captured ex-King Joseph's potty and King Ferdinand's artwork was the 14th Light Dragoons, albeit under the command of a Tenth Hussar. The 14th were, as already noted, only part of the Cavalry Brigade tasked with pursuing the French, which explains why the two drinking vessels were taken by men from other light cavalry Regiments.

Silver beaker taken from the coach of King Joseph Bonaparte

Water glass & wicker carrier, taken from the coach of King Joseph Bonaparte

Marshal Jourdan's Baton (Vitoria, 1813)

Not content with capturing the Eagle of the French 8th Infantry Regiment of the Line at the Battle of Barrosa (*see* p.85), and being peripherally involved in the possible capture of the 22nd's Eagle at Salamanca (*see* p.88), the fearsome Irishmen of the 87th Regiment of Foot[8] liberated the baton of the luckless Marshal Jourdan in the immediate aftermath of the Battle of Vitoria.

Jean-Baptiste Jourdan had started life as a Private in the French Royal Army in 1778, and had risen to become one of the most successful commanders of the French Revolutionary Army and the *Grande Armée*, until he met with Wellington at Vitoria and lost not only the battle, but also his Marshal's baton.

The title Marshal of France, styled Marshal of the Empire under

8. Later the Royal Irish Fusiliers

Napoleon I, was the second of two military honorifics awarded to distinguished French Generals for exceptional achievements. The more senior rank, which was only rarely awarded, was Marshal General of France, a distinction which during the First French Empire was awarded only to Marshal Soult. Both appointments also carried with them the ceremonial status and designation of a Great Dignitary of the Empire.

As in the United Kingdom where, until recently and in contrast to France, Field Marshal was a military rank rather than an honorary appointment, a French Marshal carried a baton which was presented to him by the Head of State. In the case of Marshal Jourdan, he had received his from the hands of the Emperor Napoleon. Less elaborate than their British equivalents, a Marshal's baton of the First French Empire was a blue velvet-covered staff decorated with gold-embroidered Imperial eagles. In addition, at either end of the baton were gold collars, stamped with the Paris assay and duty marks for the period, in the case of Marshal Jourdan's baton, 1798–1809. Around the top collar in capital letters was the Latin inscription: *Terror belli, decus pacis* (terror in war, ornament in peace). And, around the bottom collar, in script, was the Marshal's name and the date of the presentation: *Jean Baptiste Jourdan Nommé par l'Empereur Napoléon Maréchal de L'Empire le 29 Floréal Anno 12e'* (19th May 1804).

Although a Marshal's baton did not have the same emotional significance as a regimental Eagle, they were nonetheless highly prized by their owners and were usually carried by them when in uniform. It is quite surprising, therefore, that Marshal Jourdan left his baton on the battlefield of Vitoria. It was picked up by Private Paddy Shannon of the 2nd Battalion of the 87th, who found it on a pile of abandoned baggage, still in its red-morocco-leather case. Unlike the dramatic circumstances in which Captain Wyndham scooped the Spanish Royal picture collection after the same battle, according to the 82nd's regimental history no heroics were involved, and the baton was in due course passed to General Marquess of Wellington, who in turn forwarded it to Lord Bathurst with a covering letter dated 22nd June 1813, which read in part:

Marshal Jourdan holding his baton

Marshal Jourdan's baton.
Royal Collection Trust © Her Majesty Queen Elizabeth II 2018

Cartoon lampooning the loss of King Joseph's sceptre & Marshal Jourdan's baton

I send this despatch by my A.D.C. Captain Freemantle whom I beg leave to your Lordship's protection. He will have the honour of laying at the feet of H.R.H. The Prince Regent … Marshal Jourdan's baton of a Marshal of France [*sic*] taken by the 87th Regt.

The Prince Regent was delighted with the gift, which unlike his bomb and despite its suggestive shape, did not excite ribaldry in the media. On 5th July 1813, he wrote back to Wellington:

> You have sent me among the Trophies of your unrivalled Fame, the Baton of a French Marshal and I send you in return that of England. The British Army will hail it with enthusiasm while the whole Universe will acknowledge those valorous Exploits, which have so imperiously called for it …

which must have seemed like a very fair exchange to Wellington. It is worth noting that, in addition to the extraordinary spoils of war acquired during and after the Battle of Vitoria, its legacy also includes Beethoven's Opus 91, otherwise known as 'Wellington's Victory'.

CHAPTER 12

RETREAT FROM MOSCOW (1812)

From Moscow to Salisbury

Napoleon's looted Russian dispatch case (Ashmiany, Belarus, 1812)

While Wellington was advancing ever deeper into Spain and ever higher up the ranks of the British peerage, Emperor Napoleon was making the worst mistake of his entire career: the invasion of Russia on 24th June 1812. A bare five months later, he was in retreat from Moscow. As Napoleon was presiding over this disaster, his enemies in Paris, led by Claude-François de Malet, seized their opportunity and attempted a *coup d'etat* on 23rd October. It failed and the conspirators were summarily shot, but Napoleon was badly rattled.

Princess Catherine Voronzov, Countess of Pembroke by Sir Thomas Lawrence

Between the 26th and 29th November the remnants of the *Grande Armée*, reduced from a frontline strength of 685,000 men in June to just 27,000, fought a stiff rear-guard action near Borisov, which enabled Napoleon and his frost-bitten troops to cross the River Berezina, thereby avoiding a Russian trap and total annihilation. By the time he got to Vilnius on 5th December, Napoleon decided that his rightful place was in Paris. Following the example set by his brother Joseph, he abandoned his travelling coach in the snow, and clambered aboard a much faster, horse-drawn sleigh. Thirteen days later he was in Paris, having travelled an average of 100 miles a day.

A spoil of war of this disastrous campaign lies in a small display case in a corridor at Wilton House in Wiltshire, the seat of the Earls of Pembroke. As listed in their archives, this piece of loot is described as:

> A Russian cut-steel-mounted and Karelian birch dispatch case of rectangular form, with its spandrels and centre decorated with florets within a channelled border of waved stylised foliage and florets, with a tan leather-hinged lower section.

But why should this Russian briefcase qualify for inclusion in a book

Retreat from Moscow

about British-acquired spoils of war? A clue lies in the engraved-silver plaque on the reverse of the case: *Etui trouvée dans la voiture particulière de Bonaparte pendant la retraite de la grand armée Française entre Smolensk et la Beresina en 1812.* (A dispatch case found in the personal carriage of Bonaparte during the retreat of the French Grand Army between Smolensk and the Beresina in 1812.)

Given its origin, it is probable that this obviously expensive business accoutrement was not brought to Russia by Napoleon, but was looted by him (or one of his Staff) while he was in Moscow, almost certainly – for all the shops were closed – from within the Kremlin. There exists the possibility that it was given to Napoleon when he met Tsar Alexander I at Tilsit in 1807, but the Russian Imperial coat-of-arms, which would have been a feature of any such gift, is absent. It is reasonable to assume, therefore, that it is a Napoleonic spoil of war, which was in turn looted or reacquired by the pursuing Russians.

But how did it end up in a stately home in southern England? The answer lies in the Pembroke archives, which state that it was given by General (later

Wilton House

Field Marshal) Prince Mikhail Semyonovich Vorontsov, the Commander of a Russian Grenadier Division, to his sister, Ekaterina (Catherine),
the second wife of the 11th Earl of Pembroke.

When Mikhail and Ekaterina were children and adolescents, their
father, Count Semyon Vorontsov, served as the Russian Ambassador in
London from 1785 to 1800. Vorontzov senior, who was a committed Anglophile although he never learned to speak English, remained in London
on retirement from the Russian diplomatic service, until his death in
1832. He was buried in the Pembroke family vault, and the road in St
John's Wood where he lived was (and remains) named in his honour,
albeit spelt Woronsow.

Meanwhile, Mikhail had returned to Russia to join the army, rose
through the officer corps, and ended up a Divisional General shortly
before Napoleon invaded. Vorontzov fought at the Battle of Borodino in
September 1812, during which his composite Grenadier Division was
reduced from 4,000 to 300 men, and he was wounded. However, he
recovered in time to lead a new Grenadier Division in pursuit of the
retreating French, and although he failed to capture the ogre, he did
manage to rescue his looted Russian briefcase.

CHAPTER 13
WAR OF 1812 (1812–1815)

The Lost Honours of the United States of America

As a result of the momentous events taking place on and around the continent of Europe, Britain's war with its former colonial possessions in North America, which raged intermittently from 1812 to 1815, has tended to be somewhat overshadowed and its origins forgotten. The burning of much of Washington DC, and in particular the White House (then known as the President's Palace), is about the only event that most Englishmen can remember. Memories of the conflict on the other side of the Atlantic are somewhat naturally sharper, and the loss of at least ten Colours to the British has not been forgotten.

Although by 1812 the young United States had a thirty-five-year-old treaty with France, and a lingering, romanticised sympathy for the French Revolution, the country was not bound to join France in a European war. With no love for Napoleon's Imperial ideas, the Americans managed to sustain a position of neutrality. In 1803 they had doubled their landmass, with the acquisition of Louisiana from Imperial France for $15 million.

The Capture & Burning of Washington

The War of 1812 was therefore not specifically a war in support of the French, but had its own multiple origins. These included British attempts to restrict United States trade with French-occupied Europe, the Royal Navy's impressment of American seamen, and the US's ambition to expand northwards into British-held Canada.

Following the United States' declaration of war on the United Kingdom on 18th June 1812, the conflict was fought in three theatres. At sea, warships and privateers on both sides attacked their opponents' merchant

General William Hull

Major General Sir Isaac Brock

1. Later the 1st Battalion The Welsh Regiment

2. Eight years later, the future American Civil War General, William Tecumseh Sherman, was named after the Shawnee chief – presumably with unintentional baptismal irony

ships, whilst the Royal Navy blockaded the Atlantic coast of the United States to halt the Americans' export trade. Meanwhile, minor land battles took place on the United States-Canadian border, with the capture of Canada the US objective and the capture of New York that of the British. Further south, the British also attempted to capture the US capital, Washington, DC.

The Treaty of Ghent was signed on 24th December 1814. However, it was only ratified by the British three days later and by the Americans on 17th February 1815. The delayed US ratification is significant with regard to the British capture of the Colours of the 2nd Regiment of Infantry (*see* p.114). It resulted in no gains or losses for either side, other than captured warships and Colours, and the war ended as a score draw. It did, however, achieve one thing. Since then, despite a near miss in 1861, the United States and the United Kingdom have not fought a war against each other.

The Regimental Colour & the National Colour of the 4th Regiment of Infantry (Fort Detroit, 1812)

In the early months of 1812, as the tension with Britain increased, the US government decided to form an army which could secure the former Northwest Territory against the much-feared Native Americans, who had been incited to harass the United States by the British. These troops were also intended to reinforce the outpost of Detroit, which had a peace-time garrison of only 120 soldiers. The command was placed in the hands of Brigadier General William Hull, an ageing veteran of the American Revolutionary War. Hull's Army consisted initially of three Regiments of Ohio Militia, who were badly equipped and ill-disciplined, but these troops were soon joined by the 4th US Regiment of Infantry, taking the garrison to approximately 2,500.

Facing them on 15th to 16th August 1812 were the numerically inferior forces of Major General Isaac Brock, whose 1,500 soldiers, consisted of the 41st (Welch) Regiment of Foot,[1] and a contingent of Britain's Native American allies under the Shawnee leader, Tecumseh.[2]

Brock, who must have been an unusually enterprising General, had received intelligence that Hull's forces were suffering from low morale and a deep fear of the Native Americans, whom they believed to be hell-bent on rape, torture and worse. Brock decided to play on these fears. Rather than launch an all-out assault on Fort Detroit with his numerically inferior force, he put in place a cunning plan to make it appear to the Americans that they were facing not only a significant number of British regulars, but also hordes of slavering, tomahawk-wielding Native Americans. The British played on the Americans' fear of the Indians by arranging for a misleading letter to fall into Hull's hands. The letter asked that no more Indians be allowed to proceed from Fort Mackinac, as there were already 5,000 at Amherstburg and supplies were running short. Meanwhile, the British troops were told to light individual fires instead of one fire per unit, thereby creating the illusion of a much larger army. They marched to take up positions in plain sight of the Americans, then quickly ducked behind entrenchments, and marched back out of sight to repeat the manoeuvre. The same trick was carried out during meals, where the line would dump their beans into a hidden pot, and then return out of view to re-join the end of the line. The bluff worked, and after an opening salvo accompanied by blood-curdling war cries from the Native Americans, Hull raised the white flag in double quick time. For the price of just two wounded men, General Brock captured Fort Detroit, was dubbed the 'saviour of Upper Canada' and made a Knight of the Bath, while the 41st Regiment acquired both the National and the Regimental Colours of the 4th US Infantry Regiment and the unique battle honour: 'Detroit'.

In due course the American Colours arrived in London, where they were laid at the feet of the Prince Regent. Sometime later, they were hung in the Chapel at the Royal Hospital Chelsea, where they remained until the 8th March 1961 when they were handed over, without their staffs, to The Welch Regiment, who deposited them in their museum in Cardiff Castle, now known as Firing Line: the Museum of the Queen's Dragoon Guards and The Royal Welsh. Although by now very fragile, these first spoils of the War of 1812 were in pristine condition when they were captured, doubtless because the siege, if such it can be called, was over so quickly. They were still in a very good state when Captain John Ford illustrated them for his *Flag Book* in 1840.

The National Colour of the 4th Regiment is blue, with the United States Eagle at its centre; above the Eagle's head are fourteen gold stars and beneath its talons is a scroll with the regimental title. The Regiment's Colour is much simpler, being a plain white flag with the letters 'US' within a wreath, in the centre of a gold-edged blue scroll bearing the regimental title.[3]

Although the originals are now in Wales, copies of both flags still hang above the heads of the Chelsea Pensioners in the Great Hall at the Royal Hospital, while on the panelling below, the word DETROIT can be found,

Tecumseh of the Shawnee

National Colour of 4th Regiment ©*Royal Hospital Chelsea*

3. In Jonathan Riley's book, *A Matter of Honour: The Life, Campaigns and Generalship of Isaac Brock*, the 4th's National Colour is correctly illustrated, but the Regimental Colour is not

along with all the other battle honours of the British and Imperial Armies since Tangier (1662–1680). These are doubtless effective aids to the Pensioners' digestions as they munch their way through their meals.

The Colour of a New York Regiment of Militia (Queenstown Heights, 1812)
On 13th October 1812, at the Battle of Queenstown Heights, in modern-day Ontario province, Major General Sir Isaac Brock, unaware that he had been knighted for his devious deception plan at Fort Detroit two months earlier, was once again the British hero-of-the-hour. Sadly, he did not live to see the capture of another American Colour. This time it was a dark blue flag bearing the arms of New York State. It belonged to one of the units of the New York Militia, whose 16th, 17th, 18th, 19th and 20th Regiments attacked the British position, in company with the 6th, 13th and 23rd US Regiments of Infantry. These 6,000 American troops who led the invasion of Canada were under the command of Major General Stephen Van Rensselaer, a militia General who was the leading Federalist candidate for the governorship of New York, either or both of which facts may account for the large presence of the New York Militia on the battlefield.

4. Later the Royal Berkshire Regiment

Facing the American invasion on the Heights above the Niagara River were the Grenadier Company of the 49th (Hertfordshire) Regiment of Foot,[4] which Brock had formerly commanded, a Flank Company of the 2nd Regiment of York Militia, known as the York Volunteers, a detachment of the 41st Regiment of Foot with a three-pounder gun, and a war party of Native Americans.

Death of General Brock at the Battle of Queenstown Heights, 13th October 1812

In the first phase of the attack, some of the New York Militia Regiments crossed the river, climbed the Heights, and captured the British artillery emplacement which was guarding the crossing. Worried that the Americans, with the British artillery out of action, would move the rest of their troops across the river, Brock ordered an immediate counter-attack on the position by the 49th and personally led the charge on foot. The assault was halted by heavy New York Militia fire, and to Brock's dismay some of his men started falling out of the line. 'This is the first time I have ever seen the 49th turn their backs!' Brock yelled at them. 'Surely the heroes of Egmont will not tarnish their record!' This did the trick, the ranks promptly closed up, and Brock pressed forward with his attack, despite being wounded on the wrist. Unfortunately for him, and in an echo of Nelson at Trafalgar, a colourful sash, given to him eight weeks earlier by Tecumseh after the Siege of Detroit, made him a conspicuous target. When a New York Militiaman stepped forward from a thicket and fired at him, Brock fell dead with a musket ball through his heart.

General Roger Sheaffe

Following his death, the British attempt to recapture the gun position continued, but was ultimately unsuccessful. However, all was not lost and the British made a tactical withdrawal to await reinforcements, whilst the Americans made a chaotic attempt to complete the crossing of the river, this time unopposed. Frustratingly for General Van Rensselaer, his troops had again been thoroughly rattled by the war cries of Britain's Native American allies, clearly audible from across the river, and they refused to get into the boats. He then ordered the civilian boatmen to cross the river and retrieve the New York Militia units from the Heights, but they too refused.

The British counter-attack on the stranded New Yorkers was made by the Light Company of the 41st, accompanied by Native Americans of the Mohawk tribe and Chippewa militiamen, all led by General Roger Sheaffe. After firing a volley this mixed force charged, with the 41st yelling 'Avenge the General!' and the Mohawks uttering their fearsome war-cries. This was too much for the New York Militia, who fled off the Heights, leaving behind their Colour, which was duly seized by a Chippewa militia-man and later presented to Sheaffe.

Unfortunately for the New Yorkers, not only did they lose their Colour, but they also found when they got to the river bank that there was no way for them to cross back onto American soil. With no means of evacuating his men, and with the Mohawks screaming for scalps following the deaths of two Chiefs, Lieutenant Colonel Winfield Scott, the US commander on the ground, feared a massacre and decided to surrender. The first two American officers who tried to do this were hacked to death by the Mohawks. Even after Scott had personally waved a white flag (actually, a white cravat belonging to one of his colleagues), over-excited Native Americans continued to fire from the Heights into the crowd of New York Militiamen on the river bank below.

Unlike many other flags that were on display at the Royal Hospital, the

Colour of the New York Militia
©*Royal Hospital Chelsea*

Colour of the Kentucky Regiment
© *Royal Hospital Chelsea*

New York Militia Colour was not returned to the unit which captured it, as there were no recognisable successors-in-title to the Chippewa Militia. Instead, it was handed into the care of the National Army Museum, when it opened next to the Royal Hospital Chelsea in 1971. However, as with the Colours of the 4th US Regiment of Infantry, a copy is still in the Great Hall of the Royal Hospital, with the battle honours DETROIT and NIAGARA on the panelling below.

A Colour of the Kentucky Regiment (1813?)

According to the records of the Royal Hospital Chelsea, Flag No 44, which until the 1970s hung in the Chapel, was that of a Kentucky Regiment captured in 1812. White, with the Eagle crest of the United States at its centre, only one tattered half of the Colour remained when it was depicted by Captain Ford in the *Flag Book*. If the obverse bore a clue as to its precise regimental identity, it was not recorded. That is all that is known for sure; however, the available historical evidence from other sources would seem to indicate that the date and/or the attribution are, at least in part, wrong.

The Kentucky regimental Colour, which showed considerable signs of battle damage, was in all probability that of a Kentucky Volunteer Regiment. It was almost certainly lost to the British in the notorious Second Battle of the River Raisin (also known as the Battle of Frenchtown), which was the next significant conflict in the Americans' hopelessly optimistic war-strategy for retaking Fort Detroit, expunging the memory of Queenstown Heights, and seizing Canada. Fought on 22nd January 1813 by the US against British, Canadian and Native American forces, it was the biggest battle for Kentucky forces in the War of 1812, and it ended with a notorious and bloody massacre.

On 18th January, the Americans had forced the retreat of the British and their Native American allies from Frenchtown (now in Monroe County, Michigan), which they had earlier occupied in a relatively minor skirmish. On hearing that the Americans had recaptured the town, Brigadier General Henry Procter, commander of the British forces around Detroit, marched with his troops from Fort Malden and crossed the frozen Detroit River into Michigan.

Procter's 1,400-strong force comprised 597 men of the battle-hardened 41st Regiment of Foot, the Royal Newfoundland Fencibles [*sic*], the Canadian Essex Militia, and approximately 800 Native Americans drawn from the Shawnee, Potawatomi, Ottawa, Chippewa, Delaware, Miami, Winnebago, Creek, Sauk, and Fox tribes. Command of this fearsome Native American war party was in the hands of Chiefs Roundhead and Walk-in-the-Water. Facing the British were 1,000 men of the 1st and 5th Regiments of Kentucky Volunteers and the 1st Rifle Regiment of Kentucky Volunteers.

Proctor halted his men about five miles north of the River Raisin, where they engaged the 1st and 5th Regiments of Kentucky Volunteers with frontal musket volley fire and enfiladed artillery fire. The Kentuckians, who were guarding the approach to Frenchtown, almost immediately broke and ran. The American commander, General James Winchester, sent orders to the 1st Rifle Regiment in Frenchtown to reinforce the Volunteers, but the orders never reached them. Under fire from three sides, the men of the Kentucky Volunteers legged it towards Ohio, with Chief Roundhead and his posse in hot pursuit. Although the Kentuckians tried to rally three times, they were eventually surrounded on a narrow road, where more than 200 were shot, tomahawked and scalped, and 150 men, including General Winchester, were captured. Chief Roundhead stripped Winchester of his uniform before he turned him over to the British; this was the origin of the legend that the General was captured in his nightshirt. The remaining Americans were scattered and in no position to fight; those who surrendered were duly tomahawked to death.

General James Winchester

Despite the rout in the field, the 1st Rifle Regiment continued to hold out in Frenchtown until they ran out of ammunition. Proctor demanded that Winchester, by this time a prisoner-of-war, order his men to surrender. At first the American General refused, but eventually a British officer under a flag of truce gave the beleaguered Riflemen a written order from Winchester to surrender. They in turn refused and decided to fight to the death, rather than trust the Native Americans. It was only after three hours more fighting that they finally ran up a white flag. Three hundred Riflemen had been killed and five hundred were taken prisoner.

Following this victory, General Proctor decided that the wise move would be to withdraw immediately back across the border, marching the uninjured prisoners with him through the snow and leaving the wounded behind in Frenchtown. On the morning of 23rd January, the Native Americans set fire to the buildings in which the wounded were lying and hacked to death those who escaped from the inferno; the rest died in the flames. The Native Americans also killed all the stragglers from Proctor's column. This senseless slaughter of so many men of Kentucky, including

River Raisin Memorial

Major General Robert Ross

5. Later The King's Shropshire Light Infantry

General William Winder

many leading citizens of the State, horrified Americans, but perversely led many more Kentuckians to enlist for the war under the rallying cry: 'Remember the River Raisin!'

The River Raisin Massacre may also explain why the 41st Regiment of Foot did not lay claim to the Kentuckians' Colour. There is no copy of the Colour now hanging at the Royal Hospital; and as this engagement was never awarded a battle honour, it does not appear inscribed on the Great Hall's panelling.

The Colour of 68th Regiment James City Light Infantry & the Standard of 1st Hartford Dragoons (Bladensburg, 1814)

In the early years of the War of 1812, the majority of the fighting on land was on the US-Canadian border, where British, Canadian and Native American troops repeatedly prevented, through better leadership and fear of a scalping, an American invasion of Canada. However, with the Peninsular War at an end by the middle of 1814, the United Kingdom had the military resources to take the initiative. A large force was sent to Canada to prepare for a march on New York, and a smaller force of 4,500 men, under Major General Robert Ross, was designated for an attack on Washington. Amongst Ross's forces was the 85th Regiment of Foot,[5] which had fought throughout the Peninsular War, crossed the Pyrenees, and ended up in Bordeaux, where it was brought back up to strength, prior to embarkation for the United States.

Major General Ross's Army left Bordeaux on 1st June 1814, crossed the Atlantic to New England via Bermuda, and landed unopposed in Chesapeake Bay on 20th August. From there it marched, with the same determination its men had shown in Spain, straight towards the newly-established US capital, Washington. By midday on 24th August, Ross's army, led by the light infantry including the 85th, was approaching the village of Bladensburg. Clearing a rise in the road they saw an American Army, under General William Winder, drawn up on a hillside on the far side of the river Anacostia, barring the route to the newly-built US capital. Winder's Army was accompanied by US President Madison and most of his government. Mrs James Madison had been left behind in the President's Palace to supervise the preparation of a victory banquet for forty.

Estimates put Winder's force at around 6,500 men, drawn from inexperienced local Militias, supported by sub-units from the US Continental Army, including the Virginia-recruited 68th US Regiment of Infantry (James City Light Infantry) and the 1st Regiment of Light Dragoons (also known as the Hartford Light Dragoons), the latter fighting as infantry, as they had done – despite their cavalry designation – from the date of their formation in 1808, and as they were to do until their disbandment in 1815.

The engagement which followed lasted for three hours, with the British light infantry leading the attack. This determined and successful assault by the Peninsular-seasoned troops on Winder's largely amateur Army opened the road to Washington and resulted in the capture by the 85th of the Colours of the James City Light Infantry and the Standard of the dismounted Hartford Light Dragoons.

As illustrated in the *Flag Book*, the US Light Infantry Colour was white with the bald-headed eagle crest of the United States, below which were scrolls, on the upper one of which were the words '68th Regiment' and below it 'James City Light Infantry'. The obverse was more interesting. It depicted Liberty holding a US flag, with her foot on the belly of a portly male figure, who she has just stabbed; a crown lies on the ground behind him. There was also a motto: '*Tyrannos pedibus calco*' (liberty treading the tyrant underfoot). The dying man was either King George III or the Prince Regent, probably the latter given the size of his belly.

The Light Dragoons Standard is blue, fringed with tassels and with a variant of the US crest at the centre, the Regiment's name on a scroll beneath and the somewhat quaint motto for a fighting unit of: 'Touch Me Not'. Quaint that is, unless it is a contraction of the Scots Guards motto, 'Nemo Me Impune Lacessit', which translates as, 'No one touches me with impunity', sometimes rendered in the barrack room as: 'If you bash me, I'll bash you back'.

There are no official accounts of the capture of either flag by the 85th. Fortunately, however, once again the *Flag Book* provides an interesting anecdote. The Reverend George Robert Gleig served with the 85th at the Battle of Bladensburg, subsequently entered the Church, and rose to be Chaplain to the Royal Household, Chaplain General of the Armed Forces, and Chaplain Emeritus of the Royal Hospital Chelsea from 1834 to 1836. Captain Ford recorded that a report in the *United Service Journal* stated:

Mr Gleig when serving in the 85th & being engaged at Bladensburg in the United States stepped in the excitement of the moment over the very Flag in question. The Subaltern, who was as eminent for zeal and spirit in his martial

Colour of 68th Regiment (James City Light Infantry)
© Royal Hospital Chelsea

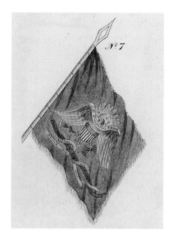

Standard of the 1st or Hartford Light Dragoons *© Royal Hospital Chelsea*

Dolley Madison

Rev George Gleig

vocation as he is distinguished for the best endeavours of a Protestant Pastor, had received a musket ball in the thigh just before coming to the Flag [of the James City Light Infantry], and a soldier who closely followed him was hit in the ankle when in the act of picking it up. It now hangs in sight of his pulpit, as 'emeritus' Chaplain of the Royal Hospital.

As the dismounted Light Dragoons were probably serving alongside the James Towners, their Standard was almost certainly captured at the same time. In any event, the Governor at the Royal Hospital Chelsea had no doubt as to which Regiment had captured the flags when he handed both to The King's Shropshire Light Infantry on 28th September 1947. These spoils of war can still be seen in the Regiment's museum in Shrewsbury Castle, whilst the battle honour BLADENSBURG is inscribed on the panels of the Great Hall at the Royal Hospital Chelsea.

There is however an ironic coda to this story. Following the capture of the US flags, the gallant 85th – presumably at their light infantry pace of 140 to the minute – marched on to Washington. They arrived at the President's Palace that evening, although not before Dolley Madison had managed to save a portrait of George Washington, by ordering her husband's personal slave to rip it out of its frame and roll it up. The President's chicken banquet, still warm on the table when the 85th burst into the Palace, and his sideboard groaning under the weight of fine wines, fared less well. They were consumed by the hungry and thirsty light infantrymen, before they looted the table silver, ransacked the President's wardrobe for clean shirts, and then torched the building. The President's Palace was faced with stone, which was badly blackened by the smoke from the ensuing blaze. The only way to repair this defacement after hostilities ended, short of re-facing the whole building, was to paint it white, hence the White House. So, the name of one of the world's most famous buildings was brought about by the post-prandial actions of what was to become The King's Shropshire Light Infantry.

Now for the ironic but unintentional symmetry of a later event. On 25th August 1992, the Regiment's museum in Shrewsbury, in which were displayed the two trophies of Bladensburg, was firebombed by the IRA, which was itself part-funded by Irish Americans. The resulting smoke irreparably blackened the white James City Light Infantry Colour, to the point where it is now impossible to detect the designs on it. However, the formerly white Colour – like the President's Palace – survived the flames, albeit in a significantly altered state.

far left
National Colour of 2nd Infantry
Regiment (No.8 in the *Flag
Book*) © *Royal Hospital Chelsea*

left
Regimental Colour of 2nd
Infantry Regiment (No.16 in the
Flag Book) © *Royal Hospital Chelsea*

The Disgraced Colours of the 2nd Regiment of Infantry (Fort Bowyer, 1815)
Although the Royal Hospital's *Flag Book* is an invaluable pictorial and
historical record of Colours captured by the British Army, it is not always
entirely accurate. This is particularly the case with two US Colours listed
in the book, both belonging to the US 2nd Regiment of Infantry. The first
is Flag 8, formerly in the Chapel, a blue National Colour which Captain
Ford had noted as being 'taken by General Brock on the frontier'. This is
not possible, as the 2nd Regiment served only in Alabama during the
War of 1812. The second is Flag 15, formerly in the Great Hall, a white
regimental Colour, which Captain Ford correctly identified as belonging
to the 2nd Regiment. However, he stated its date of capture as 'unknown',
and noted that the 2nd Regiment served at Fort Bayo, a place that does
not exist.

In fact, the 2nd Regiment of Infantry was the garrison of Fort Bowyer
(not Bayo), near Mobile, Alabama, which was the site of two engage-
ments fought either side of the Battle of New Orleans. The first Battle of
Fort Bowyer, in September 1814, was designed to unlock the approach to
the harbour of Mobile, the capture of which would have enabled the
Royal Navy to block Louisiana's profitable export trade with France.
The assault failed and led the British to try and capture New Orleans
instead. When this also failed in mid-January 1815, the British switched
their attention back to Fort Bowyer, where the defences had since been
strengthened and its garrison increased. US General Andrew Jackson
was so confident that he rather foolishly declared that 'ten thousand men
cannot take it'. In the event a considerably smaller number of British
soldiers managed the feat.

The successful British force, under the command of Brigadier General
John Lambert, comprised the 4th (King's Own) Regiment of Foot, 21st

General Andrew Jackson

6. Later the King's Own Royal Regiment, the Royal Scots Fusiliers and the Essex Regiment, respectively.

(Royal North British Fusilier) Regiment of Foot and 44th (East Essex) Regiment of Foot.[6] Amongst the officers serving with this force was Ensign (later the aforementioned Reverend George Robert) Gleig, who had also fought at Bladensburg, where he tripped over the Colour of the James City Light Infantry, which later fluttered over his pulpit at the Royal Hospital.

Eschewing an attack from the sea preceded by an infantry land assault, which had failed so badly the year before, Lambert decided to lay siege to the Fort deploying heavy artillery on the landward side with naval gunnery support from the sea. The siege bombardment commenced on 9th February 1815 and by the 12th the US garrison had run up a white flag. Accounts differ as to what actually happened, but it seems that the barrage of British artillery fire so rattled the garrison that morale collapsed and mass drunkenness ensued, to the point where Major William Lawrence, the Governor of the Fort, had no option but to agree to unconditional surrender, which must have included relinquishing the Colours of the inebriated 2nd Regiment.

Strangely Gleig, who wrote extensively and frankly about his combat experiences in the United States, made no mention of the 'capture' of these Colours; neither did the Royal Hospital ever ascribe their acquisition to any of the British Regiments involved. There is, however, an explanation as to why these Colours are not on display in a regimental museum and why Fort Bowyer is not emblazoned as a battle honour on the panelling of the Great Hall at the Royal Hospital Chelsea. The War of 1812 had actually ended six weeks *before* with the Treaty of Ghent, albeit that the Treaty was formally ratified by the USA the day following the assault on Fort Bowyer. Which begs a further question: why, when this emerged a few days after the battle, were the Colours not returned to the 2nd Infantry Regiment? The answer is that, immediately following the end of the war, the Regiment lost its identity and its alcohol-vulnerable soldiers were merged into the 1st Regiment of Infantry and so had no need of their old Colours.

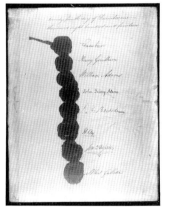

Signatures on the Treaty of Ghent

Other US trophies of the War of 1812

In addition to the United States Colours already described, there were three further American flags from the War of 1812 in the collection of the Royal Hospital Chelsea: two regimental Colours and a ship's Ensign. Unfortunately, Captain Ford's illustrations in the *Flag Book* do not show to which Regiments the Colours, or to which ship the Ensign, belonged.

Nor are there any explanatory notes appended, beyond a comment next to the Ensign, stating that it should have been sent to Greenwich Hospital, the Royal Navy's equivalent of the British Army's Royal Hospital at Chelsea.

Given the nature of warfare, in which aeroplanes are shot down and ships sunk, it is inevitable that the majority of spoils of war were captured by the Army. The relative paucity of naval trophies is further accounted for by the practice of captured merchant ships being sold for Prize Money and ships-of-the-line being pressed into the service of their captors. This was the case with five US Navy ships that were taken by the British during the War of 1812.

The first of the five

USS *Nautilus*, a fourteen-gun brigantine converted from a schooner launched in 1799, had the dubious distinction of being the first ship lost on either side during the War of 1812. On 17th July 1812, whilst cruising off the coast of New Jersey, USS *Nautilus* was attacked by a British Squadron and captured intact. Re-crewed with British tars and re-named HMS *Emulous*, she was soon back in business, capturing a number of American privateers and merchantmen. At the end of the war, HMS *Emulous* was sent to Deptford where she was laid up. Eventually, in August 1817, the British Admiralty sold her for the princely sum of £900.

USS *Nautilus*

Scuttled not captured

USS *Adams* was a purpose-built twenty-eight-gun frigate, laid down in 1797 and launched on 8th June 1799. Like USS *Nautilus*, *Adams* was later converted to a sloop, although the process, which involved cutting her in half and adding fifteen feet to her length, was somewhat more drastic. By the end of 1812, having survived her nautical surgery, she was re-launched, but was unable to leave Chesapeake Bay due to the British blockade. There she lay for the whole of 1813 until she finally managed to slip out to sea on 18th January 1814, crossed the Atlantic, and captured five merchantmen off the African coast, before returning to Savannah, Georgia, in April.

The following month, *Adams* once again set sail, this time for the waters off the British Isles, where she captured five more merchant ships, narrowly avoided being captured herself, briefly captured a sixth merchantman which was released when a brace of British warships arrived on the scene, and then set a course back across the Atlantic.

Near the end of her homeward passage, *Adams* ran aground on the Isle au Haut on 17th August 1814 and was seriously damaged. Skilful seamanship and a rising tide managed to re-float the ship, and despite heavy leaking, she limped into harbour at Hampden, Massachusetts. There, on 3rd September 1814, during the Battle of Hampden, she was scuttled and set ablaze to prevent capture by a British squadron.

Captured by the Irish
USS *Eagle* was originally a merchant sloop, but she was acquired by the US Navy in 1812, re-fitted for war and stationed on Lake Champlain on the US-Canadian border, where she was part of the naval force blockading the British advance from Canada. Most unusually for a ship, she was captured on 3rd June 1813 by the British 100th Regiment of Foot (Prince Regent's County of Dublin Regiment), a short-lived unit raised in 1808 and disbanded in 1818. The action, which lasted three-and-a-half hours, took place on the Sorrell River near Ile aux Noix on the Canadian side of the lake.

Taken into British service, and with deliberate irony re-named HMS *Finch*, she accompanied the British expedition that burned the arsenal and storehouses at Plattsburg, New York. However, this was to be the highpoint of her service under a British Ensign. On 11th September 1814, at the Battle of Lake Champlain, she was ordered to engage the USS *Preble*, a sloop of seven guns. But as she did so, the schooner USS *Ticonderoga* shot away her rigging and *Finch* ran aground near Crab Island, where a small American shore battery commenced firing on her. Unable to free herself, and with two men wounded, her commander, Lieutenant William Hicks, struck the colours. After a refit, she re-joined the US Navy under her original name, only to be sold in July 1815.

Having a whale of a time
USS *Essex* was a thirty-six-gun frigate, which in the first four months of the war captured ten prizes off the US coast. She then set her compass to south, crossed the Equator and rounded Cape Horn in heavy gales, arriving at Valparaíso, Chile, on 14th March 1813, having seized two British whaling schooners *en route*. Over the next five months *Essex* captured a further thirteen British whalers.

In January 1814, she returned to Valparaíso, where she was trapped for six weeks by HMS *Phoebe*, a thirty-six-gun frigate and the eighteen-gun sloop-of-war HMS *Cherub*. Eventually, on 28th March 1814, *Essex* made a break for the open seas in very heavy weather, lost her main topmast, and was engaged by the British just north of Valparaíso. For the next two-and-a-half hours, despite the longer-range guns of the British and two major fires on *Essex*, the Americans managed to hold them at bay. Eventually, with her crew reduced by half, fifty members having jumped overboard and swum for the shore, *Essex* was forced to surrender.

USS *Essex*

Because *Essex* was stored and provisioned for six months, she was sent to England with a skeleton crew. Arriving there in November, she was absorbed into the Royal Navy as HMS *Essex*. Sadly, that was the end of adventurous times for *Essex*, for despite being up-gunned, her next role was to act as a troop ship. But that was not the end of her degradation. From 1823 to 1837 she served as a prison hulk in Ireland and was finally sold, for £1,230, in 1837.

A causus belli

USS *President* was one of the original six three-masted heavy frigates of the fledgling US Navy. On 16th May 1811 her Captain mistakenly identified HMS *Little Belt* as HMS *Guerriere*, which had recently impressed an American seaman, and commenced a short engagement. Although the incident was resolved (albeit to neither party's satisfaction), it nonetheless fanned the flames that led to the War of 1812.

During the war, to the outbreak of which she had been a major contributing factor, *President* sailed across the North Atlantic, and up the English Channel, as far as Norway. Along the way, she captured the armed schooner HMS *Highflyer* and numerous merchant ships. By February 1814, however, *President* was back in New York harbour, where she remained, blockaded by a British Squadron. In January 1815, unaware that the Treaty of Ghent had been signed, she made a break for freedom.

On the evening of 14th January, *President* set sail but quickly ran aground, causing considerable damage to the ship and necessitating a return to base. However, the wind direction made this impossible, and *President* had no choice but to head out to sea and hope to dodge the

USS *President* in action with
HMS *Belvidera*

blockade. Two hours later she was spotted and a twenty-four-hour engagement ensued with the Royal Navy, in which *President* was captured, escaped
and captured again. After a dangerous voyage to England, during which
she lost her masts in a gale, *President* entered British service and was
twice up-gunned, before being broken up in 1818 on the discovery that
she was falling apart with rot.

A fishy tale

Now lodged together in the Institute of Jamaica are the jaws of a shark
and the ship's papers of an American merchant brig, the *Nancy*, captured
in 1799 by HMS *Sparrow*. The *Nancy*'s cargo was claimed as a prize by the
Sparrow's Captain Hugh Whylie RN, but when the claim came before the
Court of Vice-Admiralty in Jamaica, the *Nancy*'s Captain Thomas
Briggs was able to show from the ship's manifest that his ship was not
carrying contraband and therefore should be released. That would have
happened had a colleague of Captain Whylie's not mentioned to him that
he had recently hooked and gutted a large shark, in the belly of which
were a set of ship's papers. On examination, they turned out to be those

of the *Nancy*, and proved incontrovertibly that some of the cargo was indeed contraband and that the papers lodged with the Court by Briggs were false. Truth is often stranger than fiction.

Engagement between
USS *Enterprise* and HMS *Boxer*

In the interests of the special relationship, it is worth recording that the War of 1812 also produced spoils of war for the USA. These include a cannon belonging to HMS *Boxer*, which was lost to the American USS *Enterprise* at the Battle of Monhegan in September 1813. It now resides in a store room at Portland City Hall, where it has been since it was donated to the Maine Historical Society in 1894. Despite the fierceness of the engagement, the only fatalities were the opposing Captains – Lieutenant William Burrows USN and Commander Samuel Blyth RN – who were buried side-by-side in a single grave in Portland's Eastern Cemetery on Munjoy Hill.

CHAPTER 14

THE HUNDRED DAYS
(1815)

Souvenirs of the Battle of Waterloo

By early 1814, following defeats in Spain and Germany at the end of the previous year, France had been successfully invaded by the forces of the Sixth Coalition, an alliance consisting of Britain, Austria, Prussia, Russia, Portugal, Sweden, Spain, and several small German states. On 11th April 1814, the Treaty of Fontainebleau was signed by representatives of France, Austria, Russia and Prussia, ending Napoleon's rule and sending him into exile on the Mediterranean island of Elba. Although Britain was not a signatory to this treaty, it was a party to the Treaty of Paris, signed on 30th May 1814. Under the Fontainbleau agreement, Napoleon was allowed to keep his titles, although not his thrones, save that of Elba.

Napoleon arrived at Elba's capital, Portoferraio, on 4th May. Ten months later, he was bored to tears with ruling the tiny state. Separated from his wife and son, and deprived of the allowance guaranteed to him by the Treaty, he was also aware of rumours that he was about to be banished to St Helena in the South Atlantic. On 26th February 1815, with only 700 men, Napoleon escaped from Elba. After two days at sea, he

The Battle of Waterloo, 18th June 1815

128

Cartoon depicting Napoleon's banishment to Elba

landed on the French mainland at Golfe-Juan and headed north. Marshal Ney, who had thrown in his lot with King Louis XVIII, declared that he would bring Napoleon back to Paris in an iron cage.

There is no more telling illustration of the attitude of the French to Napoleon's return to France than the daily reports of his progress from Elba to Paris, published in the French government newspaper, *Le Moniteur Universel*:

> The *anthropophagus* [a mythical cannibal] has come out of his den …
> The Corsican ogre is about to land at Golfe Juan …
> The tiger has arrived at Gap …
> The monster lies at Grenoble …
> The tyrant has crossed Lyon …
> The usurper has been seen sixty leagues from the capital …
> Bonaparte advances at a great pace but will never enter Paris …
> Tomorrow Napoleon will be under our ramparts …
> The Emperor has arrived at Fontainbleau …
> Yesterday evening His Imperial & Royal Majesty took up residence at his
> Tuileries Palace surrounded by his loyal subjects

Napoleon returns to France, landing at Golfe-Juan

By 20th March, Napoleon was once again on the Imperial French throne, with Marshal Ney (who had again turned his coat) and some

The Battle for Hougoumont,
print after the painting by
Denis Dighton, 1815

50,000 soldiers of the old *Grande Armée* at his back. By the end of May, Napoleon's troops-under-arms had swelled to nearly 200,000 and *L'Armée du Nord* was ready to march to meet the forces of the Seventh Coalition, which had been rapidly assembled to put the Emperor back in his cage. Consisting of an alliance between the United Kingdom, Austria, Spain, Portugal, Prussia, Russia, Sweden, Holland, Saxony, Bavaria, Würtemburg, Switzerland, Hanover, Nassau, Brunswick, Sardinia, Liechtenstein, Denmark, and Naples, the Seventh Coalition pledged to field 150,000 troops against the French Emperor.

Napoleon's strategy for dealing with the Coalition was simple: he had to defeat them piecemeal before they could join forces and overwhelm him. His first move was to knock out the British-Allied forces south of Brussels, led by Field Marshal the Duke of Wellington, before they could link up with Marshal Blücher's Prussians. Speed was the essence of this plan. At first, all went well: on 15th June, at Charleroi, Napoleon drove a wedge between his enemies, following this up the next day by defeating the Prussians at Ligny. At the same time, Marshal Ney and the left wing of *L'Armée du Nord* fought Wellington's Anglo-Allied army at the crossroads of Quatre Bras, preventing them from coming to the aid of the Prussians and driving the British back towards Brussels. On the 17th, Napoleon, in pursuit of his strategy, split his forces and sent Marshal Grouchy after the Prussians, while he advanced on Wellington's defensive position near the village of Waterloo.

Hougoumont: a lock plate & several bricks (Waterloo, 1815)
On 18th June 1815 at Waterloo, one hamlet and two farm houses anchored Wellington's position: on his left flank was the garrisoned building of Papelotte; at the centre, the farmhouse La Haie Sainte; and on his right flank the fortified buildings of the Château d'Hougoumont. Defending the latter, under the overall command of Lieutenant Colonel James Macdonnell of the Coldstream Guards, were the 1st Battalion of the 2nd Nassau Regiment, elements of the 1st (Hanoverian) Brigade, the Light Company of the 2nd Battalion of the 3rd Regiment of Foot Guards, two Light Companies from the 1st and 2nd Battalions of the 1st Regiment of

Foot Guards,[1] and the Light Company of the 2nd Battalion of the Coldstream Guards under the command of Captain Henry Wyndham of Vitoria fame, who had recently transferred into the Coldstream.[2]

The French, led by Napoleon's brother Jérôme, commenced an assault on the Château at about eleven o'clock. Although this managed to clear the surrounding orchards, the farmhouse complex was not breached until 12.30 pm when Sous-Lieutenant Bonnet, known as 'Le Gros' on account of his enormous size, led an assault on the north gate, and wielding an axe broke through it. French troops streamed into the farmyard and a bitter hand-to-hand battle ensued. Colonel Macdonnell quickly realised that if the north gate, which was a choke point for the French, could be closed, the situation might yet be saved. Leading a party of ten men, including Wyndham, Ensigns James Hervey and Henry Gooch, Corporal James Graham and his brother Private Joseph Graham, Company Sergeant Majors Charles McGregor and Ralph Fraser, Sergeant Joseph Aston, and Private Joseph Lester, the feat was achieved, the gate was closed, and those French trapped in the farmyard were all slaughtered, save for a lone drummer boy. Wellington later remarked that 'the success of the battle [of Waterloo] turned upon the closing of the gates at Hougoumont'.

In addition to being the man who slid the bar of the north gate back in place, Corporal James Graham saved the life of the badly-wounded Wyndham, by shooting a sniper who was about to fire at him from the top of the wall, and then rescued his own injured brother from the flames of the farm's burning barn. When Wellington was asked by the Rev John Norcross, Rector of Framlingham, who the bravest man at Waterloo had been, he nominated Corporal Graham. On receipt of this opinion, Norcross awarded Graham a pension of £10 per annum, but it only lasted for two years, terminating with the vicar's bankruptcy.

Fighting continued around the Château all afternoon, but even heavy French shelling, which set the complex alight, was unable to dislodge the Guards. By seven o'clock in the evening, the building and its defenders had become the stuff of several legends and gave rise to a number of very British traditions.

The first of these relates to the Wyndham family. Constance, Lady Leconfield, sister of the 5th Earl of Rosebery and wife of Henry Wyndham's nephew, Henry, 2nd Baron Leconfield, as châtelaine of the family's country seat, Petworth House in Sussex, would constantly complain that no Wyndham had ever shut a door since Uncle Henry had shut the gate at Hougoumont. The Wyndham

1. Later the Scots Guards and the Grenadier Guards

2. As a Guards officer, Wyndham enjoyed the double rank unique to the Brigade of Guards, whereby he was accorded the pay and privileges of two ranks higher, thus making him a Captain in the Guards but a Lieutenant Colonel in the wider Army. This was an arrangement that did not – to the chagrin of current Guards officers – survive the Army reforms of the late-nineteenth century

Jérôme Bonaparte, King of Westphalia by Sarcy

New North Gate at Hougoumont, made from an oak on the Wyndham's estate at Petworth, 2015.

connection with Hougoumont persists to the present day. When a decision was taken to restore the buildings as part of the Waterloo 200 Commemorations in 2015, the present Lord Egremont donated new north gates made by the Petworth Estate carpenters from a 200-year-old oak grown on the estate, where his great-great-great-uncle Henry Wyndham had been born.

The original lock plate of the Hougoumont north gates is not in Belgium, from where it was removed after the battle, but on display in the Guards Museum at Wellington Barracks in London, complete with the following legend engraved on a silver plate:

> Lock from the Principal Gate at Hougomont [*sic*].
> Acquired from the Londesborough Collection. 1888.
> Presented by Colonel W Fox-Pitt late Grenadier Guards.
> To the Officers of the Brigade of Guards.

Albert, 1st Baron Londesborough, was only ten at the time of Waterloo and was later commissioned into the Royal Horse Guards, a Regiment which fought at Waterloo, but not at Hougoumont. Londesborough was, however, an avid collector, who accumulated a substantial collection of militaria and items of archaeological interest. These were all described in a book published in 1857 and then exhibited in Dublin in 1872, before being dispersed at auction by his heir in 1888. Unfortunately, neither the book nor the exhibition catalogue explains how he acquired the Hougoumont lock plate; and Lord Londesborough's papers, which might have provided the answer, were destroyed after his death in 1860.

The Guards Museum also has sections of Hougoumont's wooden gate and the lock's keeper chain. In addition, as Gareth Glover's book, *Waterloo in 100 Objects*, records, there is a brick from the orchard wall in a private collection, and The Royal Green Jackets Museum in Winchester has a fragment of the balustrade that edged the orchard. According to the museum, this sat unnoticed in the Regimental Headquarters of The Royal Green Jackets,[3] being used as a door stop until 2014, although how it got there is a mystery.

More interestingly, and certainly the stuff of legends, are the Hougoumont bricks that are the eponymous items at the centre of the Grenadier Guards' and Coldstream Guards' traditions of 'Hanging the Brick'.[4] Of the two Regiments, the Coldstream ceremony is marginally the less boisterous. Just before Christmas every year, the Hougoumont brick is

3. Later The Rifles

4. The Life Guards ceremony of the same name has no connection with any battle (*see www.householdcavalry.info*)

paraded around the barracks by the members of the Sergeants & Warrant Officers Mess wearing fancy dress, while the Regiment's junior ranks attempt (usually unsuccessfully) to steal it. Once back in the Mess, it is hung from a tall frame and whoever touches it has to buy a round of drinks for everybody. The act of contact with the brick takes the form of a violent game of basketball crossed with Rugby League, with the ball in the shape of the involuntary head of a junior officer, whose ranks only ever enter the Sergeants & Warrant Officers Mess by invitation for this expensive humiliation.

The Grenadiers' ceremony – which, initially, is similar to that of the Coldstream, but appears to exclude the officers – is best described, in a necessarily edited version, by an anonymous Grenadier, on the Army Rumour Service (www.arrse.co.uk). This account, even post-editing, is not for the faint-hearted:

> The event of hanging the brick begins at around midday with Officers Mess v's Sergeants & WOs Mess sport. Afterwards, the Sergeants & WOs Mess form up at the Guard Room in fancy dress and parade a brick which was taken from Hougoumont Farm during the Battle of Waterloo. They have to parade the brick around camp and into the Mess. The Lance Corporals and Guardsmen are tasked with stopping them. If they succeed in getting the Brick to the Corporals Mess then the Sergeants & WOs Mess get the beers in, but it's not that simple. The last time we held Hanging the Brick we had blokes in hospital after being 'filled in' by a Non-Commissioned Officer with a hockey stick, one Lance Sergeant was hit in the face with a sink and there were sheep guts thrown around with gay abandon. There were also rumours that some Companies had blokes keeping buckets of piss in their utility rooms for weeks, filling them up ready to be used on the big day. There were some cracking videos on Facebook and YouTube shortly after and it did look like a riot, sadly these appear to have been removed. It is good to settle old scores with no come back, though we have been banned from wearing any balaclavas or any other form of mask to hide our faces.

The fact that, for over 200 years, successive Grenadier and Coldstream Commanding Officers have been willing, at Christmas, to unleash the Lords of Misrule, without a risk to discipline for the rest of the year, is a tribute to the unique ethos of the Guards. As King Edward VIII noted in his memoirs: 'The Guards Division was a great club, and if it was tinged with snobbishness it was the snobbishness of tradition, discipline,

King Louis XVIII in Coronation robes by Gerard

5. Now the Royal Scots Dragoon Guards

The Capture of the Eagle of the 45th Regiment of Infantry

perfection and sacrifice. They were the shock troops of the British Army; their prestige was purchased in blood'. This is why no other non-Guards Regiment's Commanding Officer would dare risk allowing a Hougoumont brick to be hung, even if they had one.

The Eagles of the 105th & 45th Regiments (Waterloo, 1815)
Following Napoleon's exile to Elba, King Louis XVIII commanded that all the Imperial Eagles of the *Grande Armée* be destroyed and replaced with Bourbon Colours, of white silk embroidered with gold fleur-de-lys. Accordingly, only a very small number of Imperial Eagles survived. On his return from Elba, Napoleon immediately reversed this instruction, but the new Eagles were of a lesser quality, with the birds having closed beaks and being set in a more crouched posture. So short indeed was the time between Napoleon landing in France in February 1815 and the Battle of Waterloo in June that some Regiments had to carve rather than cast the Eagle finials, often quite crudely, and paint the Colours that hung below on canvas.

Two of the new gilded bronze Imperial Eagles, of the 45th and 105th Infantry Regiments of the Line, were captured at Waterloo from Count d'Erlon's I Corps by the British heavy cavalry under the command of Henry, 2nd Earl of Uxbridge. Later in the day he lost his leg, and after the battle was created Marquess of Anglesey. The story of the capture of the Eagle of the 45th by the 2nd (Royal North British) Dragoons,[5] known as the Scots Greys because they only rode grey horses, is relatively straightforward, as is its aftermath.

At Waterloo, the Scots Greys were part of the Union Brigade, a formation of heavy cavalry Regiments held in reserve by Wellington. The Brigade was deployed against d'Erlon's Corps, when the latter attacked the left wing of the Anglo-Allied position at around one o'clock. The Scots Greys' charge – actually a quick walk, not a gallop as depicted in Lady Elizabeth Butler's dramatic painting *Scotland Forever!* – broke through to the centre of the French infantry as it was forming into line. In the brisk hand-to-hand fighting that followed, the 45th's Eagle was seized by Sergeant Charles Ewart. He later somewhat laconically described the action:

It was in the first charge that I took the Eagle from the enemy: he [the Ensign carrying the Eagle] and I had a hard contest for it; he made a thrust at my groin, I parried it off and cut him down through the head. After this a lancer

left to right
Eagle finial of the 45th
Regiment of Infantry

The Colour of Eagle of the 45th
Regiment of Infantry

The Cravat from the Eagle of
the 45th Regiment of Infantry

came at me; I threw the lance off by my right side, and cut him through the chin and upward through the teeth. Next, a foot soldier fired at me and charged me with his bayonet, which I also had the good luck to parry, and then I cut him down through the head; thus ended the contest.

The French Ensign carrying the Eagle was actually Lieutenant Pierre Guillot, who survived the battle, so the identity of the man cut-down by Ewart is a mystery. In any event, to prevent the Eagle being recaptured, Ewart was ordered to leave the battle and take it to Brussels immediately. The Eagle became a prized possession of his Regiment and is now on display in the museum of the Royal Scots Dragoon Guards at Edinburgh Castle. Ewart was granted a commission in 1816, being promoted to the rank of Ensign. He died in 1846 and was buried in the New Jerusalem Chapel graveyard in Salford. His grave was later paved over and forgotten until 1936, when it was rediscovered. Two years later, his body was exhumed and reburied by his old Regiment on the esplanade of Edinburgh Castle, just yards from the Eagle he captured – and a pub named after him.

The Capture of the Eagle of
105th Regiment of Infantry

In the 200 years since the Battle of Waterloo, from time-to-time, the Scots Greys have been asked by the French to return the Eagle of the 45th. The same answer is always given: 'Come and get it.'

The story of the capture of the Eagle of the French 105th Infantry Regiment of the Line by the 1st (Royal) Regiment of Dragoons (known as The Royals) is less straightforward and still resonates today. That it

was captured during the charge against d'Erlon's Corps is not in question; it is the identity of the Royal responsible which is still hotly disputed.

One version of the story is that Captain Alexander Clark led his Squadron of The Royals around the French flank, caught sight of the Eagle and made to capture it. Later, writing to his sister and including some significant inaccuracies about the Eagle, Clark recounted how he ran the French Ensign through the right side above the hip, and then again through the body, but was unable to grab the Eagle, which fell across the horse of Corporal Francis Stiles. Stiles, in a separate account, claimed that Captain Clark had ordered *him* to capture the Eagle. What is not in dispute is that Clark then sent Stiles to the rear with the trophy.

So seriously was the dispute taken that an enquiry was ordered by The Royals' Commanding Officer, which lasted until 1816. During the enquiry, Stiles called upon the evidence of Lieutenant George Gunning of The Royals, who had been present at the time and who confirmed in writing to the enquiry that it was he who had ordered Stiles to capture the Eagle. It would seem that Stiles' account was believed, for he was rewarded for the capture, being made a Sergeant and later an Ensign.

To further confuse matters, Gunning later claimed that it was he who killed the French Ensign, but French service records of the period show that the Frenchman, Jean Chantelat, actually survived the battle, albeit that he had been shot in the leg. To confuse matters even further, claims have been made by another Union Brigade Regiment, the 6th (Inniskilling) Dragoons,[6] that one of their Sergeants was responsible. The truth will never be known, although it seems probable that Stiles took the Eagle, Gunning killed an officer next to it (who was not the Ensign to the Eagle), and Clark ordered Stiles to take the Eagle to safety.

Whatever the *actualité* of the matter, Clark was having none of Stiles' or Gunning's claims, and over the next twenty-three years he made ten official complaints reasserting his right to be recognised as the man who captured the Eagle of the 105th. The descendants of both men continue to contest their competing claims to the present day. Meanwhile, the Eagle was kept by The Royals and adopted as the Regiment's cap badge. Following the amalgamation of The Royals with the Royal Horse Guards (The Blues) to form The Blues and Royals in 1969, the trophy continued to be worn as a sleeve badge. The Eagle itself was, somewhat controversially, presented to the National Army Museum in 1971 by the Colonel of The Blues and Royals, Field Marshal Sir Gerald Templer.

6. Not to be confused with the 5th Dragoon Guards with which the Regiment amalgamated in 1922 to form the 5th Inniskilling Dragoon Guards, later becoming the Royal Dragoon Guards

Marengo (Waterloo, 1815)

On the march from Paris to his nemesis, the portly Napoleon travelled in a carriage, but as the supreme master of public relations, he abandoned his wheels prior to the battle. The sight of the Emperor cantering through the lines of his men on a small, pale grey charger must have done much to raise the morale of the *Armée du Nord* in June 1815.

However, unlike Wellington, who spent seventeen hours in the saddle of his charger *Copenhagen* during the Battle of Waterloo, Napoleon, who was an indifferent horseman and was allegedly suffering from piles, was on foot or seated at a campaign desk for most of the battle. Nonetheless, the abiding and iconic image of the Emperor on the battlefield is of his stocky figure, in a grey greatcoat topped with his signature bicorn hat, mounted on his favourite charger, *Marengo*, a twenty-two-year-old, 14.1 hands, light grey Arabian stallion. Judging from the many inkwells, snuff boxes and paperweights allegedly made from his hooves, *Marengo* must have had at least eight legs. The question as to which of these equine souvenirs is genuine can be answered by provenance and empirical evidence.

For a start, whether or not the eight-times wounded *Marengo* was Napoleon's favourite charger is a moot point, as is the question raised by Jill, Duchess of Hamilton in her book *Marengo: The Myth of Napoleon's Horse* concerning the horse's actual identity. These questions arise because Napoleon had more than fifty horses in his personal stables, including several greys. However, it is well established that a pale grey Arabian carried his master at the Battle of Marengo in northern Italy, in the Peninsular, at the Battles of Austerlitz, Jena and Wagram, throughout the Russian campaign, and at Waterloo.

At Waterloo, following the collapse of the Imperial Guard and the resultant retreat of the *Armée du Nord*, the pale grey Arabian believed to be *Marengo* was again wounded, this time in his near rear quarter, and was left where he fell 'in the hollow road in advance of the French position'. Meanwhile, Napoleon took to his travelling coach which was itself later abandoned. Unlike his Imperial master, who made it safely back to Paris, the injured *Marengo* was found by Lieutenant William Petre, 11th Baron Petre, of the 6th (Inniskilling) Dragoons, who recognised the Imperial brand-mark on his hind quarter, saved him from the battlefield scavengers who would

Napoleon on *Marengo* at Waterloo

have swiftly turned the horse into *Beef Marengo*, and nursed him back to health. When Lord Petre returned to England he brought *Marengo* with him, and put the horse, with its saddle and bridle, on public display at the Waterloo Rooms, 94 Pall Mall, London. Admission to see and pet *Marengo*, who was advertised as 'so gentle that the most timid Lady may approach him without fear', was one shilling for adults and sixpence for children and servants.

In 1824, having passed the horse around between various relations, Lord Petre sold *Marengo* to Captain John Julius William Angerstein of the 1st Guards, a grandson of the Russian-born John Julius Angerstein, who himself may have been the illegitimate son of Empress Anna of Russia. Whatever his antecedents, the elder Angerstein was Chairman of Lloyds of London, a rich slave-owner, and – somewhat contradictorily – a leading abolitionist. He was also founder of the Lloyd's Patriotic Fund (a very well-endowed grant-making trust for wounded servicemen, still in existence today), and was chairman of the public collection made for veterans of Waterloo and their families. A connoisseur and prolific art collector, some of Angerstein's pictures were purchased after his death in 1823 by the government for £57,000 (2020: £6.6 million), to form the core of the National Gallery's collection.

Angerstein's grandson William put *Marengo* to stud at his property, New Barns near Ely, with a stud fee of £50 (2020: £5,400). Although the stallion sired two colts and a filly, none of them performed well on the turf.

Marengo's hooves

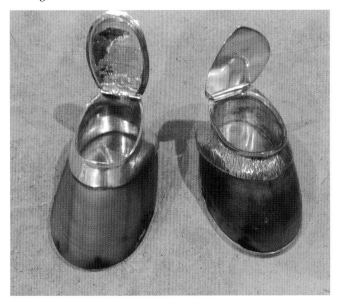

This disappointment notwithstanding, *Marengo* was allowed to see out his days in clover at Angerstein's country seat, Weeting Hall in Suffolk, dying in 1831 at the advanced age of thirty-eight, outliving his Imperial master by ten years, but not *Copenhagen*, who died in 1836.

However, unlike *Copenhagen* who was buried on Wellington's country estate at Stratfield Saye in Hampshire, Angerstein sent *Marengo*'s remains to the London Hospital, where his skeleton was articulated and then put on display at the Royal United Services Institution, less his two front hooves. Some ten years later Angerstein, by now a Guards Colonel (and an Army Lieutenant

General), had these two hooves shod with silver and converted, appropriately given the Emperor's addiction to the tobacco product, into snuff boxes, albeit by different silversmiths and at different dates.

One snuff box, with silver mounts by Mortimer & Hunt and hallmarked 1841, was retained by the Angerstein family at Weeting Hall, complete with a lock of *Marengo*'s mane. In 1897, with the Angerstein fortune in steep decline thanks to race horses and the card table, their heavily-mortgaged house was re-possessed by Norwich Union. The hoof then apparently disappeared, until in 1999 it was rediscovered by an Angerstein descendant, wrapped in a plastic bag in a kitchen drawer far from Suffolk. This hoof is currently on loan from the family to the Household Cavalry Museum at Horse Guards in London. Of the two snuff box hooves, it is the plainer, bearing only the single legend 'MARENGO' on the lid and naturalistic engraving of horse hair on the silver fetlock.

The other hoof, with silver mounts and a gold lid, is simpler in design and hallmarked 1840. However, the edge of the silver shoe and both sides of the gold lid are covered with engraved information, which establishes its history beyond doubt. This hoof was given by Angerstein to the Officers of the Brigade of Guards, along with a lock of *Marengo*'s hair. It is kept at the Officers Mess of The Queen's Guard at St James's Palace, where at luncheon every day it is placed in front of The Captain of The Queen's Guard.

Given the impeccable provenance of these two hooves, it can be stated with some confidence that many if not all the other *objets* claiming to be *Marengo*'s hooves are imposters. However, whether or not the skeleton (now at the National Army Museum) and the two hooves featured here are actually those of *Marengo*, or those of another Imperial charger present at Waterloo, is another question altogether.[7]

7. Collectors of military-historical trivia may be interested to know that both of *Marengo*'s converted front hooves were reunited for the first time in 175 years for the photography in this book

Napoleon's carriage, pocket book & cloak clasp (after Waterloo, 1815)
Although the identity of Napoleon's Waterloo carriage has never been in doubt, the circumstances as to how it was put on display in London are not entirely clear. That it was abandoned by the fleeing Emperor and seized by Major Baron von Keller, a Prussian infantryman, is an established fact.

There are conflicting accounts as to what happened next. According to a contemporary report in the *Monthly Magazine* (1816): 'It was taken by the Prussians, sold to government, and re-sold or lent to Mr Bullock as a

Bullock's Museum of Natural Curiosities, Piccadilly

Prussian trophy.' This is confirmed in part by the catalogue for a Cambridge University Library exhibition in 2016, which included items from the carriage. In that catalogue, it is stated that the British government bought the *equipage* for 3,500 guineas and then put it on display at the London Museum in Piccadilly. However, the *Literary Panorama* (1815) averred that: 'The splendid carriage taken at the Battle of Waterloo … was sent as a present to the Prince Regent, with the four horses which were attached to it, and a French driver accompanied it.' The driver had sustained serious wounds to his arm when the carriage was seized, leading to its later amputation, which must have made driving the vehicle thereafter almost impossible.

Whichever account is correct, it is certain that the carriage came to England. It is also well-established that it went on display in 1816 at Mr Bullock's Museum of Natural Curiosities at the Egyptian Hall, Piccadilly, where it created a sensation. Queues of gawpers flocked to see the coach and sit where the Emperor had once parked his imperial rump. The vehicle was described in *Ackermann's Repository* of 1816:

> The exterior of the carriage is, in many respects, very like the modern English travelling chariots. The colour is a dark blue, with a handsome bordure ornament in gold … the Imperial arms are emblazoned on the bullet proof panels of the doors. It has a lamp at each corner of the roof, and there is one lamp fixed at the back which can throw a strong light into the interior … the under-carriage and wheels are painted in vermillion, edged with the colour of the body, and heightened with gold …
>
> On the outside of the front windows is a roller-blind made of strong painted canvass [*sic*]: when pulled down, this will exclude rain and snow, and therefore secure the windows and blinds from being blocked up, as well as prevent the damp from penetrating… The interior deserves particular attention; for it is adapted to the various purposes of a kitchen, a bed-room, a dressing-room, an office, and an eating-room… Among the gold articles are a tea-pot, coffee-pot, sugar-bason [*sic*], cream-ewer, coffee-cup and saucer, slop-bason [*sic*], candle-sticks, wash-hand-bason [*sic*], plates for breakfast, &c. Each article is superbly embossed with the Imperial arms, and engraved with his favourite N.; and by the aid of the lamp, anything could be heated in the carriage …

Beneath the coachman's seat is a small box about two feet and a half long, and about four inches square; this contains a bedstead of polished steel, which could be fitted up within one or two minutes … a small mahogany case containing the peculiar necessaire of the ex-emperor [presumably his commode] … nearly one hundred articles, almost all of them solid gold; a liquor-case; and a writing desk.

This sumptuously appointed vehicle must have been similar to that of ex-King Joseph Bonaparte, captured after the Battle of Vitoria in 1813 (*see* p.81). Once the London public had had their fill of the Imperial conveyance, by command of the Prince Regent the carriage went on a tour around the United Kingdom. By the time it returned to London, Mr Bullock had banked in excess of £26,000 from the entry price (2020: £2.5 million).

After the tour, the carriage and its contents were disposed of at auction. Having passed through various hands, they were sold to Madame Tussaud's in 1842, where they continued to be a significant money-spinner as part of a special exhibition about Napoleon, advertised as follows in *The Times* in 1843:

Napoleon's Mameluke burnous.
Royal Collection Trust © Her Majesty Queen Elizabeth II 2018

Napoleon's celebrated military carriage, taken at Waterloo… his watch, gold snuff box, ring, one of his teeth, the instrument that drew it, tooth-brush, Madras worn in exile, dessert service used by him at St Helens, counterpane stained with his blood…

Madame Tussaud and Son's Exhibition, Bazaar, Baker-Street: open from 11 till dusk, and from 7 till 10. Great room, 1s; Napoleon relics and chamber of horrors, 6d.

Napoleon' travelling desk set.
Royal Collection Trust © Her Majesty Queen Elizabeth II 2018

The juxtaposition of 'relics' with the 'chamber of horrors' may not be accidental, as Napoleon remained a revered hate figure in British culture for much of the nineteenth century. The 'boneyman' was often substituted for the 'bogeyman' in tales told to frighten children.

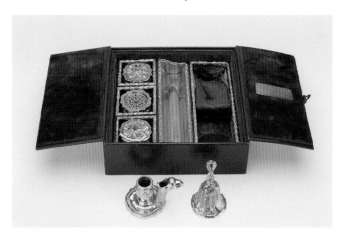

In 1925 a fire destroyed Madame Tussaud's, and as *The Times* reported, Napoleon's carriage was reduced to 'scrap iron'. Fortunately, many of the items captured from Napoleon's baggage train at Waterloo

Napoleon's pocket book

8. Now, following successive amalgamations, The Light Dragoons

Napoleon's greatcoat clasp

are held in other collections, most notably the Royal Collection at Windsor Castle. The latter is particularly rich in Napoleonic artefacts captured at Waterloo. These include a travelling desk set and a heavily silver-embroidered, scarlet, Mameluke burnous used by Napoleon as a dressing gown, which was presented to the Prince Regent by Marshal Blucher. The Prince Regent was an obsessive collector of Napoleana, a great admirer of the Emperor, and indeed was later convinced that he had led a charge of his Tenth Hussars at Waterloo. When, as King George IV, he asked Wellington to confirm the fact, the Iron Duke, never a fan of his obese and deluded sovereign, replied tactfully and with his tongue firmly in his cheek: 'I have often heard Your Majesty say so.'

Two Napoleonic items acquired at Waterloo and held in separate collections are in all probability connected. The first is a pocketbook and the second is a gold cloak clasp in the form of Imperial bees, joined by an 's' or serpent link.

The pocketbook was taken from Napoleon's carriage by Corporal Henry Rolfe of the 15th (The King's) Regiment of (Light) Dragoons (Hussars),[8] almost immediately after the carriage had been seized by the Prussians. As the story goes, a patrol of the 15th was in hot pursuit of the retreating French, when it came across the abandoned carriage. Corporal Rolfe leaned from his saddle, and through the open window of the carriage grabbed what he described as the Emperor's grey cloak, in an inside pocket of which he found a pocketbook embroidered with beads and lined with green silk. This item of clothing was more probably Napoleon's iconic grey greatcoat, as cloaks do not have pockets and the Emperor never wore one on the battlefield.

Although the Prince Regent would probably have loved to add this highly personal souvenir of Napoleon to his collection, Rolfe told no one what he had taken and retained the pocketbook until his death in 1871, when it passed to his wife. She in turn gave it to a friend, who passed it on to Captain James Gordon of the 15th Hussars. In due course, it was given to the Newcastle Discovery Museum, where staff recently discovered that it contained two notes. The first is a brief hand-written obituary of Henry Rolfe, recalling his role at the Battles of Vitoria, Toulouse and Waterloo. The second, written by Captain Gordon, records the pocketbook's provenance from Waterloo until it came into his possession in 1895. What is not recorded was the fate of Napoleon's greatcoat the collar of which, like all military greatcoats, was secured by a chain link between two bosses, in this case a pair of gold bees which were Napoleon's personal symbol.

The clasp was discovered by one of Wellington's ADCs, Major Hon Henry Percy of the 14th Light Dragoons.[9] Percy was a grandson of the Duke of Northumberland and an Old Etonian. He had fought with Moore at Corunna, and then with Wellington in the Peninsular Campaign, until he was captured during the retreat from Burgos in 1812 and held as a prisoner-of-war in France for two years. At Waterloo, Percy was one of only three of Wellington's Staff who was not wounded, although his horse was shot from under him. Wellington therefore selected him to take the Waterloo Dispatch – the document announcing the victory – and the two captured French Eagles to London, and to lay them at the feet of the Prince Regent.

What Percy was later careful *not* to lay at the acquisitive Regent's bulging pumps in London was Napoleon's greatcoat clasp, which he had cut from a garment he had found lying on the ground by the abandoned Imperial carriage. It is not being unduly fanciful to assume that the grey greatcoat from which Corporal Rolfe removed the Emperor's pocket-book was, moments later, found and despoiled by Major Percy. It is worth noting, as additional evidence of the Imperial provenance of the pocketbook and the bee clasp, that cavalry greatcoats were (and are still) referred to by cavalrymen as 'cloaks', even though they have sleeves, and both Rolfe and Percy were cavalrymen.

Like the pocketbook, the bee clasp was retained by Henry Percy until his early death in 1825. It can now be seen in the Museum Room at Levens Hall, Cumbria, the seat of the Bagot family, along with other Waterloo spoils of war and memorabilia, including the Iron Duke's campaign bed. Wellington's niece, Lady Mary Wellesley-Pole, had married Sir Charles Bagot in 1806, although this does not explain how Henry Percy's bee clasp passed to her family. Perhaps he, or one of his two illegitimate sons, gave it to the Duke, who in turn gave it to his niece, in the same way he had given Tipu Sultan's ring to her sister Emily (*see* p.62).

Marshal Ney's snuff box (Waterloo, 1815)
Napoleon, who was a snuff addict and consumed up to three kilos of the tobacco product a month, re-popularised the habit of taking snuff after it had fallen out of fashion during the Revolution. With its revival came the production of ornate and valuable snuff boxes.

Ney's snuff box
© *Green Howards Trust*

Ney's snuff box, a bibelot given to him by the Emperor as a sign of his esteem, probably after the Retreat from Moscow, is of high quality. It was made by Pierre-André Montauban, a leading French goldsmith, much patronised by the Emperor, and now best known for his Italian micro-mosaic-mounted boxes. Approximately five inches long, the snuff box was designed for table rather than for pocket use. Oval in form, the side is decorated with a floral pattern on a peacock blue enamel background, laid over 20.5 carat gold, and interspersed with Napoleonic bees. The base is decorated with stars, while the image of the Emperor enamelled on the lid is in the style of a painting by Jacques-Louis David, dated 1812. It depicts Napoleon at the Tuileries Palace, in the undress uniform of the Chasseurs à Cheval of the Imperial Guard.[10]

This ornate snuff box was taken from Ney's carriage after the Battle of Waterloo by an unknown Guardsman, and given as a souvenir to Captain (later Colonel) William Cameron of the 1st Regiment of Guards. Cameron lost his arm during the battle, a fact which dispels the myth that he seized the bibelot from Ney's carriage. The snuff box was subsequently bequeathed by Cameron to his son Abney, an officer in the 19th Regiment of Foot.[11] On his death in 1877, he bequeathed it to the Officers Mess of his old Regiment, from where it found its way in due course to the Green Howards Museum in Richmond, Yorkshire.

As for the original owner, Marshal Michel Ney, 1st Duke d'Elchingen and 1st Prince de la Moskva, was the prototypical French revolutionary and Napoleonic soldier. Of *petit bourgeois* stock, Ney was born in 1769 on the Franco-German border, the son of a successful barrel cooper; in consequence of these facts he was bilingual, reasonably well-educated, trained as a lawyer, and became a civil servant in the Department of Mines & Forges, a job of which he quickly tired. In 1787, he exchanged his *chapeau melon* for a hussar trooper's busby and soon saw action, gaining accelerated promotion through the ranks of non-commissioned officers. On the abolition of the Bourbon monarchy in 1792, Ney was granted an officer's commission, something previously denied to him as he was not an aristocrat. By March 1799 Ney was a General of Division, and in 1804 he was given his Marshal's baton by Napoleon.

Known to his troops as 'the red faced' – he had red hair and a ruddy complexion – Ney was described by Napoleon as the 'bravest of the brave'. Frequently wounded, he distinguished himself in all the Napoleonic conflicts and commanded with great bravery the rear guard of the *Grande Armée* on its disastrous retreat from Moscow. This earned him the

10. Presentation gold snuff boxes with images of the Emperor are rare; in England, the only other one on public display, which depicts Napoleon in coronation robes, is part of the Gilbert Collection at the Victoria & Albert Museum in London

11. Later the Green Howards

soubriquet of 'the last Frenchman on Russian soil', and in all probability the snuff box. However, his ambition and sense of self-preservation led him to head the Marshals' Revolt of April 1814, which demanded the Emperor's first abdication.

With Napoleon on Elba, the institutions and nobility of the First Empire abolished, and King Louis XVIII in the Tuileries Palace, Ney accepted a Bourbon peerage and a Bourbon Marshal's baton from his new monarch; but before long he had turned his coat again. During the Waterloo Campaign, Ney commanded the left wing of the *Armée du Nord*, tasked with routing Wellington at Quatre Bras, while Napoleon dealt with the Prussians at Ligny. Although successful at this first engagement, at Waterloo Ney unleashed a disastrous and unsupported mass cavalry attack on the British artillery and infantry squares, without a direct order from Napoleon. For reasons which are still debated, Ney's massed ranks of charging cavalrymen missed the Allied guns, which they could easily have spiked and thereby disabled, with a significant consequent impact on the outcome of the battle. When his horsemen broke on the cavalry-proof British infantry squares, they fell like waves against a sea wall. This disaster notwithstanding, during the battle Ney had five horses shot from underneath him, and he ended Waterloo on foot, leading the last French infantry charge shouting: 'Come, see how a Marshal of France dies!'

That, however, was not to be his fate. With Louis XVIII once again on the throne, Ney was arrested on 3rd August 1815 and eventually tried for treason by the Chamber of Peers. On 6th December, he was found guilty and sentenced to be shot by firing squad the following day. Brave to the last, Ney refused to wear a blindfold and demanded the right to give the order to fire. This he did with the words: 'Soldiers, when I give the

Execution of Marshal Ney

command to fire, fire straight at my heart. Wait for the order. It will be my last to you. I protest against my condemnation. I have fought a hundred battles for France, and not one against her ... Soldiers, fire!'

Since that fateful day neither Ney's descendants, who became extinct in the male line in 1969, nor the Grenadier Guards, still very much in existence, have ever laid claim to the snuff box, which still has pride of place in the Green Howards Museum.

The Wellington Monument & Canova's Napoleon (after Waterloo, 1815)
Captured enemy cannons, of both the naval and military variety, have often been recycled to produce both large and small memorial objects. Possibly the largest of these is the eighteen-foot-high bronze statue of Achilles, the hero of the Trojan War, which stands atop the thirty-six-foot-high Wellington Monument at the south-western corner of Park Lane in London. This monumental statue was the work of the renowned sculptor, Richard (later Sir Richard) Westmacott, who cast the figure using thirty-three tons of captured Napoleonic French bronze cannon barrels.

Wellington Monument, Park Lane

The nude, virile figure of Achilles, sword and shield in hand, but armour discarded, was based by Westmacott on one of the Roman sculptures of the Horse Tamers on the Quirinal Hill, Rome; however, Achilles' head, and as wags at the time claimed, a certain other appendage, were modelled on that of the notoriously amorous Duke of Wellington. Ironically, the two statues of the Horse Tamers in Rome had earlier been earmarked by Napoleon as spoils of war, but had proved too large to remove to France.

Located just behind Apsley House, Wellington's London home, the erection of the monument was commanded in the name of King George III, in the aftermath of the Battle of Waterloo. At the time, the King was confined to Windsor Castle, deaf, blind, and afflicted with dementia that was so advanced he was incapable of knowing or understanding that he had been declared King of Hanover in 1814, that Napoleon had been defeated in 1815 or that his own wife had died in 1818.

In 1822, two years after George III's death, Achilles was finally unveiled. It was the first statue to be installed in Hyde Park, and the first male nude to be on public display in London since Roman times. Despite the fact that the statue had been funded to the sum of £10,000 (2020: £1,250,000) by a prim group of upper-class women known as the Ladies of England, the proportionally modelled flaccid phallus and ample scrotum caused such moral outrage that a sizeable fig leaf had to be bolted into place soon after the Union flag had been tugged away to reveal the statue in all its glory. Despite this prudery, much controversy still resulted, pitching the sculptor's supporters against his fiercest critics.

A cartoon of the statue by George Cruick-

Cruickshank cartoon of the Wellington Monument

shank, entitled *Backside and Front View of the ladies fancy man, Paddy Carey*, was published in July 1822. In it, a crowd of spectators are admiring the statue of 'O'Killus Esq – Erected in Hide [*sic*] Park, in Honor [*sic*] of the Waterloo Man & his Soger Men'. Speech bubbles above the crowd include comments such as: 'Do you think it will stand the weather? Bless you, it will stand anything; My eyes, what a size!' And as two ladies, arm-in-arm, gaze upwards, one exclaims: 'La! They must be a brazen set of jades to stick up such a thing [slang for penis] in public – what is it meant for?' Her companion replies: 'I understand it is intended to represent His Grace after bathing in the Serpentine & defending himself from an attack of Constables'.

The controversy was further fuelled by the installation in the entrance hall at Apsley House of Canova's Carrara marble, nude colossus of Napoleon, which was most definitely surplus to the restored Bourbon government of King Louis XVIII. In 1816 it was purchased by the British government for 66,000 francs, and the Prince Regent duly presented it to the Duke of Wellington. Fortunately for the prudes, there was no need for Wellington to cover-up Napoleon's *bijoux de famille*, as they already sported an elaborately carved fig leaf. However, for many years Napoleon's outstretched right arm was used by the Duke and his guests as a convenient limb on which to hang their umbrellas. One dreads to think what they might have used as a brolly hook had the fig leaf not been in place.

Statue of Napoleon by Canova at Apsley House

Trumpets & Spoons

The 18th Hussars' silver trumpet (Waterloo, 1815, and after)

It seems entirely appropriate from every point of view that, in the aftermath of the Battle of Waterloo, the 18th (King's Irish) Regiment of (Light) Dragoons (Hussars)[12] should have purchased a silver cavalry trumpet as a memento of the battle. It was bought with part of their prize money from spoils of war, in this case the sale of many captured French cavalry horses. At Waterloo it is estimated that, within the two-and-a-half-mile-wide battlefield, more than 30,000 cavalry horses faced each other. To understand the scale of this equine presence on the battlefield, if all of these chargers had been ordered into a single rank, knee-to-knee, the line would have stretched for twenty-three miles.

Unlike Household Cavalry trumpets, which were and are relatively long, with the trumpet tube only looping around once, the 18th's trumpet has three overlapping loops of tubing. From them hangs a scarlet silk brocade trumpet banner, elaborately embroidered in gold thread with British

12. Later the 13th/18th Hussars and now The Light Dragoons

18th Hussars' Waterloo trumpet

national symbols, a royal crown and the Regiment's title. The curious arrangement of the tube has the practical effect of making the trumpet not much longer than a bugle, but it also makes it rather odd-looking.

Hardly had the trumpet been delivered to the 18th, than the Regiment was disbanded in 1821, as was recorded in an exchange of letters between the ex-Adjutant of the 18th, Captain Standish O'Grady, and Major General Sir Hussey (later Lieutenant General 1st Baron) Vivian:

New Bridge Barracks, Sept 10, 1821

My dear Sir Hussey

I have been deputed by the Officers of the 18th Hussars, to present you with a silver trumpet, purchased with the Waterloo prize money, and intended as a memorial of that victory.

This corps is now disbanded. Its officers separate, perhaps to meet no more. But they are anxious that the 18th Hussars should still live in the memory of one, whom they always so highly respected. They avail themselves, therefore, of their last opportunity, to present to you this testimonial of that victory, to which it was their fortune to be led by you; not only to recall the glorious recollections by which it was surrounded, uniting as it does their achievements with your fame, but also to convince you that while you gained their admiration as a soldier, you failed not to obtain their hearts as a friend.

It gives me infinite pleasure to be the bearer of this gift, conscious that the sincerity with which it is given, as well as the moment at which it was bestowed, will gain for it a real value in your estimation.

Believe me, my dear Sir Hussey,
Most faithfully yours
Standish O'Grady

To which Sir Hussey replied very fulsomely, including the following edited highlights:

Truro, September 20, 1821

My dear O'Grady

… That a Regiment, to which I had such reason to be attached, for it having served so much under my orders, and which I have ever found so patient under privations, so cheerful in all difficulties, so ready to obey, and so willing to follow; a Regiment, than which does not exist in his Majesty's service one more loyal, or more brave, should be disbanded, could not but affect me with the most heartfelt regret; that the officers should, at the moment of their separation, perhaps to meet no more! have remembered my poor services towards, and with them, gives rise to feelings, to which no language can do justice.

I hope that, notwithstanding their dissolution as a body, you will be able to make known to the officers, how much I am gratified by this last kind testimonial of their regard, to which my only claim was, an earnest endeavour at all times to unite the conduct of a friend with the duty of a soldier…

Believe me ever, my dear O'Grady,

Most faithfully yours,

Hussey Vivian

Major General Sir Hussey Vivian

The central character in this saga, Major General Sir Hussey Vivian, was an experienced and trusted leader of cavalry. By 1815, he was in command of the 6th Brigade of Cavalry, which included the 18th Light Dragoons, a Regiment which had distinguished itself in Vivian's Brigade in the earlier Peninsular War.

At Waterloo, Vivian's cavalrymen were positioned on the Allies' left flank. In the late afternoon, Wellington ordered Vivian to move to support the centre of the Allied line, which was under pressure from Napoleon's Imperial Guard. Vivian's Brigade swept aside the legendary Frenchmen, and then had the distinction of making the very successful and final cavalry charge of the day, against the French troops positioned between Hougoumont and La Haie Sainte. Vivian was rewarded for this action with the thanks of both houses of Parliament and his appointment to the Prince Regent's newly instituted Royal Guelphic Order. The Emperors of Austria and Russia invested him with the Order of Maria Theresa and the Order of St Vladimir respectively.

After hostilities had ceased, Vivian remained in France, along with the 18th Light Dragoons, as part of the Army of Occupation. In 1816 – and this may be one reason why he was remembered so fondly by the Regiment – Vivian was censured by the Duke of Wellington for failing to report a disturbance in a French theatre caused by officers of the 18th. In the British Army of 1816, the blood of friendship was clearly much thicker than the water of duty.

The Regiment was re-formed in 1858 as the 18th Regiment of (Light) Dragoons, and again renamed the 18th Hussars in 1861. On the 10th September 1880, the fifty-ninth anniversary of the disbandment of the old Regiment, the trumpet was returned to the care of the 18th by Vivian's son, Charles, 2nd Baron Vivian, 'believing that in this record of glorious deeds the memory of his father who led the Regiment to victory on many occasions will ever be cherished in the corps whose admiration he secured'. The trumpet, along with the Regiment's historical collection, is now in the care of the Discovery Museum in Newcastle-upon-Tyne.

The Tenth Hussars' Waterloo trumpet

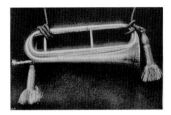

Tenth Hussars' Waterloo trumpet

The gorgeously uniformed and socially exclusive Tenth Hussars also used their Waterloo prize money to acquire a silver trumpet, actually a bugle. Following the appointment in 1796 of the Prince of Wales as its Regimental Colonel, the Tenth became the most fashionable Regiment in the British Army, not least because the Prince re-officered the Regiment with his friends. These included London's leading arbiter of taste, the exquisite George Bryan 'Beau' Brummell. Captain Brummell, who largely shirked his regimental duties, did not serve with the Tenth at Waterloo, having resigned his commission when the Regiment was posted temporarily to Manchester in 1798, on the (doubtless) witty grounds that he 'refused to serve abroad'.

Like the 18th Hussars, the Tenth at Waterloo were in Hussey Vivian's 6th Brigade of Cavalry, a fact commemorated by the engraving on their trumpet: 'Purchased by desire of the soldiers of the Tenth or Prince Regent's Own Royal Hussars with part of the prize money arising from the enemy's horses captured by their brigade under the command of Major-General Sir H. Vivian K.C.B. at the Battle of Waterloo, 18 June 1815'.

Following several regimental amalgamations to form The King's Royal Hussars in 1992, the Tenth's Waterloo memento, less elaborate and unembellished with an embroidered trumpet banner, remains in their Officers Mess.

Chisholm's spoons

Less grand, but probably more practical than the Hussars' trumpets, is a set of Fiddle pattern silver spoons by Charles Dalgleish of Edinburgh, bearing the hallmarks for 1817 and 1818. The set comprises a salt spoon, a table spoon and a serving or 'hosh' spoon (specially made for serving stews), all engraved with the initials 'SC', the Chisholm family's crest, and on the reverse in a flowing script, the words 'Waterloo Prize Money'.

These spoons were purchased by Assistant Surgeon Stewart Chisholm of the Ordnance Medical Department, the forerunner of the Royal Army Medical Corps. Chisholm left the Army on half-pay in 1817, but returned to the Ordnance Medical Department for active service in Canada in 1837. In 1855 he was promoted to Staff Surgeon (1st Class), and he retired in 1858 with the rank of Senior Surgeon in the Royal Artillery and Deputy Inspector General of Army Hospitals.

In 1815 an Assistant Surgeon's rank was equivalent to that of an infantry Lieutenant. Accordingly, Chisholm received £34.14.9 (2020: £3,000) from the Waterloo prize money fund. Given that the three spoons would have cost only a small fraction of this sum, and there are two different date stamps on the spoons, it is a reasonable assumption that they formed part of a larger service which has since been sold or dispersed. The three surviving spoons are now in the National War Museum in Edinburgh Castle.

Wellington's State Funeral Carriage (1815 & 1852)
When the Duke of Wellington was given a State Funeral in 1852, the authorities decided to outdo the magnificence of Nelson's obsequies, by constructing an even more ornate funeral car for the late Field Marshal, Duke and Prime Minister. This proved to be an embarrassing mistake: spectators thought that it was grotesque and the media ridiculed it mercilessly. For instead of wood, Wellington's six-wheeled mobile catafalque

Wellington's Funeral Car

was made of bronze cast from French cannons captured at Waterloo.

Under the direction of Queen Victoria's husband, Prince Albert, this monstrosity, which cost £12,500 (2020: £1.7 million) was assembled in the incredibly short time of eighteen days, by six foundries employing more than 100 men. On completion, it weighed in excess of ten tons and required twelve horses to pull it. In spite of this significant horsepower, it got stuck in the mud of The Mall, where sixty policemen

had to be deployed to free it. On arrival at St Paul's Cathedral, the mechanism for transferring the coffin off the funeral car failed, and it took more than an hour to get Wellington's remains from the bier onto the shoulders of the waiting Guardsmen.

However, unlike Nelson's funeral car, which succumbed to woodworm and dry rot, Wellington's bronze funeral car can still be seen at his country house at Stratfield Saye in Hampshire.

CHAPTER 15

FIRST ANGLO-ASHANTI WAR
(1823–1831)

Sound the Trumpet

An elephant tusk trumpet (Nsamankow, 1824)

A trumpet of an altogether different type to those purchased with Waterloo prize money was captured in West Africa in 1824, during the First Anglo-Ashanti War. Unlike the Waterloo instruments (*see* p.147), which are made of silver, the Ashanti one is made from the tusk of an elephant and is covered in shagreen (fish skin), with the mouthpiece set into the side of the tusk, rather than at the tip as with a European trumpet. According to contemporary accounts, it was an object much venerated by the tribesmen from whom it was captured on 21st January 1824.

The cause of the First Anglo-Ashanti War in West Africa, of which there were to be four more before the end of 1901, was slavery. Not, however, the protection of the trade by the British, but the determination of the Ashanti that the British should not abolish the highly profitable business of selling their own kith and kin to the United States and elsewhere. The spark which ignited the flame, as so often before and after, was the kidnap and murder of an African Sergeant, who was serving with the British-led Royal African Corps. This was followed by an early victory for the Ashanti, when they led a small British punitive expedition into a trap, which in turn led to a much larger colonial force of 3,000 men being dispatched to quell the West Africans, under the command of the British Governor, Brigadier General Sir Charles MacCarthy. Unfortunately for him, MacCarthy was over-confident, and made the cardinal errors of dividing his forces and allowing them to march carrying minimal ammunition, errors that were later repeated by the British in the Anglo-Zulu and Boer wars.

MacCarthy's own column of only 500 soldiers made contact with the 10,000-strong Ashanti Army at Nsamankow, with disastrous consequences for both him and Britannia's honour. In addition to under-estimating the Ashanti's war-fighting capabilities, MacCarthy mistakenly believed that

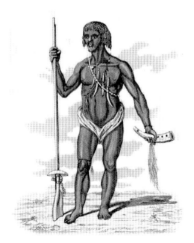

Ashanti soldier holding an elephant tusk trumpet

The Defeat of the Ashantees, at the Second Battle of Accra, 7th August 1824

the Ashanti army contained several disaffected groups whose Chiefs would defect. To achieve the desired defections, and in what now seems an almost unbelievable move, he instructed his band to play *God Save the King.* The Ashanti responded by beating their war drums and blowing their trumpets, while their ranks held firm.

Fighting started shortly thereafter, with the two sides separated by a sixty-foot-wide stream, which the Ashanti attempted to cross, using felled trees as bridges. Initially the British picked them off. However, as MacCarthy should have predicted, his civilian native bearers carrying most of the military stores fled on hearing the distant gun fire, and so it wasn't long before the ammunition ran out. At which point, the Ashanti poured across the river, quickly over-ran MacCarthy's position, and slaughtered the British-led column. Only twenty managed to escape, one of whom must have acquired the Ashanti trumpet at some point, although how and why he had the presence of mind to hold onto it during his headlong flight is not recorded.

MacCarthy, along with his Colonial Secretary, J T Williams and Ensign Wetherell of the 2nd West India Regiment, also attempted to escape. The Governor was wounded by Ashanti gunfire, and then either killed by a second shot or took his own life in preference to being captured. Ensign Wetherell was killed whilst trying to defend MacCarthy's body. Williams, however, was luckier (up to a point), when he was recognised by an Ashanti Chief, for whom he had earlier done a favour.

Instead of being decapitated and filleted, the Colonial Secretary was taken prisoner. For several months, he shared a locked hut with the severed heads of MacCarthy and Wetherell, which the Ashanti – who had previously eaten the Governor's and the Ensign's hearts at a victory banquet – kept as spoils of war.

This was not, however, the end of the affair for MacCarthy's decapitated head. Once the flesh and brains had rotted away or been consumed by flies, the bare skull was removed to the Ashanti capital, Kumasi, where it was lined in gold and used as a ceremonial drinking-cup by successive Ashanti Kings. Despite the best efforts of later British punitive expeditions, for whom the skull had achieved iconic status, it has never been recovered. In the meantime, the Ashanti's trumpet has been on display at the National Army Museum since 1963.

CHAPTER 16

SINDH CAMPAIGN (1843)

Princely Discomfort

The Amir of Sindh's alabaster chair (Sindh, 1843)

The precise details as to how the Peninsular War veteran, Major General (later General) Sir Charles Napier, acquired the Amir of Sindh's chair in 1843, or indeed to which of the Amirs it belonged, are not known. However, in 1926 Napier's granddaughter presented the chair to the 22nd Regiment of Foot,[1] part of the Anglo-Indian force led by her grandfather to supress the Muslim rulers of Sindh in north-west India (now Pakistan). The Regiment subsequently donated the chair to the Cheshire Military Museum in Chester.

1. Later the Cheshire Regiment and now the 1st Battalion of the Mercian Regiment

Encampment at Jummuck

Alabaster chair of the Amir of Sindh & other trophies of the campaign

The reason for the punitive expedition, which as so often before in British Imperial history led to the annexation of the territory, arose from the actions of the Sindhi Amirs in the wake of the Anglo-Afghan War of 1839 to 1842. Faced with the tempting target of regular British camel trains trekking between India and Afghanistan, these chieftains had done their

General Sir Charles Napier in native dress

level best to disrupt, with considerable violence and bloodshed, the British East India Company's lines of communication. Napier's expedition, including the 22nd, set out from Bombay with orders merely to put down the rebels. What followed was the conquest of the whole of Sindh Province. Napier achieved this through victories at the Battles of Meeanee and Hyderabad, at both of which his forces were outnumbered ten-to-one. Six Amirs surrendered and Mir Sher Muhammad, known as the Lion of Sindh, was routed. Napier had clearly greatly exceeded his mandate from the Governor-General of the Bombay Presidency, Lord Ellenborough, but his conquest was not reversed until Indian Independence in 1948.

On completion of his mission, Napier was alleged to have despatched to Ellenborough the cryptic message, '*peccavi*', the Latin for 'I have sinned', a fairly obvious pun for a Classicist to decrypt. However, so the story went, there was a shortage of Classically-trained Staff officers in Bombay, and for some days the acquisition of another jewel for the future Crown Imperial went unrecognised. The exposure of the intellectual shortcomings of the British Staff officers in Bombay was given its first public airing, to the undisguised delight of the Classics Double Firsts in the Foreign Office, in 1844, in the satirical magazine, *Punch*, when the pun appeared as the caption to a caricature of Napier. Unfortunately for lovers of Army and Civil Service myths, the true author of the joke was a certain Catherine Winkworth, who submitted the pun to *Punch*, which then printed it as a factual report.

CHAPTER 17

CRIMEAN WAR (1853–1856)

The Cannons' Roar

The Crimean War of 1853 to 1856 was the first major conflict on the European continent to involve British troops since the end of the Napoleonic Wars in 1815. It exposed brutally the sclerotic state of the post-Waterloo British Army, as well as producing a number of interesting spoils of war. It also gave birth to the historical icons of the Charge of the Light Brigade, and the nurses, Florence Nightingale and Mary Seacole. Without taking away any of the credit rightly garnered by those involved in the creation of these legends, the first was a gross act of command ineptitude, leavened only by the incredible bravery of the British light cavalry soldier. The second arose through the sheer bloody-mindedness of a largely untrained nursing manager, based in a hospital not in the Crimea, but across the Black Sea on the Turkish coast at Scutari. The last was a myth involving a mulatto boarding (and, probably, bawdy) house keeper of Scottish-Jamaican ancestry, who opened the British Hotel at Balaclava as 'a mess table and comfortable quarters for sick and convalescent officers'. Although she did indeed venture selflessly onto the battlefield to tend the wounded, she has since been mythologised as an angelic black nurse.

Emperor Napoleon III

The Charge of the Heavy Brigade at Balaclava, 25th October 1854

Almost as misunderstood as the legends of the 'Gallant Six Hundred', 'The Lady with the Lamp' and the 'Greatest Black Briton' were the origins of the war, which were deliberately but thinly veneered with noble aims. The apparent *causus belli* was a dispute between the Russians and the French, over the right to protect the Orthodox and Catholic Christians, and the Christian Holy Sites, within the

General Lord Raglan

Marshal Armand-Jacques
Leroy de Saint-Arnaud

Ottoman Empire. The real reasons were the ambitions of France's Emperor Napoleon III to avenge his uncle Napoleon I, and restore the grandeur of France; Russia's determination to seize Constantinople and so open up the Mediterranean to its Black Sea Fleet; and the United Kingdom's perennial obsession with Russian threats to the route to India and India itself. To further complicate matters, the French and British were determined that Russia should not gain territory in the Balkans and Near East at the expense of the moribund and decaying Ottoman Empire, otherwise known as the 'Sick Man of Europe'.

The war started not in Russia's Crimea, but after preliminary Russo-Ottoman skirmishes in the Balkans and the Caucasus, followed by a Russian advance across the Danube river, which marked the northern Ottoman border. In June 1854, an Anglo-French force under the command of General Lord Raglan and Marshal Armand-Jacques Leroy de Saint-Arnaud landed at Gallipoli. They then marched north to Varna to block any Russian march south towards Constantinople. The invasion never happened and the following month the Russians withdrew north. This should have been the end of the matter, but war fever had been whipped up by the media in London and Paris, with Karl Marx joking, 'there they are, the French doing nothing and the British helping them as fast as possible'. As a consequence, the respective governments were obliged to cast around for a further military objective.

Their eyes fell on the Russian naval port of Sevastopol on the Crimean Peninsula. The politicians agreed that its destruction would be both a worthy objective, and would satisfy the jingo journalists and the demands of their citizens at home. This decision set in train the second phase of the Crimean *bellum*, with even less *causus* than the Iraq War of 2003 and without the benefit of a 'dodgy dossier'. In September 1854, the Anglo-French armies, along with some Ottoman military units, were loaded back onto naval transports, which sailed across the Black Sea. They landed at the ill-omened Calamita Bay, on the south-west coast of the Crimea peninsula, some thirty-five miles from Sevastopol.

At the Battle of the Alma on 20th September, the French and British launched an uphill frontal assault on well dug-in Russian positions and broke through. By nightfall the British cavalry could have been in the lightly defended port city of Sevastopol, potentially bringing the war to a quick close. But Raglan vacillated, while his fifty-six-year-old French opposite number was dying of stomach cancer. The moment was lost, and by October the Franco-British forces were facing two ways, besieging

Sevastopol, while also defending themselves from Russian forces determined to
relieve the siege and sever the only Franco-
British line of re-supply at the fishing village
of Balaclava. The battles which followed,
most notably Balaclava on 25th October
1854 and Inkerman on 5th November, were
inconclusive in terms of ending the war. This
only happened after an extremely harsh
winter, in which thousands died of disease
and hypothermia, followed by a protracted
siege, which finally ended on 9th September
1855 with the fall of Sevastopol and the con-
sequent destruction of the Russian fleet and its docks over the winter.

Siege of Sevastopol

Unusually for a nineteenth-century conflict, perhaps because the port
city was a fortress without a palace, there was no post-action Prize Auction
of the spoils of war. However, the fortress and port were stripped of everything
that could be moved. Thousands of tons of serviceable cannons, mortars,
munitions, granite blocks, grain, and even the massive lock gates were
meticulously recorded, divided between the victorious allies, and shipped
home, as evidenced by the papers of the British naval Commander-in-
Chief, Rear Admiral Lord Lyons, which are now in the Duke of Norfolk's
archives at Arundel Castle in West Sussex. Some of the larger cannons
and mortars are still on display at various British military establishments,
including the Royal Military Academy Sandhurst and the Royal Hospital
Chelsea; the location of the lock gates is unknown.

In the meantime, individual officers were allowed to acquire anything of
value that was unserviceable or easily transportable. John Deane, an
underwater explosives expert-turned-salvage-man, had been sent to the
Crimea by the Admiralty to sabotage Russian naval ships. On the orders
of the Commander-in-Chief, Major General Sir William Codrington, he
was redeployed after the conflict to salvage discarded Russian military
items from the creeks around Fort Paul and Sevastopol, and from the
Great Redan and the 'Valley of Death'. This is confirmed by various letters
in the archives at Arundel Castle, including some to and from Lord Lyons.
In one of these exchanges of letters, Deane states that he has assembled a
collection of 'relics and trophies … in Sevastopol', including an assortment
of gun barrels, wheels from gun carriages and other non-operational
materiel, which he proposed fashioning into wall trophies, and which he

Admiral Lord Lyons

suggested distributing to senior officers. In the same letter, Deane offered Lord Lyons first pick, but the Admiral later declined, and instead ordered that some of the trophies be boxed up and shipped to Queen Victoria and the Prince Consort at Osborne House on the Isle of Wight.

The Quadrangle, Arundel Castle

The Arundel Collection

The Victorian Gothic vastness of Arundel Castle in Sussex, and the verdant parkland surrounding it, are unlikely places to find Crimean spoils of war, particularly as Henry Fitzalan-Howard, 14th Duke of Norfolk (1815–1860) didn't serve in the Crimea. Nonetheless, there are in the castle three Russian bronze bells in an arcaded vault, a Russian ship's figurehead in the Smoking Room, an eighteenth-century bronze gun barrel lying in long grass at the foot of the Keep, and an ancient Greek altar in the park. All of these, with the exception of the figurehead, have been given a Sevastopol provenance, and were traditionally believed to have been part of a presentation of spoils of war to Queen Victoria. The truth is otherwise.

The probable reason that Admiral Lyons declined to take pieces from Deane's Sevastopol collection, and why the pieces at Arundel Castle were *not* part of Queen Victoria's Sevastopol loot, was that Lyons had already acquired these particular spoils of war from an earlier Crimean naval engagement at Berdyansk. This naval port was a major Russian re-supply point on the Sea of Azov, behind the Russian lines and well to the north-east of Sevastopol. It was attacked successfully on 26th May 1855,

Russian gun barrel at Arundel Castle

by a Squadron of fifty-seven English and French ships, under the command of Lyons' son, Captain Edmund Moubray Lyons, aboard HMS *Miranda*. The allied naval campaign caused a significant reduction in supplies reaching the besieged Russian troops at Sevastopol.

One of Deane's letters to his girlfriend back in England, a transcription of which is now in the Arundel archives, describes a diving operation he carried out at Berdyansk in July 1855, during which he recovered several cannons and a bronze bell from vessels sunk by Edmund Lyons' force. It seems likely that one of the cannons, the bell, and the gilded figurehead of the Russian warship – the flagship of the Russian Rear Admiral Wolff, which was destroyed by Edmund Lyons at Berdyansk – were presented to Lord Lyons by Deane or acquired from him by Lyons. It also seems probable that they were acquired as trophies of Captain Edmund Lyons' triumph in the Sea of Azov, rather than from the scene of his death. For tragically, during a night attack on Sevastopol on 18th June 1855, the promising Captain Lyons was fatally wounded and died of wounds on 23rd June 1855, an event which his father probably had no wish to mark with *memento mori* from the fallen port city.

At some point after the Battle of Berdyansk, Lord Lyons also took possession of an ancient Greek altar, in the form of a stubby carved marble column, and three seventeenth-century church bells. These items may also have been acquired through Deane, although there are no records to that effect. On the plinth that now bears the altar in Arundel Park, there is a plaque which states that it was 'found in the museum at Sevastopol', although there is no record of a Sevastopol museum containing ancient Greek artefacts. It is more probable, given the association of Edmund Lyons with the destruction of the coastal battery at Kertch, the fortress town which guarded the entrance to the Sea of Azov, that the bells were taken from an Ionic-style mausoleum, which housed the tomb of a Governor of Kertch. Similarly, the ancient Greek altar may have come from an adjacent Doric-style museum, both buildings being co-located on Mount Mithridates, above Kertch. The museum was reported, in a contemporary letter written by the Crimean War photographer, Robert Fenton, to contain a 'valuable collection of ancient sculpture' that was 'sacked by the troops' after the fall of Sevastopol, which seems reasonably conclusive as to the provenance of the altar. The *bas relief* image of the Madonna and Child on the bells is consistent with them being part of the embellishment of a grand Christian tomb. But why did these trophies come to Arundel Castle? The answer is that the 14th Duke of Norfolk had married Augusta

Russian bell

Greek altar

Figurehead from the Russian ship, *Maloditz*

Lyons, the daughter of Lord Lyons and sister of the late Edmund, in 1839. The Norfolks' family seat was therefore an appropriate setting for these Azovian *triumphi spolia* of the deceased Captain.

The Sevastopol Chairs (1855)

Russian chair found at Sevastopol

1. Now the Royal Dragoons

2. Later the Connaught Rangers

The nineteenth century was a particularly fecund time for the acquisition of chairs by the British Army. The capture by Major General Sir Charles Napier of the deeply uncomfortable alabaster seat of the Amirs of Sindh in 1843 (*see* p.155) was followed, at the end of the Crimean War, with two further acquisitions of furniture by British Regiments.

As a curtain-raiser to the fall of Sevastopol, the British launched two determined assaults on the Russian defensive position, Bastion No 3, better known as the Great Redan. The first assault on 18th June 1855 failed. The second on 8th September succeeded, the Russians retreated, and the port city fell the following day, after a 337-day siege. The Great Redan's fortifications were not simply gun emplacements, but contained offices, stores, accommodation and Officers Messes. Within one of these, Lieutenant Thomas Lewis Hampton of the 5th (Princess Charlotte of Wales's) Dragoon Guards [1] found a polished Russian, Biedermeier-style, birchwood drawing room or library chair, on brass casters with scrolling arms, a swab cushion and a curved backrest. Doubtless more comfortable than the camp chairs to which he was accustomed, Hampton took this piece of Russian domestic furniture for his own use. How it ended up in the Cheshire Military Museum is not recorded, but it now sits only yards from the Amir's grander but altogether less comfortable seat, and next to a label declaring it to be a 'spoil of war'.

Two hundred miles to the south of Chester, in London's National Army Museum, there is a Russian campaign chair taken from Sevastopol, but of an altogether different design to that captured by Lieutenant Hampton. Made from turned, ebonised wood with an upholstered seat and back, the throne-like upright armchair on casters can be collapsed without tools into a flat-pack for transportation, a reverse take on the products of IKEA, which it pre-dates by approximately ninety years. It was acquired by an officer of the 88th Regiment of Foot, [2] and remained in the Officers Mess until their successor Regiment was disbanded on Irish independence in 1922. The upholstered seat and back are actually modern. The original back was leather-covered, with the top embroidered in silver thread, with the name and date: 'SEBASTOPOL [*sic*] 1855' within a laurel wreath. This back was removed by Colonel Jourdain in 1906 and donated in 1956 to what would become the National Army Museum in 1971; the rest of the chair came to the museum in 1978, with its seat, back and arms upholstered in vinyl, of all things.

Bath's missing cannons

Bath is best known for its waters, its social history, and its architecture, but not its bellicosity. There is no military museum in Bath, and the War Memorial was not unveiled until 3rd November 1927, after much controversy and debate. It therefore comes as something of a surprise to discover that Bath's city fathers went to considerable trouble to obtain a pair of bronze cannons from the War Office, which had been captured from the Russians after the fall of Sevastopol.

In the wake of the end of the siege, some of the larger Russian artillery pieces embellished British military establishments, and were also put on display in selected cities around the United Kingdom. Bath was not one of these, which is why Mayor Robert Cook lodged a petition for the cannons with the Secretary of State for War, Lord Panmure.

Russian cannon in Bath's Royal Victoria Park

Once the War Office had agreed to release two Russian gun barrels, Bath's elders decided on the site of the Victoria Monument, an elaborate obelisk on the western side of the Royal Victoria Park, as a suitable position for the guns. At this time, the park was privately run by a committee, which readily agreed to the installation, and Wednesday 9th September 1857 was fixed for a grand ceremonial inauguration. The event, which happily fell on the second anniversary of the fall of Sevastopol, was extensively reported by *The Illustrated London News*. In the gushing prose of the day, the *ILN*'s correspondent somewhat breathlessly recorded that:

> The weather was remarkably fine. The bells rang out merrily from the various churches, while a running cannonade of feux de joie announced that a festival of no ordinary interest was at hand.

The cannon barrels arrived at Bath Quay, re-mounted on iron gun carriages paid for by the Pickwick Ironworks of Bath, but made at Woolwich Arsenal. They were then slung onto two red, cloth-covered brewer's drays and decorated with laurel wreaths. The first dray was pulled by a team of eight grey horses and the second by eight bays, all of whose harnesses were decorated with tiny flags, rosettes and wreaths of flowers, 'in keeping with the holiday spirit and character of the day'.

Installation of the Russian cannons, Bath

The horse-drawn drays duly set off for the Royal Victoria Park, led by an elaborate 'trophy' of flags and shields bearing the names of the bloody Crimean battles, and followed by a civic and military procession. This consisted of the Deputy Mayor (the Mayor was off sick) and the Aldermen; the committees of the Royal Victoria Park and the Hanoverian Band (which was also on parade); a phalanx of military and naval officers; a party of Crimean War invalids in Bath to take the waters; the Band and a mounted detachment of the North Somerset Yeomanry; two Companies of '*pensioners*' (presumably from the Royal Hospital Chelsea); the Staff and recruiters of the 2nd Somerset Militia with their Fifes & Drums; and a rear guard of a second mounted detachment of Yeomanry.

Mid-way along Royal Avenue the procession halted and the guns were formally handed over by the Deputy Mayor to the care of the Royal Victoria Park Committee. Short speeches were made by Mr Williams of the Pickwick Ironworks and a Crimean War veteran, Major General Willes of the Royal Marines. The guns and their vast escort then trundled on to the Victoria Monument, which had been flag-draped and garlanded for the occasion, and was surrounded by soldiers of the Somerset Militia and the West Somerset Yeomanry. To the immediate east and west of the balustrading surrounding the column, two stone platforms had been constructed on which the guns were to rest. What followed next is best described by the *ILN*:

> The ceremony of dislodging the guns from the cars and depositing them on the stone platforms … was performed … by the West Somerset Yeomanry, amidst the almost breathless silence of the multitude, who watched with no little admiration and interest this novel, and apparently difficult, operation and when it was accomplished the welkin [the sky] rang with a hearty simultaneous shout of triumph.

But this was by no means the end of the installation: gunners stepped forward, and in defiance of health and safety, fired the Russian guns, which were loaded with blanks. Whilst the flash, roar and smoke from the cannons filled the air, the pensioners and the Militia let off their muskets, and the Bands played the National Anthem. As the final notes died away, the Parade Commander, Captain Haviland of the North Somerset Yeomanry, called for three cheers for The Queen from the assembled thousands. So concluded the 'inauguration of the Russian trophies at Bath'.

The Russian guns, and two neat stacks of cannon balls, remained in place in the Royal Victoria Park into the twentieth century, as evidenced by a photograph of soldiers of the 2nd Wessex Royal Engineers posing on one of them in 1915. Despite the city declining the offer of a First World War tank, the Russian guns survived *in situ* until December 1941, when with the Bath Parks' Committee's approval, they were dismantled and removed to a scrap-metal yard, along with much of Bath's irreplaceable Georgian architectural ironwork, prior to being melted down and converted into munitions for use against the Germans.

2nd Wessex Royal Engineers posing with a Bath cannon

However, it has recently emerged that the guns were not consigned to a furnace, although their actual fate remains a mystery. One *Bath Chronicle* account claims with some authority that they were dumped in the Gloucester & Sharpness Canal as part of the foundations for Sharpness Docks. Another account in the same newspaper avers that in 1946 one of the cannon barrels was delivered by a gardener and his fourteen-year-old assistant to a house 'near the Hare & Hounds pub on Lansdowne Hill', the second was taken by the same team 'to a house on Widcombe Hill', and the cannon balls were 'delivered to a house in the Royal Crescent'. Given the size and weight of the cannons, this is an extremely unlikely explanation, and it probably refers to the delivery of some much smaller ordnance scrap. This theory is confirmed by an extensive leafleting of both Lansdowne and Widcombe Hills, carried out recently by the author, which achieved a nil return.

Newcastle cannon

Another non-military establishment which acquired a Russian cannon in the same year as Bath is the Staffordshire town of Newcastle-under-Lyme. Now proudly guarding the entrance to the Brampton Museum & Art Gallery, a bronze plaque next to the gun provides the following information:

> The Russian cannon, which dates from 1840 was captured at the end of the Crimean War in 1856. It stood in Stubbs Walks from 1857 until it was moved to its present position in 1965. It was repaired & restored in 1986. The cannon weighs 2.3 tons and fired a 36lb shot.

The Newcastle-under-Lyme cannon self-evidently not only survived the call for bronze during the Second World War, but has also been cherished by the town. This is in stark contrast to the fate of its larger brothers in Bath, a much richer but considerably less bellicose city.

CHAPTER 18

INDIAN MUTINY (1857–1858)

Mutinous Mementos

On 10th May 1857, Indian soldiers of the 3rd Bengal Light Cavalry mutinied in the garrison town of Meerut. As the original mutineers trotted the sixty or so miles to the old Mughal capital of Delhi to re-instate the last Mughal Emperor, the ageing Bahadur Shah Zafar, the revolt rapidly spread to other Anglo-Indian cantonments along the Ganges Valley. Within a matter of days, the Indian Mutiny was a bloody fact.

At first the British were severely wrong-footed by the uprising, and before long their principal garrisons at Lucknow and Cawnpore were under siege. By 8th June other units of the British and the British East India Company's armies, principally located in the hill stations, had deployed two columns, which converged on Delhi, intent on its recapture. After routing a large but disorganised rebel force at the Battle

Massacre in the boats at Cawnpore

of Badli-ki-Serai, six miles west of Delhi, the Company force took up a position on the northern ridge overlooking the city. Here, for the next three-and-a-half months, they were alternately besiegers and besieged.

Hindu Rao's table (Delhi, 1857)

The principal strong point on the Delhi Ridge was a large house belonging to a rich merchant called Raja Hindu Rao, a Maratha nobleman loyal to British rule and related to the royal ruler of Gwalior. When the shooting started Hindu Rao very sensibly vacated his mansion, leaving his property and all its contents to the tender mercies of the Sirmoor Rifles,[1] under the command of Lieutenant Colonel Charles Reid. During the siege, the Gurkha Battalion was supported from time to time by Companies of the Guides Infantry and the 60th Regiment of Foot.[2] Over the next three-and-a-half months, all three Regiments took heavy casualties, resulting in them being granted the unique privilege of embellishing their tunic collars with blood-red piping.

1. Now the Royal Gurkha Rifles

2. Also known both as the 60th Rifles and The King's Royal Rifle Corps, and now, following many amalgamations, The Rifles

Many of these casualties were treated for their wounds on an ebonised-mahogany dining-room table, consisting of three pedestals with eight leaves. Recent research has determined that the table was made from West Indian mahogany, probably shipped to Madras as ballast in the early 1800s. Once in India, the wood was turned into a table by native craftsmen in Calcutta, who fashioned the lumber into a reasonable approximation of the then popular Regency style.

In the aftermath of the eventual re-capture of Delhi on 21st September, Colonel Reid ordered that the makeshift operating table be divided up and retained by the three Regiments as a trophy. The Guides and the 60th Rifles each took a section with a pedestal, leaving the Sirmoor Rifles with six leaves and the third pedestal.

Over the next 150 years the tops (but not the bases) were stripped back to the original mahogany. Recently the Gurkhas consulted an expert at the Victoria & Albert Museum, who determined that the tops had always been ebonised, and a decision was taken to restore the black finish to their portion of the table. In the 1920s, the precise date is uncertain, the 60th Rifles somehow lost their piece of the table and were generously given a replacement by the Sirmoor Rifles, thus reducing the latter's holding to five leaves (and no pedestal). This necessitated their adaptation as a wall decoration, in which condition they now hang in the entrance of the Officers Mess of The Royal Gurkha Rifles.

Raja Hindu Rao

Raja Hindu Rao was not the only Indian aristocrat to lose a table at this time. In 1858, following the fall of the fortress at Jhansi, a vast, 36-leg dining room table was acquired from the palace of Rani Lakshmibai, the last ruler of Jhansi, by the 3rd Bombay European Regiment.[3] The rebellious Rani, whose princely state had been absorbed into the East India Company in 1853, had personally led her troops against the British. She was killed on 17th June 1858 by a Trooper of the 8th (King's Royal Irish) Hussars in the immediate aftermath of the Battle of Kota-ki-Serai.

On the disbandment of The Leinster Regiment in 1922, the table was consigned for safe keeping to the Army Council until it was dissolved in 1964. The table then passed to the National Army Museum, where it remained until 2007 when it was acquired by the Royal Asiatic Society.

3. Later the 109th Regiment of Foot which, in 1881, became The Leinster Regiment. The current Vice Chairman of The Leinster Regiment Association is Sir Anthony Weldon Bt, the publisher of this book

A Pearl Earring (Delhi, 1857)

When Delhi eventually fell to the British on 21st September 1857, the contents of Bahadur Shah Zafar's palace were auctioned, as was the custom. Amongst the spoils of war on offer was jewellery that had belonged to the Emperor Bahadur's four consorts, including a large and elaborately-made Mughal-style pearl, ruby and diamond earring. This was purchased by Captain Sir Edward Campbell of the 1st Battalion of the 60th Regiment of Foot.

Campbell was uniquely well placed to acquire the earring as, in advance of the final assault on Delhi, he had been appointed to be the Prize Agent 'in charge of the legalised looting of the captured city'. He would therefore have had sight of all the spoils to be auctioned before they were put up for sale. In a curious twist, he may also have already seen the jewel hanging from the ear of one of Bahadur's wives, while he was courting his own future wife, Georgiana, who was the second daughter of the British Agent at Bahadur's Court in Delhi.

Georgiana's father, Sir Thomas Metcalfe, was against the proposed union, as he thought that Campbell was too poor to support his wife in the manner to which he thought she should be accustomed. Campbell, who was deeply in love with Georgiana, went on hunger strike until her father relented. They married in 1853, only ten days before Sir Thomas died in mysterious circumstances, possibly as the result of being poisoned by Bahadur's third and favourite wife, Zinat Mahal. Zinat was the *de facto* ruler of Delhi and may have had Sir Thomas murdered in revenge for his part in the exclusion of her only (and Bahadur's fifteenth) son from the

Emperor Bahadur II, the last Mughal Emperor

somewhat meaningless Imperial succession. No images exist showing Zinat Mahal wearing the Campbell earring, but it would be a beautiful and ironic piece of symmetry if it could ever be proved that she had possessed it.

Once order was restored in India, and the 60th had returned to their cantonment, Campbell gave the earring to his wife, with whom it remained until her untimely death giving birth to her thirteenth child in 1872. Following this tragic event, the Mughal jewel passed to her daughter, and it is now on loan from the family to The Royal Green Jackets (Rifles) Museum in Winchester.

Zinat Mahal

The Delhi Purple Sapphire (Cawnpore 1857)

Lying in a display case in The Vault, the precious stones gallery at London's Natural History Museum, is a large faceted purple gemstone in an elaborate silver setting. By any standards, it is a curious piece of jewellery, but not half as curious as its history. For this is the so-called 'thrice-cursed' Delhi Purple Sapphire, a sinister souvenir of the Indian Mutiny, and according to the museum's website, one of its most treasured possessions.

Tales of cursed gemstones are a commonplace of Victorian action-adventure fiction and Hollywood films of the *Indiana Jones* genre, with the curses usually arising from the theft of the stone in question from an oriental temple statue. In order to determine whether the legend of the Delhi Purple Sapphire is the origin or the end product of one of these romances, it is necessary to review the recorded facts.

According to an account written by Edward Heron-Allen, which accompanied the stone when it was gifted to the Natural History Museum, it was looted from the Temple of Indra in Cawnpore by Colonel William Ferris, following the relief of the city by the British on 16th July 1857. According to Heron-Allen, Ferris was a Bengal Cavalry officer in the Army of the British East India Company, and Indra is the Hindu God of weather and (appropriately) war. History does not relate whether or not the Colonel prised the stone from the head of the God, but he apparently returned with it to England.

From that point on, it appears that the Colonel's fortune and health deteriorated, as did those of his son, Surgeon Lieutenant Colonel J E C Ferris of the Indian Medical Service, who so the story goes inherited the unset stone, actually an amethyst and not a sapphire. In a bid to rid himself of the curse, the younger Ferris gave the amethyst to a friend, who subsequently committed suicide, but not before bequeathing the stone back to Ferris. In a final bid to recover his health and his wealth,

The cursed Delhi Purple Sapphire

169

Edward Heron-Allen,
'the Black Boy Scout'

Ferris then gave the stone to Edward Heron-Allen. A wealthy polymath, Rosicrucian, and keen supporter of the Boy Scout movement, Heron-Allen was a friend of Oscar Wilde, an author of supernatural fiction (under the pseudonym of Christopher Blayre), and a man who preferred to dress in black. His penchant for black clothes included a specially sanctioned Scout uniform, which led to his nickname of the 'Black Boy Scout'. He was also a practicing lawyer, with an interest in violins, Persian literature and the occult.

Unfortunately for Heron-Allen, the change of ownership did not, apparently, evade the curse. However, its new owner was familiar with the ways of the Eastern occult and took a succession of measures to neutralise the stone's baleful influence. First, he had it set in a double-headed snake ring, which he claimed had belonged to an eighteenth-century English magician known as Heydon the Astrologer. This ring was then 'looped up with Zodiacal plaques and neutralised between Heydon's magic Tau and two amethyst scaraboei of Queen Hatasu's period, brought from Thebes'. In the view of *savants* of the occult these were powerful charms, and despite the presence in his library of a naked Hindu Yoga who 'haunted the stone' in an attempt to secure its return, according to Heron-Allen they did the trick until 1901.

But when the talismanic setting started to lose its power, Heron-Allen was prevailed upon to give the stone to a lady friend, who was duly 'overwhelmed with every possible disaster' and returned the stone to him. With this development, a rational person might have arranged for the amethyst to be returned to Cawnpore. Not so Heron-Allen, who threw it into the Regent's Canal, only for it to be returned to him three months later. Somewhat unkindly, he then gave the stone to an opera singer friend, who promptly lost her voice and never sang again.

Fearing that the curse might have an adverse effect on his new-born daughter, Heron-Allen finally encased the Delhi Purple Sapphire in seven boxes (a significant number in occultist circles), and in October 1904 deposited it with his bank with instructions that the box was not to be opened until thirty-three years after his death (another significant astrological number). Along with the stone, he also left a letter which detailed the history of the cursed stone and the misfortunes that had fallen upon all who had possessed it, since it had been taken from the Temple of Indra in 1857.

In 1944 (only a year after his death), Heron-Allen's daughter, who had self-evidently survived the curse thanks to her father's timely deposit of the stone in his bank, presented the Delhi Purple Sapphire and her father's account of the stone's history to the Natural History Museum, along with a warning against any of the museum staff handling it. Since when the stone, one of the top exhibits in The Vault, appears to have lost its evil powers, although not its grisly reputation. Given this utterly fantastical tale, could the legend of this cursed spoil of war have been fabricated in whole or in part by Heron-Allen? The answer lies in a pseudonymous fictional short story he published in April 1921, entitled *The Purple Sapphire*. In a significantly expanded form and with altered names and places, this tale replicates the account Heron-Allen attached to the stone when he deposited it at the bank in 1904.

Further proof that the tale of the 'thrice-cursed' Delhi Sapphire is nothing more than an elaborate Heron-Allen fantasy-turned-hoax, perpetrated successfully on one of London's best-loved museums, has been established by Peter Ferris, the three-times great-grandson of William Ferris, who holds the family's extensive archives. Whilst confirming that his ancestor was in the Indian Army, although William served with the 12th Native Infantry not the Bengal Cavalry, and that Heron-Allen was the family's lawyer, Mr Ferris states unequivocally that the 'curse' visited on his family had nothing to do with a 'purple sapphire' and everything to do with Surgeon Lieutenant Colonel J E C Ferris's addiction to alcohol and his abuse of substances from his own medical supplies. Furthermore, there is no mention in William Ferris's will of a valuable gemstone (the semi-precious amethyst is of little value); and there is no evidence that it was looted from a temple. In fact, it probably never belonged to the Ferris family, as it is clearly a stone that was cut and polished in Europe; and in all probability, that particular link with the Ferris family was fabricated by Heron-Allen in order to give the elaborate story a veneer of truth.

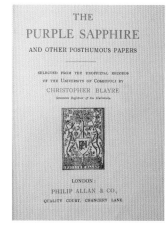

Heron-Allen's book, *The Purple Sapphire*

The skull of Havildar Alum Bheg

In early 2018, BBC News went into moral overdrive with the discovery that a skull, in the possession of a couple living in Essex, was that of an executed Indian mutineer called Havildar Alum Bheg. Much politically correct copy was expended on what should be done with the cranial remains, the rights and wrongs of the Indian Mutiny itself, and the barbarity of the way in which Havildar Alum Bheg had been executed for his brutal and senseless crimes. No editorial whatsoever was devoted to

Mutineers blown from guns at Peshawar

the gruesome fate of his innocent victims, whose suffering must have been considerably more prolonged than the instant and explosive disintegration of the Havildar, when he was blown from a cannon.

Readers can judge for themselves the merits of the case by reading the following note which was lodged in one of the eye sockets of the jawless skull:

Skull of Havildar 'Alum Bheg,' 46th Regt. Bengal N. Infantry who was blown away from a gun, amongst several others of his Regt. He was a principal leader in the mutiny of 1857 & of a most ruffianly disposition. He took possession (at the head of a small party) of the road leading to the fort, to which place all the Europeans were hurrying for safety. His party surprised and killed Dr Graham shooting him in his buggy by the side of his daughter. His next victim was the Rev. Mr. Hunter, a missionary, who was flying with his wife and daughters in the same direction. He murdered Mr Hunter, and his wife and daughters after being brutally treated were butchered by the road side.

Alum Bheg was about 32 years of age; 5 feet 7 ½ inches high and by no means an ill-looking native. The skull was brought home by Captain (AR) Costello (late Captain 7th Dragoon Guards), who was on duty when Alum Bheg was executed.

The present whereabouts of the skull are unknown.

CHAPTER 19

SECOND OPIUM WAR
(1856–1860)

Treasures from the Old Summer Palace

A gold-plated snuff box & other knick-knacks (Peking 1860)

On 19th May 2011, an Imperial Chinese gold-plated snuff box was offered for sale anonymously at a Woolley & Wallis auction in Salisbury, along with a number of other items. All were spoils of war from the looting and sacking of the Old Summer Palace in Peking in 1860.

But why were British troops on the rampage in Peking in 1860? The answer is trading rights, the most important of which was the right to import vast quantities of Indian-grown opium for Chinese consumption. This was a trade to which the Qing dynasty (1644–1912) was opposed, not because it cared that its subjects were as high as Chinese kites on the powerful narcotic, but because it created a significant imbalance in its previously favourable balance of trade account.

The disputed and illegal importing of opium first reared its bleary-eyed head as a *causus belli* in 1839, when the Imperial Chinese government rejected a British proposal to legalise the trade. Emperor Daoguang

The King's Dragoon Guards in action near Peking, 21st September 1860

Emperor Xianfeng

James Bruce, 8th Earl of Elgin

1. Earlier in the nineteenth century, Elgin's father, the 7th Earl, purchased the so-called 'marbles' from the Parthenon frieze in Athens from the Ottomans, which are now in the British Museum

appointed one of his Court officials, the scholar Lin Zexu, to solve the problem. He did so by the simple expedient of abolishing all imports of the drug, a decision which he backed up by confiscating without compensation 20,000 chests of opium (approximately 1,210 tons) from British warehouses. He then banned all further trade of any sort and confined foreign merchants to their quarters.

The British government, although not officially denying China's right to control imports of the 'blue smoke' as it was known, objected to this unexpected seizure and used its overwhelming naval power to make the point. Negotiations ensued, enforced by British naval cannon, and in 1842 the Chinese reluctantly signed the Treaty of Nanking, bringing the First Opium War to an end. Britain was granted an indemnity and extraterritoriality, the five treaty ports of Shanghai, Canton, Ningpo, Fuchow and Amoy were opened to foreign merchants, and Hong Kong Island was ceded to the British in perpetuity.

However, on other points, including the opium trade and the establishment of diplomatic representation in Peking, China prevaricated. By 1856 both sides were preparing for another armed confrontation. The spark that ignited this box of firecrackers was struck by the Chinese, who impounded an illegal opium trading vessel, the *Arrow*, which unfortunately (and quite illegally) happened to be flying a British flag. What ensued is probably one of the more curious episodes in the history of British, French and Chinese diplomacy and conflict.

In a nutshell, after bombarding Canton, where the *Arrow's* Chinese crew were being held, the British and the French governments informed the Emperor Xianfeng, fourth son of Emperor Daoguang who had been humiliated in the First Opium War, that they were determined to establish embassies in Peking, as mandated in the terms of the Treaty of Nanking. To that end, the Europeans announced that they were sending a heavily-armed diplomatic mission from the coast, under the leadership of James Bruce, 8th Earl of Elgin,[1] and Baron Jean-Baptiste-Louis Gros.

The Chinese responded with an invitation to the mission to come to Peking, opposed it every step of the way, and then imprisoned, tortured and killed in quite horrific circumstances an Anglo-French negotiating team. On all counts this perfidy, and its barbaric aftermath, was viewed very badly by Lord Elgin and his French counterpart, who ordered a rapid advance on Peking. When the hideously mutilated corpses of the negotiators were uncovered, they ordered the destruction of the Emperor's Summer Palace in retribution.

The Yuanming Yuan (The Garden of Perfect Brightness), as the Old Summer Palace was known, was the private residence of the Qing Emperors. It covered 860 acres, and included hundreds of halls, pavilions, temples, galleries, gardens, lakes and bridges. The buildings of this pleasure complex housed thousands of Chinese antiquities and artefacts, some of which were up to 3,600 years old. The value of the contents of the Summer Palace before its destruction is incalculable, but destroyed it was by English and French troops. Fortunately, wholesale British looting – the French were more intent on wanton wrecking – saved many works of art from the flaming buildings, which burnt for three days.

View of the Yuan Ming Yuan

Included in the force that seized Peking and helped with the pillage of the Summer Palace were four Troops of the 1st King's Dragoon Guards,[2] amongst whose number was Captain James Gunter. Nothing is known about how precisely Captain Gunter acquired the Qing dynasty, gold-plated snuff box encrusted with seed pearls and enamel, along with other pieces, including a yellow jade dragon pendant carved in the 'archaistic' style, a tiny white jade cup and saucer carved with stags, two white jade vases, and a watch which was a gift to the Emperor from King George III, all of which were offered for sale on 19th May 2011.

2. Now 1st The Queen's Dragoon Guards

The value of antiquities is considerably enhanced if their original provenance can be established. In the case of Captain Gunter's snuff box, this was put beyond doubt by the inscription inside the lid: 'Loot from Summer Palace, Pekin, Oct 1860, Captain James Gunter, King's Dragoon Guards.'

Consequently, instead of a pre-sale estimate of £10,000, which it would have had without this inscription, the snuff box sold for £400,000 to a Chinese buyer. Gunter's other items looted from the Old Summer Palace fetched a further £1.5 million. The anonymous sellers are known to retain in their possession further Gunter loot, including ivory chopsticks, jade boxes, wind

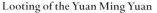

Looting of the Yuan Ming Yuan

Looty, **painted by Friedrich Wilhelm Keyl, 1861**

© *Royal Collection Trust*

3. Later the Duke of Edinburgh's (Wiltshire) Regiment and, following several further amalgamations, The Rifles

chimes, and a small jadeite belt hook worth an estimated £2,000,000.

These treasures are but some of the many thousands of items taken from the Old Summer Palace that remain in royal, regimental, national and private collections. These may include a collection of chinoiserie acquired by Captain (later Major General) Charles Gordon, which are now in the Royal Engineers Museum at Chatham in Kent. The collection includes a large Imperial couch with dragon carvings, and a Cantonese export-ware games table. Gordon was present at the sacking of the Old Summer Palace, and afterwards remained in China on the British Staff. In 1862, he was appointed to command the Chinese Emperor's 'Ever Victorious' Army, which quashed the Taiping Rebellion the following year. As he disapproved of the destruction of the Old Summer Palace, it is possible that he may have acquired some or all of his Chinese collections during this period, rather than at the sacking of the palace.

Without question, five Chinese lapdogs (probably Pekinese) belonging to the Chinese Empress were also liberated by British troops. Two of these dogs were given to the Duchess of Wellington, another pair were given to the Duchess of Richmond, and one was presented to Queen Victoria by its captor, Captain John Hart Dunne of the 99th (Lanarkshire) Regiment of Foot.[3] So pleased was the Queen with her gift that she named the dog Looty, had it painted by Friedrich Wilhelm Keyl, and installed it at Windsor Castle, where it lived for a further eleven years.

In his memoirs, Captain Hart Dunne left an interesting insight into looting and a brief account of his acquisition of *Looty*:

Lay down very tired, and with the conclusion that plundering a palace was, after all, anything but an amusing occupation. It brings out the worst passions in one's nature – avarice and covetousness amongst others. Everyone is dissatisfied with what he has got, because he thinks someone else has done better; and I believe everyone feels more or less lowered in his estimation, by the inward knowledge of what his feelings are on the occasion… I have been able to retain a good many trifles that I bought in the French camp, also a pretty little dog, a real Chinese sleeve dog. It has silver bells round its neck. People say, it is the most perfect little beauty they have ever seem.

Queen Victoria clearly agreed with this assessment of *Looty*.

CHAPTER 20

ABYSSINIA EXPEDITION (1867–1868)

An Elephantine Auction

In 1868, an Anglo-Indian army of 13,000 soldiers, 26,000 camp followers and 40,000 pack animals (including forty-four elephants) took three months to slog 400 miles south through the inhospitable terrain of Abyssinia. The route took them from Zula on the Red Sea coast to the hill-top fortress of Magdala. The purpose of this Imperial expedition, which Alan Moorehead described in his book *The Blue Nile* as proceeding 'from first to last with all the decorum and heavy inevitability of a Victorian State banquet', was to rescue two English missionaries, five representatives of the British government, and the wife and child of one of the latter from the clutches of Emperor Tewodros II, the country's Coptic Christian ruler, who claimed descent from King Solomon and the Queen of Sheba.

Emperor Tewodros II

The British camp at Magdala

1928 faked photograph of the
Drum of Gold

Despite considerable opposition along the route, the campaign was entirely successful. Following a brief siege of the Abyssinian capital, the prisoners were released unharmed between 10th and 12th April, and Britannia's honour was restored at the cost of only two dead and eighteen wounded. Emperor Tewodros, who had only imprisoned these people in a misplaced bid to secure British military support against a domestic insurrection, did the honourable thing and blew out his brains with a pistol given to him in happier days by Queen Victoria. Tewodros' body was cremated and his ashes buried inside a local church, which was guarded by soldiers of the 33rd Regiment of Foot.

However, this was not only a rescue but also a punitive expedition. Its commander, General Sir Robert Napier, who was later created Baron Napier of Magdala for his victory, ordered the looting and burning of the fortress on 13th April, in accordance with the then custom and practice of war. The Anglo-Indian troops, as in so many other victorious aftermaths, gathered up many historical artefacts, which were then sold at a Prize Auction. Many were taken back to the United Kingdom, later to be displayed in the British Library, the British Museum, and in the museums and Messes of the participating Regiments.

Emperor Tewodros' Drum of Gold (Magdala, 1868)
This largely forgotten paragraph of British Imperial history has, however, left a mystery that remains unsolved to the present day. Amongst the spoils seized was an item known as Emperor Tewodros' Drum of Gold. The regimental folklore of the 33rd Regiment of Foot alleges that this silver (not gold) musical instrument was found by Bandsman Thomas Dunn of the 33rd, during the official looting. Dunn was determined that it should join the Band's array of drums, and so hid it in his quarters under a greatcoat. This tactic might have worked, had not one of the late Emperor's officials complained about its theft, with the result that it had to be surrendered to Sir Robert Napier. However, far from organising its return or placing it in the Prize Auction, Napier, who must have been in a Solomonic mood, ordered that it should be divided and shared in equal sections between the three British Regiments which had taken part in the campaign: the 4th (King's Own) Regiment of Foot, the 33rd (or Duke of Wellington's) Regiment of Foot, and the 3rd (Prince of Wales's) Dragoon Guards.[1] These parts remained separated until 1928, when they were temporarily re-united and photographed to accompany an article about the drum in

1. The successor Regiments today are, respectively, the Duke of Lancaster's Regiment, the Yorkshire Regiment and the Royal Scots Dragoon Guards

Individual parts of the Drum of Gold

The Lion & the Rose, the journal of The King's Own Royal Regiment, at that time the successor Regiment of the 4th.

So far, so good. But in 1997 the three sections of the drum, all of which have been historically authenticated, were again temporarily re-united to mark the re-opening of The King's Own Royal Regiment Museum in Lancaster. To the dismay of the three Regiments, it was discovered that the parts would not fit together, the centre section being far smaller than it appeared to be in the 1928 photograph. It was then discovered that the photograph had been manipulated to make the pieces fit. Despite extensive further enquiries, and in the absence of anyone left alive who could recall the events of either 1868 or 1928, the question as to why the centre section of the drum owned by the 33rd didn't fit remains unresolved. Although an officer of the Regiment, who wishes to remain anonymous, has a theory:

> I suspect that when the officers, in a fit of Imperial hubris, decided to melt down the other drum captured at Magdala to create the Abyssinia Cup as a twin to the Cornwallis Cup the then silver member got in a muddle and took the wrong drum for melting. This would explain perhaps the mismatch in sizes. Reinforcing this suspicion is the fact that the script on the small plate taken from the original 'melted' drum and attached to the rear of the Abyssinia Cup is in the same style as that on the other two end sections, whereas that on our extant drum is in a different style. Sad, but too late to worry about it now.

Indeed – and it is news to many that there was a second drum…

An Emperor's Crown, 'The Glory of Kings' & a lock of Imperial hair (Magdala, 1868)
So great was the Abyssinian haul of spoils placed on sale at the Prize Auction that it required fifteen elephants and nearly two hundred mules

Captain Speedy and Prince
Alamayu of Abyssinia

2. In the course of researching this
book, I unearthed another case of
voluntary repatriation of spoils of
war by the Victoria & Albert
Museum which is covered in the
chapter on the Third Anglo-
Burmese War (*see* p.185)

Lord Granville

to transport the lots to the plain of Dalanta below the burning fortress.
Among the crowd at the auction was Captain Tristram Speedy, who had
lived in Abyssinia and worked with the Emperor from 1861 to 1863.
During the Expedition, he acted as one of General Napier's advisers and
translators, and afterwards was appointed guardian of Tewodros' son,
Prince Alamayu, by Queen Victoria. Captain Speedy's widow donated
her husband's extensive collection of Abyssinian clothes, jewellery, and
artefacts to the British Museum in 1912. The donation included a *very*
large number of Abyssinian trousers. Unfortunately for this book, none
of these were spoils of war, although some of the other items in his collection may have been acquired by Speedy in the two-day sale.

The Prize Action included hundreds of historical manuscripts collected
by the late Emperor, as well as his Imperial regalia. Of particular significance
in the history of spoils of war, and the current debate about repatriation,
are the Emperor's crowns and a book called *The Glory of Kings*.

It is a firmly held article of faith in Britain, and a precept of international
law, that museums do not have to repatriate spoils of war or other items
(such as the Parthenon Marbles), providing that they were legitimately
acquired. It was and remains the view that officially conducted Prize Auctions legitimised the subsequent ownership of items so acquired, and they
cannot therefore be challenged. That notwithstanding, one of the Emperor's crowns, *The Glory of Kings*, and most recently a lock of Tewodros'
hair, were in due course returned to Abyssinia/Ethiopia, under circumstances that inform the current debate, particularly the pains to which
officials went (until recently) to ensure that no precedents were set.[2]

The first to be sent back to its country of origin was *The Glory of Kings*,
a fourteenth-century account of the origins of the Solomonic line of the
Emperors of Abyssinia. Part of a collection of 359 books bought for the
British Museum at the Prize Auction, it was not just an Abyssinian
Almanac de Gotha, but the document that established the legitimacy of
the Emperor to the throne of Solomon and the Queen of Sheba. So
precious was it to Imperial legitimacy that it had been kept by Emperor
Tewodros under his pillow, where it was found by Napier's soldiers after
his untimely suicide.

The book had already been catalogued by the British Museum, when
Queen Victoria and Lord Granville, the British Foreign Secretary, received
a letter from one of Tewodros' successors in 1872. Emperor Yohannes IV
had sided with the British during the dispute with Tewodros, and the

Foreign Office was keen to maintain good relations with him. In the letter, the new Emperor asked the Queen and the Foreign Secretary to find for him the *Fetha Nagast*, otherwise known as *The Glory of Kings*, as 'my people will not obey my orders without it'. Lord Granville appealed to the Trustees of the British Museum. There ensued a considerable debate about the inalienability of the museum's collection, largely driven by a desire not to inadvertently open a hornet's nest at the centre of which were the Parthenon Marbles, until it was discovered that there were in fact *two* copies of the book, one distinctly inferior to the other.

Queen Victoria

Somewhat typically, it was the inferior copy which was sent back to Emperor Yohannes in 1872, with a covering letter from Queen Victoria. It is to date the only legitimately acquired spoil of war to have been repatriated by the British Museum to its country of origin. Yohannes carried the book with him everywhere, and it was in his campaign tent (presumably under his pillow) when he was mortally wounded by Mahdist Sudanese forces at the Battle of Gallabat in 1889. Initially his book was thought to have been lost, but in 1904 the Emperor Menelik II of Ethiopia (as Abyssinia was by then more commonly known) agreed to show it to the French envoy, Hugues Le Roux, who thought it contained 'the delicious perfume of [the Ethiopian people's] most cherished traditions' and, more prosaically, the stamp of the British Museum and an inscription which confirmed its authenticity:

This volume was returned to the King of Ethiopia by order of the Trustees of the British Museum, Dec. 14th 1872, J Winter Jones, Principal Librarian.

Raguel Church, Addis Ababa

Imperial Solomonic rule of the African country continued on and off, presumably thanks to their possession of *The Glory of Kings*, until the abolition of the monarchy in 1975. Despite the subsequent murderous culling of the Imperial Family by Ethiopian revolutionaries, there is still an heir to King Solomon and the Queen of Sheba, the Eton- and Oxford-educated Crown Prince Zera Selassie. However, he does not keep *The Glory of Kings* under his pillow, as it is currently in the Raguel Church in Addis Ababa, which may account for why Prince Zera doesn't have the Imperial Ethiopian throne either.

The saga of the return of the Imperial Ethiopian Crown is no less fraught, some might say devious, but is of a more

Regent of Ethiopia Haile
Selassie

recent date. In 1923 Ethiopia was admitted to the League of Nations. In 1924, the Ethiopian Regent, the future Emperor Haile Selassie, embarked on a tour of the Middle East and Europe, including – somewhat as an after-thought and at very short notice – a State Visit to the United Kingdom.

It is customary on such occasions for Britain's ruling sovereign, at that time King George V, to present a suitable gift to his visiting opposite number, usually in the form of a senior Order of Chivalry, such as the Garter. However, the Regent was only *in loco imperatrix* for Emperor Menelik II's daughter, the Empress Zewditu. Unfortunately, there existed no sufficiently august British Order that could then be given to a woman, and it was thought potentially insulting to give any lesser Order not so debarred. This left the Royal Household and Foreign Office at a loss to know what to do. The situation was made worse by the fact that the last Empress Regnant of Ethiopia had been the Queen of Sheba, believed to have ruled in the tenth century BC, so there were no recent precedents on which they could fall back.

As the other countries already visited by the Regent had been lavish with their gifts for the Empress, real concern had started to set in when someone in the Foreign Office had a bright idea. Why not present the Ethiopian Empress Zewditu *in absentia* with Emperor Tewodros' crown, then on display, with an accompanying solid gold chalice, at the Victoria & Albert Museum? This proposal was given the enthusiastic support of Prime Minister Ramsay MacDonald, a socialist who was probably not averse to there being one less crown in England, and who was in any event also the Foreign Secretary. A letter was duly dispatched to the Board of Education, the government body then in control of the V&A.

However, a complication then arose: there were, it emerged, *at least two* Ethiopian crowns in the museum's collection. One crown, which was the inalienable property of the V&A, had been presented to the museum by HM Treasury in 1872. It had been acquired by Professor Richard Holmes, a British Museum manuscripts curator attached to the Abyssinia Expedition, who had seized it, along with the chalice and an amulet, half-an-hour after the capture of Magdala and long before the Prize Auction. Once back in England, these and many other Abyssinian objects taken by Holmes were deposited with national museums. This three-tiered crown, not dissimilar to a Papal tiara, was made of solid gold, and required an Act of Parliament to release it from South Kensington.

The second, a 'barbaric' and distinctly inferior crown, was made of gold-plated silver and paste, somewhat in the manner of a stage 'prop', and

Prime Minister & Foreign
Secretary Ramsay MacDonald

belonged not to the V&A, but to the Secretary of State for India from whom it was on loan. The gift of the 'barbaric' crown to the Empress would therefore not compromise the rules relating to the repatriation of items in museum collections, and Britain's heritage would be only very minimally depleted. Besides which, reasoned the officials, if the British government didn't know that there were two (or more) crowns, why would the Ethiopians? This would therefore allow the King to present the theatrical prop rather than the real thing. Anyway, the Board of Education was clear: they certainly had no wish to set an unfortunate precedent, and either didn't know about the return of *The Glory of Kings*, or had conveniently forgotten the fact. If the government wanted to give the Ethiopian Empress the better of the two crowns, and wanted it there and then, the whole matter would have to be dropped.

An Abyssinian Crown at the Victoria & Albert Museum, London

This focussed Ramsay MacDonald's mind and a letter was rushed to the India Office requesting the release of the 'barbaric' stage prop. The Secretary of State for India duly gave his consent to the transfer, and the distinctly inferior crown was packed up in time for King George to be able to tell the Ethiopian delegation that 'We are returning to you the crown of Emperor Tewodros'. A year later it was handed to the Empress Zewditu in an impressive ceremony in Addis Ababa where, presumably, it remains to this day.

In a recent blog, the present Director of the Victoria & Albert Museum has stated that the crown returned to Ethiopia was probably that of Emperor Tewodros' widow, Queen Terunesh, who died a month after her husband in British captivity. Following her death, her 'dress and jewellery' were sent to the Secretary of State for India at the India Office in London, and in 1869 were given to the V&A.[3]

An Abyssinian Chalice at the Victoria & Albert Museum, London

By way of a *post script*, in addition to the crown still held by the V&A, there is at least one more Abyssinian crown in a British collection. It is well documented that Gerhard Rohlfs, a German interpreter attached to Napier's Expedition, acquired a crown at the Prize Auction which he sent, via the Prussian Vice Consul in Suez, to the Prussian Foreign Minister, Count Otto von Bismarck. In due course, the presence of an Imperial Ethiopian crown in Berlin came to the attention of the British Minister, probably as part of the planning for the upcoming State Visit to Britain by King Wilhelm I, during which the question of a suitable gift for Queen Victoria would have been raised. In due course this crown crossed the Channel and was given to Queen Victoria by Wilhelm I. However, it is not currently listed as part of the Royal Collection, although another Abyssin-

3. *www.vam.ac.uk/blog/muse-um-life/magdala-1868* (accessed November 2019)

ian crown belonging to Tewodros II is listed, but with the information that it was sent to Queen Victoria by General Napier, together with Tewodros II's robes, seals and slippers. The Royal Collection's catalogue states that this crown was 'Taken after [Tewodros'] defeat at the 1868 Battle of Magdala and sent by General Napier to Queen Victoria', although it does not state if Napier had acquired it at the Prize Auction.

Quite how many crowns Emperor Tewodros II and his wife possessed remains a mystery; nor is there any absolute certainty as to the number of Imperial Abyssinian crowns that were auctioned on the plain of Dalanta in 1868. That said, Count Götz von Seckendorff, a German officer attached to Napier's Expedition, reported that the Prize Auction included 'several gold and gilt crowns', and Henry Morton Stanley wrote that there were 'four royal crowns, two of which were fine specimens of workmanship, and worth a round sum of money'. If Stanley is correct, then it is probable that two of the Emperor's crowns ended up with Queen Victoria and two with the V&A, whilst that returned to Abyssinia in 1924 was *not* in the Prize Auction at all but had been acquired as described earlier.

The return of Abyssinian crowns and their book are not, however, the end of the story. Until 2019, there existed in a British collection a lock of Emperor Tewodros II's hair. It had been cut from the head of the Emperor by Captain Cornelius James, after he had executed a *post mortem* water-colour of the defeated monarch, and was held by his descendants until 1959 when it was gifted to the National Army Museum in London. In 2019, the Museum bowed to pressure from the Ethiopian government, which claimed that it wished to inter the relic with the ashes of the Emperor. Other museums must be praying that this repatriation does not add to the unfortunate precedents already set.

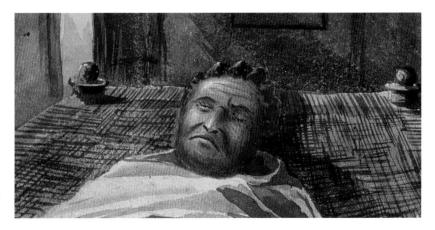

Emperor Tewodros on his deathbed by Captain Cornelius James

CHAPTER 21

THIRD ANGLO-ASHANTI WAR (1873–1874)

Gold from the Gold Coast
Items from King Kofi Karikari's palace (Kumasi, 1874)

There is a certain predictability to the *prima facie* causes of the small wars on the African continent in the nineteenth century. More often than not, it was the capture and imprisonment of Europeans. The justification for the Third Anglo-Ashanti War concerned German and Swiss missionaries, who had been captured in 1869 and were still being held at the Ashanti capital, Kumasi, in 1873.

The real reason for the short war was an Anglo-Ashanti dispute over the ownership of the port of Elmina, acquired as part of the Dutch Gold Coast by the British on 2nd April 1872. Prior to its sale, the Ashanti had received an annual payment from the Dutch for its use, but this stopped when the British took over. In January 1873 an Ashanti Army invaded the new British protectorate to try and enforce the rent arrears. This third affront to British Imperial rule by the West African Kingdom could not be allowed to pass unpunished by London, and a mixed force of British and West Indian troops, under the command of Brigadier General Sir Garnet Wolseley, was tasked with teaching King Kofi Karikari of the Ashanti a lesson he would not forget.

Unlike many of his contemporaries, Garnet Wolseley was no bumbling or sozzled aristocrat, with tactics honed on the playing fields of Eton and strategy developed at the gaming tables at White's. He was in fact 'the very model of a modern Major General', as was recognised later by Messrs Gilbert & Sullivan in their smash-hit of 1879, *The Pirates of Penzance*. Wolseley's military management and organisational skills were also epitomised by the expression 'all Sir Garnet', the Army equivalent of the Royal Navy's 'all ship-shape and Bristol-fashion', which was still in Army usage in the mid-twentieth century.

Wolseley, like Field Marshal 1st Viscount Montgomery of Alamein in

Major General Sir Garnet Wolseley, as seen in *Punch* – the very model of a modern Major General

The Burning of Kumasi

the twentieth century, believed not only that 'time spent in reconnaissance was seldom wasted', but also that proper preparation was the key to military success. Appointed to the Ashanti command on 13th August 1873, he travelled to West Africa to make his plans before the arrival of his troops. Once he had assessed the lie of the land, Wolseley decided that he needed a 160-mile-long road from the coast to the Ashanti capital at Kumasi, with fortified camps at ten-mile intervals, so that his conventional troops could move swiftly through dense, jungle terrain, crisscrossed with rivers and streams. In September 1873, Royal Engineers commenced the work of building the road, 237 bridges, a telegraph line and sixteen fully-stocked forts.

Wolseley's first troops arrived on New Year's Day 1874, clad (on his orders) in new light-weight uniforms better suited to the foetid climate than heavy scarlet tunics. On 5th January they started marching along the new road towards the Ashanti capital. The 2,500 troops consisted of three British Regiments, drawn from the Black Watch, the Rifle Brigade and the Royal Welsh Fusiliers.[1] In addition, there were two West Indian Regiments, a Naval Brigade, two native Regiments, Royal Artillery, Royal Engineers and Royal Marines. By the end of January, the road was more than half completed and Wolseley's forward positions were close to the Ashanti's outposts. Skirmishing between the two forces began, and on the last day of the month battle was joined at the village of Amoaful.

The British advanced in their conventional 'square' formation, accompanied by the bagpipes of the Black Watch. At what sounded like a thousand cats being strangled and the sight of glinting British bayonets,

1. The successor units are, respectively, the 3rd Battalion of the Royal Regiment of Scotland, The Rifles and the 1st Battalion of the Royal Welsh

the Ashanti fled, although they later mounted an unsuccessful attack on Wolseley's rear-guard. At the cost of four men killed and just over 200 wounded, the road to Kumasi was open, and Wolseley's force marched into the Ashanti's abandoned capital on 4th February.

As at Magdala in Abyssinia, Kumasi was destroyed, but not before the palace had been emptied of its contents. These included a suite of wooden furniture (for some reason a favourite, albeit modest, spoil of war for the British soldier), King Kofi Karikari's sword, and a part of one of his jewelled necklaces. All of these items were removed by members of the 2nd Battalion of the Rifle Brigade, which had been appointed – in the event unwisely – to guard the palace and its impressive contents. These spoils of war are now on display at The Royal Green Jackets (Rifles) Museum in Winchester.

Concerned about the number of sick and wounded among his troops, and lacking supplies, Wolseley decided to withdraw his army back to the coast. By the end of February, just two months after their arrival, they were on their way back to England. There Wolseley received the thanks of Parliament, along with a grant of £25,000 (2020: £2.7 million); he was also promoted to Major General, made a Knight Commander of the Bath, and advanced to Knight Grand Cross in the Order of St Michael & St George. King Kofi Karikari fared less well: he was deposed by his own people on 26th October 1874.

Sir Richard Wallace Bt

Meanwhile, and somewhat unusually, the many surviving spoils of war were not auctioned *in situ*, but were transported back to London, where they were later sold at a Prize Auction. This may have been a typically practical decision of Wolseley's, aimed at getting the best possible financial return for his men and their families. In any event, a number of lots, including gold jewellery, elaborately gold-embellished weapons, and a life-size gold face mask weighing nearly four pounds, were sold at the auction at far from bargain prices to Garrard & Co Ltd, the Crown Jeweller in London. They were subsequently acquired in May 1874 by Sir Richard Wallace, the illegitimate son of the 4th Marquess of Hertford and an avid collector of fine art, arms and armour, who had the benefit of very deep pockets. Wallace paid Garrard £500 (2020: £55,500) just for the gold mask. The Wallace Collection, including the Ashanti spoils of war, was bequeathed to the British nation by Sir Richard's widow, Lady Wallace, in 1897, and is now displayed at Hertford House, his home in Manchester Square, London.

Gold mask

CHAPTER 22

ANGLO-ZULU WAR
(1879)

Sir Henry Bartle Frere

Lieutenant General 2nd Lord
Chelmsford, 1879

Spoils of the Zulus

In 1877 Lord Carnarvon, Secretary of State for the Colonies, decided to create a federation of British colonies and Boer Republic in South Africa, similar to the recently successful political re-arrangement of the Canadian states. Sir Henry Bartle Frere was appointed as the first British High Commissioner there, with instructions to carry out this plan. Among the many obstacles to Carnarvon's aspirations was the kingdom of Zululand. To remove this impediment to the British imperial plan, Frere presented Britain's former ally, King Cetshwayo of the Zulus, with an impossible ultimatum on 11th December 1878 to join the federation and disband his army.

The aim was to provoke a war, which Frere was certain the British would win. When the ultimatum was ignored as planned, Frere ordered Lieutenant General Lord Chelmsford, a soldier most definitely not cut from the same cloth as Wolseley, to invade Zululand and give the spear-wielding tribesmen a sound thrashing, before capturing the Zulu capital at Ulundi and declaring game over. Clearly no student of previous military disasters, and doubtless holding the Zulus' military capabilities in contempt, Chelmsford made the fundamental military error of splitting his forces into three columns. What followed on 22nd January 1879 can best be described as one of the worst disasters suffered by the British Army in the nineteenth century.

The column under Chelmsford's direct command had camped at Isandlwana two days earlier, but failed to entrench or form a defensive circle of wagons. After Chelmsford had sub-divided his force again and left with about 2,500 men to seek the enemy, the main Zulu army, estimated to be about 20,000-strong, attacked the encampment at Isandlwana. The ensuing battle lasted from shortly after 11 am to about 3 pm, by which time over 1,300 of the 1,700 British and colonial troops had been massacred

188

and the Zulus had won a decisive victory. The losses included almost all of the men of the 24th Regiment of Foot,[1] who had fought back-to-back in desperate last stands, using rifle butts and bayonets when their ammunition ran out. An officer riding in advance of Chelmsford's returning forces described what he saw of the end of the battle:

Lieutenants Melvill & Coghill, dying to save the Queen's Colour at Isandlwana

1. Now part of the Royal Welsh

King Cetshwayo of the Zulus

> In a few seconds we distinctly saw the guns fired again, one after the other, sharp. This was done several times – a burst, and then a flash – flash! The sun was shining on the camp at that time, and then the camp looked dark, just as if a shadow was passing over it. The guns did not fire again after that, and in a few minutes all the tents had disappeared.

Shortly after this catastrophic episode ended, the British army achieved one of its greatest triumphs. *En route* to Isandlwana, Chelmsford had left a small force behind him to defend the mission station, military hospital and river crossing at Rorke's Drift. During an attack by 3,000 to 4,000 Zulu warriors, which began at four-thirty in the afternoon on 22nd January and continued until two o'clock the following morning, just over 150 men, most from B Company of the 2nd Battalion of the 24th Regiment of Foot, successfully defended the mission. They were eventually relieved at breakfast time by the arrival of the vanguard of Chelmsford's relief column.

This famous action, in the course of which eleven Victoria Crosses and four Distinguished Conduct Medals were won, was immortalised in the 1964 film *Zulu*. The film starred Michael Caine and Stanley Baker as the two British officers present at Rorke's Drift, Lieutenant Gonville Bromhead VC and Lieutenant John Chard VC, and featured Zulu Chief Mangosutho Buthelezi, playing his maternal great-grandfather, King Cetshwayo. By Hollywood standards, the film is a reasonably accurate account of the defence of the mission station. However, some of the details in *Zulu* are the result of dramatic licence. Most notable of these is the portrayal of Private Henry Hook as a thief and a malingerer; he was in fact a model soldier, and his elderly daughters walked out of the film's premiere in disgust at the way he was presented. There is also the misrepresentation that the 24th Regiment of Foot was a Welsh Regiment and that they sang *Men of Harlech* to keep up their spirits. At the time of the Zulu War, the 24th was largely recruited in Warwickshire and its Regimental March was *The Warwickshire Lad*. However, to be fair to the film's producers, Cy Endfield and Stanley Baker, the Regiment was renamed the South Wales Borderers in 1881 and changed its Regimental March to *Men of Harlech*.

Lieutenant Gonville Bromhead VC

The Action at the Mission Station, Rorke's Drift

The facts of the film notwithstanding, it is not surprising that when the Regiment returned home from the Anglo-Zulu War, the officers brought with them a large assortment of Zulu weapons and artefacts, some of which were used to decorate their Mess at The Barracks in Brecon, now the Officers Mess of the 160th (Welsh) Brigade. In the twentieth century, this collection of shields, spears, knobkerries and other items of Zulu origin, including beaded female modesty fringes (as prominently featured in the opening sequence of Zulu) and King Cetshwayo's ceremonial head dress, was moved to the South Wales Borderers museum, now the Regimental Museum of the Royal Welsh. This is housed in a building just outside the Brecon barrack gates, where visitors can see, displayed high up on a wall and in glass-fronted cases, the spoils of the battles and skirmishes that made up the minor, short-lived, but infamous Anglo-Zulu War.

Bromhead's Zulu weapons (Rorke's Drift, 1879)

In addition to these displays, the relatives of the only officer of the 24th who saw action at Rorke's Drift, Lieutenant (later Major) Gonville Bromhead VC, still retain a collection of weapons collected by the gallant officer off the bodies of Zulus fallen at the mission station. These include a warthog tusk armlet (possibly an *iziqu*, the Zulu equivalent of a Victoria

Zulu trophies at the Regimental Museum of the Royal Welsh

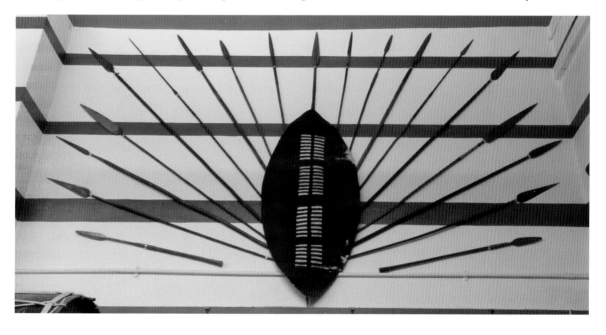

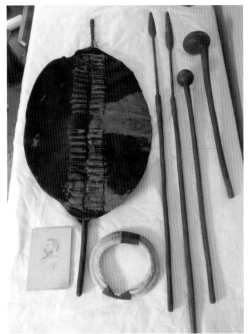

Bromhead's trophies – Zulu shield, assegais, knobkerries and an *iziqu*

Cross), a Martini-Henry rifle (taken from the British the previous day at Isandlwana), two cowhide shields, a brace of assegais, and a clutch of knobkerries, one of which was later converted into a walking stick. On his return to England from South Africa, Bromhead deposited these spoils of war at his family home, Thurlby Hall in Lincolnshire, where they joined an informal collection of other trophies acquired over the centuries by members of his warrior clan, including souvenirs of Quebec, the American War of Independence and Waterloo. However, unlike the manner in which Zulu spoils of war are displayed in the Brecon Museum, or were formerly displayed in the Officers Mess of the 24th Regiment, Bromhead's souvenirs are stored rather than displayed, in a reassuringly British way, at the family's current home. And although no longer living at Thurlby Hall, they do occasionally dig them out to show to curious house guests.

Although technically not a spoil of war, there is also in the uncatalogued Bromhead family collection a Victorian-era shabraque (saddlecloth) of a Royal Engineers Lieutenant. As no member of the Bromhead family served in that Corps, there exists the intriguing possibility that it belonged to the Rorke's Drift commander, Lieutenant John Chard VC, Royal Engineers, and was given to his second-in-command, Bromhead, as a personal souvenir of the action.

Surgeon Reynolds' operating table (Provenance uncertain) & a hospital chair (Rorke's Drift, 1879)

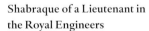

Shabraque of a Lieutenant in the Royal Engineers

Although the Officers Mess at Brecon is now devoid of Zulu weaponry, there is still a table in the entrance hall, which is widely believed to be the

former altar at the Swedish mission station at Rorke's Drift. It was on this altar that Surgeon James Reynolds VC, of the Army Medical Department, operated on the wounded and dying members of B Company 2nd Battalion of the 24th Regiment of Foot. Throughout the battle, Reynolds was accompanied by his fox terrier *Dick*, who only left his side once to bite a Zulu who came too close to his master.

In the film *Zulu*, Surgeon Reynolds, to the dismay of Pastor

Witt, orders soldiers of the 24th to clear the altar in the mission station's chapel for use as an operating table. When Witt remonstrates, Reynolds replies: 'Isn't this as good a place to be when a man is in pain?' Affixed to the leading edge of the table at Brecon is a well-worn engraved brass plate which states: 'Left to the Officers 1st Battn 24th Regiment by Maj Gen R A P Clements CB DSO 1909.'

Despite the gory legend attached to the table, it is extremely unlikely to have ever been anywhere near Rorke's Drift. There are a number of good reasons for stating this. First, although both the 1st and 2nd Battalions of the 24th Regiment of Foot served in the Zulu War of 1879, men of the 1st Battalion – of which Clements was a member – were *not* present at Rorke's Drift. It is also on the record that Clements arrived in South Africa well after Rorke's Drift, and only saw service against the Zulus at the Battle of Ulundi six months later. So, it seems unlikely that he would have bequeathed a table in 1909, apparently closely associated with the 2nd Battalion, to the 1st Battalion. Second, far from being an example of South African-Dutch, Swedish or British

The Burmese altar table

colonial carpentry, the table is clearly of oriental manufacture and probably, given the four-toed male dragon carved on each end and the overall design, a Chinese altar table. The likelihood of such a table finding its way to a Swedish mission station in rural South Africa is close to zero, particularly when it can be verified in the archives of the Church of Sweden Mission, Uppsala, that the Rorke's Drift incumbent, Pastor Otto Witt, never visited the Far East, either before or after 1879. Either way it is disqualified as a spoil of the Zulu War. So, if it is not a grisly trophy of Rorke's Drift, what is the probable provenance that qualifies this piece of furniture for inclusion in this book?

The answer is that Clements later served in the Third Anglo-Burmese War of 1885, as a Major on the Staff of General Sir Harry Prendergast VC, and it is probable that he acquired the table at the Prize Auction of the spoils from King Thibaw Min's palaces (*see* p.207). His former Regiment's knowledge that Clements had served in the Zulu War *and* that the item was an altar table, albeit a Buddhist one, may have been conflated and resulted in its incorrect provenance. It is also possible that the presence of Major

Chair from the temporary hospital at Rorke's Drift

Gonville Bromhead VC in the Burma campaign may have further unwittingly contributed to the legend of the table's provenance.

The only thing that is certain is that past officers of the 1st Battalion 24th Regiment of Foot, and present officers of HQ 160th (Welsh) Brigade, cannot be accused of profaning a Christian altar-turned-operating-table by using it as a hall table, for it is no such thing (although it is, nonetheless, an altar table for a different religion). Given the British Army's well-known disregard for such niceties, this may come as a considerable disappointment to many.

In striking contrast to Surgeon Reynolds' operating-table-that-isn't, there is in the Regimental Museum of the Royal Welsh a small, bentwood kitchen chair with turned legs and splats, the Rorke's Drift provenance of which is without doubt. Affixed to it is a plaque which states: 'This chair was in the hospital at Rorke's Drift during the battle on 22nd January 1879, removed by Major General H J Degacher CB it is presented by his nephew Major James Harter DSO MC Royal Fusiliers to the South Wales Borderers in memory of his friend Lt Col Basil Ramsden DSO MC 24th Regiment.'

Henry James Degacher was, at the time of Rorke's Drift, the Commanding Officer of the 2nd Battalion, 24th Regiment of Foot, in the rank of Lieutenant Colonel. Degacher's younger brother William was serving as a Captain in the 1st Battalion, and was killed at Isandlwana.

2. The largest award for a *single action* is eighteen, for the assault on Sikander Bagh, during the Second Relief of Lucknow (1857)

3. Royal Navy awards of the Victoria Cross were hung on a dark blue ribbon until 1918

The Victoria Cross

Although the Victoria Cross was instituted during an earlier conflict, it is appropriate to include it within the Zulu War section, as of the eleven medals awarded for the action at Rorke's Drift on 22nd-23rd January 1879, seven of them of them represent the highest number ever given to *one unit* for a single action.[2]

The Victoria Cross is a medal in the form of a plain bronze cross hanging from a dark red ribbon.[3] It was introduced on 29th January 1856 by Queen Victoria, to honour acts of valour, irrespective of rank or class, during the Crimean War, and remains the highest military decoration awarded to members of Britain's armed forces for valour 'in the face of the enemy'. The Victoria Cross is first in the 'order of wear' in the United Kingdom honours system, taking precedence over all other Orders, decorations and medals, including the Order of the Garter. By tradition, holders of the decoration, irrespective of their rank, are saluted by everyone, including the Sovereign. Since its inception, the medal has been awarded only 1,358 times to 1,355 individual recipients, three men having received it twice: Surgeon Captain (later Lieutenant Colonel) Arthur Martin-Leake VC & Bar, RAMC; Captain Noel Chavasse VC & Bar, RAMC; and his relative, Captain Charles Upham VC & Bar, 20th Canterbury-Otago Battalion, New Zealand.

There is, however, one abiding myth attached to the Victoria Cross, namely that they are struck from bronze cannon barrels captured at Sevastopol. Metallurgical research has recently revealed that the metal used for all VCs awarded *since* December 1914 has come from the cascabels (knobs) of two Chinese cannons, which were sawn off and melted down for production of the medal. The origin of these cannons is shrouded in mystery, but they cannot be those at the Royal Armouries' Fort Nelson site, as the Chinese cannon there still have their cascabels. It is possible that the cannons from which the bronze was removed may have been spoils of war from the First Opium War of 1839 to 1842 in China.[4] The invaluable lump of bronze from those cascabels, of which there remains enough to make about another 85 VCs, is kept by the Royal Logistic Corps, and can only be removed under guard. Similar metallurgical analysis shows that a different (but unidentified) gun provided the bronze for the medals issued *before* 1914.

Lieutenant (later Lieutenant Colonel) John Chard VC

4. Catriona Davies, 'Author [John Granville] explodes myth of the gun-metal VC', *Daily Telegraph*, 28 December 2005

CHAPTER 23

URABI REVOLT
(1879–1882)

Loot from Defeat & Victory

The completion of the Suez Canal in 1869, the purchase by the British of the Egyptian government's shares in the Canal in 1875, and the guarantee of Egypt's National Debt, coupled with a long-running obsession with the security of the trade route with India had a profound impact on British foreign policy towards the Middle East in general, and the governance of Egypt in particular, until the early 1960s.

The Surrender of Colonel Ahmed Urabi to Major General Drury Lowe, 1882

Although Egypt was nominally a part of the Ottoman Empire until 1918, it had in fact been a largely self-governing province since well before Napoleon ousted the Mamelukes. In the wake of the withdrawal of French forces in 1801, a war for control of Egypt was fought between the Ottomans and the Mamelukes, until the Sublime Porte appointed an Albanian, Muhammad Ali Pasha, as Wali (Governor) of Egypt in 1805.

It didn't take the new Wali long to murder the remaining Mameluke Beys, declare himself Khedive (Viceroy) of Egypt, and subjugate to his rule not only Egypt but Northern Sudan – a fruitful recruiting ground for the Egyptian Army. Muhammad Ali was followed onto the Khedival throne in 1848 by his grandson, Abbas I, who was described as 'bigoted and sensual'. He lasted only five years, until he was murdered in 1854 on the orders of his uncle, Said Pasha, who succeeded him. On the natural death of Said in 1863, another of Muhammad Ali's grandsons, Ishmail Pasha, stepped onto the bloodstained Khedival divan. He remained there until he was toppled by the British in 1879, who replaced him with his eldest son, Twefik Pasha.

216. Khedive Tewfik

During all of this period and beyond, the British interest in the affairs of Egypt was managed through the office of the British Agent and Consul General based in Cairo. This seemingly modest post became of increasing importance in Egyptian government affairs, particularly once the decision was taken to build the Suez Canal, and in parallel the country spiralled into debt and instability.

Whether it was the inept rule of the Khedive, the obvious interference in national affairs of the British Agent, or both, the fourth quarter of the nineteenth century witnessed the rise of Egyptian nationalism. This movement became a real threat to the Anglo-Egyptian *status quo*, when it fell under the leadership of a charismatic Egyptian Army Colonel of peasant origins called Ahmed Urabi, who succeeded in pressuring the Khedive to allow ethnic and peasant Egyptians to hold senior rank in the Egyptian Army. This was a serious threat to Khedival rule, but worse was to come.

In 1879, Urabi formed the Egyptian Nationalist Party, the principal aims of which were the end of both the Khedival autocracy and foreign control of the government. In a bid to keep Urabi on side, Tewfik promoted him to Bey, appointed him Under-Secretary of War, and then brought him into his Cabinet. All to no avail. Instead, Urabi used his new position to demand the creation of a parliamentary assembly, and it became increasingly clear to the Khedive and the British Agent that Urabi's ultimate goals were to dethrone the Khedive, default on the massive Egyptian National Debt principally owed to the British and the French, and seize control of the Suez Canal.

Britain and France responded with a fine example of gunboat diplomacy, by ordering their Mediterranean Fleets to Alexandria in May 1882. It wasn't long before Tewfik had moved his Court to the protection afforded by these foreign naval guns, and Urabi was in control in Cairo and, soon after that, most of Egypt. This was followed by anti-Christian riots in Alexandria on 11th June, which provided the British with the perfect excuse to intervene militarily in support of the Khedive. The French pusillanimously declined to be provoked into direct action.

The Kafr-el-Dawwar drum (near Alexandria, 1882), the Duke of Connaught's coffee pot & flag, Colonel Urabi's Koran & pistols, & Egyptian grapeshot (Tel el Kebir, 1882)

The British issued Urabi with a cynical ultimatum to remove his guns from the Alexandrian forts. Predictably, Urabi refused, and a British bombardment on 11th July reduced the fortifications to dust and body parts. This was followed up by a landing of British troops under the command of Brigadier General Sir Archibald Alison, one of Wolseley's

Armoured train at the Battle of Kafr-el-Dawwar

Ashanti veterans, in advance of the arrival at Alexandria of the main force under Wolseley's command. Alison, doubtless in pursuit of a peerage as reward for a quick end to the conflict, decided on a rapid march to Cairo in two columns, divided by an irrigation canal and the Alexandria-to-Cairo railway. Will Generals never learn? Although these two features ensured that the British marched in the right direction, they also resulted in the two columns, one including an armoured train, losing contact with each other in the failing light. Urabi's well dug-in Egyptian troops ensured that Alison met his Waterloo at the Battle of Kafr-el-Dawwar on 5th August 1882, and had to withdraw back towards Alexandria.

The engagement was hailed by both sides as a victory; Alison stated that it was merely a 'probing attack'. History has not been altogether kind to Alison. He was clearly a gallant officer, who had lost an arm at the Second Relief of Lucknow in 1857, and after the debacle at Kafr-el-Dawwar, he personally led the Highland Brigade, pistol in hand, at the Battle of Tel-el-Kebir on 13th September 1882. However, the earlier action resulted in no spoils of war for the British or a peerage for Alison, although a drum was acquired from the Kafr-el-Dawwar fortifications by the Princess Charlotte of Wales's Regiment at the conclusion of the Revolt, when the defensive position surrendered to Major General Sir Evelyn Wood on 16th September. This 'Sudanese' drum is now in The Rifles Berkshire and Wiltshire Museum at The Wardrobe, Salisbury, where it is incorrectly catalogued as having been 'taken at the surrender of Kafr el Daur [*sic*] in the Sudan'. The drum may well be Sudanese, as the Egyptian Army's recruiting area included the Sudan, but no such place as Kafr el Daur exists there.

Major General Sir Evelyn Wood

Despite the setback at Kafr-el-Dawwar, British fortunes soon changed with the arrival in Alexandria on 15th August of Lieutenant General Sir Garnet Wolseley, who immediately staged an elaborate deception designed to convince Colonel Urabi that he was going to launch a flank attack on the Kafr-el-Dawwar position. His actual plan was to attack Cairo from a base on the Suez Canal. By 20th August Wolseley had established a base at Ismailia and commenced his march along the Sweet Water Canal towards Cairo.

The Battle of Tel-el-Kebir

Prince Arthur, Duke of
Connaught & Strathearn

However, Urabi was no military slouch and swiftly established a defensive position at the Kassassin lock, which the British encountered just before dusk on 28th August. At first the British infantry were pinned down, but the timely arrival of the Household Cavalry Composite Regiment, followed by their decisive charge in the moonlight, swept all before it and established another military legend, but no spoils of war. Those had to wait until the aftermath of the decisive Battle of Tel-el-Kebir on 13th September, which ended the Revolt.

Unusually for a British victory, there was no Prize Auction after the battle or the liberation of Cairo which followed, presumably because spoils of war of any value were relatively thin on the ground at Tel-el-Kebir. More to the point, the British action had been in support of the Khedive, whose palace in Cairo doubtless held many treasures but was of necessity off limits. However, it was recorded by Captain Walter Churchward that there was unrestrained pillaging of the Egyptian's Mahsameh Camp at Tel-el-Kebir by British troops, during which boxes and mirrors in the abandoned Egyptian tents were smashed, and cushions slit open in the fruitless search for gold and jewellery. Local villagers' goats, chickens, and even Wolseley's tethered horse were looted. This went on until it was suppressed on the orders of the Provost Marshal. Wolseley's horse was eventually returned to him by a shamefaced Highlander subaltern. An interesting insight into the advance on Cairo, and a contradictory report of the opportunities for acquiring spoils of war, was given by Captain John Brocklehurst of The Blues, in a letter to his aunt:

> We had very rough work at first, very short of food for men and horses; none at all for 24 hours. When we took Mahsameh Camp, oh such loot, but I was too busy to look after it, and afterwards was too dead beat. I'd have given the Koh-i-Nor for a water melon.

Egyptian flags. *Royal Collection Trust © Her Majesty Queen Elizabeth II 2018*

There was one tent complex which did produce some spoils. This was Urabi's, which was described as containing 'beautiful carpets, tables, chairs and sofas'. There Queen Victoria's third son, Prince Arthur, Duke of Connaught & Strathearn, who was in command of the Guards Brigade, acquired Colonel Urabi's silver coffee pot, some valuable oriental rugs, and a white silk Egyptian flag embroidered with Arabic inscriptions in gold thread. From the same source Wolseley acquired Colonel Urabi's visiting card, which he sent to his daughter who had asked for 'the tip of Urabi's nose', a Koran, which he sent back to his wife, and a brace of Urabi's pistols which he presumably kept.

The current whereabouts of all of these spoils of war is unknown, although the flag which Connaught presented to his mother was photographed and painted by William Gibb at Windsor Castle in the late-nineteenth century. The Royal Collection still holds a glass-plate negative of the flag at Windsor in about 1882–1900, but the flag itself seems no longer to be in the collection. The drawing of the flag, illustrated here, was given to Queen Mary in 1935. However, there is on view in the Shropshire Regimental Museum in Shrewsbury a small stack of Egyptian grapeshot described as a 'souvenir' of the Battles of Chalouf on 20th August and Tel-el-Kebir on 13th September 1882.

Egyptian grapeshot

CHAPTER 24

MAHDIST WAR (1881–1899)

Muhammad Ahmad, known as The Mahdi

A Forbidden Trophy

The Mahdi's head (Khartoum, 1898)

While Egyptian nationalism was simmering dangerously in Cairo, Muhammad Ahmad bin Abd Allah, a Nubian religious leader of the Samaniyya sect in Sudan, declared himself to be 'The Mahdi', the messianic redeemer of the Islamic faith. This announcement, on 29th June 1881, was followed by the declaration of a Holy War on the Ottoman Empire. The Mahdi's objective was the replacement of the semi-secular Ottoman rule, from Constantinople to the source of the Nile, with a fundamentalist religious order. This was a declaration which echoes down to the present day.

From his announcement of the Mahdiyya in June 1881 until his death from typhus on 22nd June 1885, Muhammad Ahmad was unstoppable. His greatest triumphs were the destruction of an Egyptian Army under the command of Colonel William Hicks, at the Battle of El-Obeid on 5th

The Death of Hicks Pasha, by R Talbot Kelly, 1895

November 1883, and the capture of Khartoum and the murder of its
Governor, Major General Charles Gordon, on 26th January 1885. An
Anglo-Egyptian relief column, the Nile Expeditionary Force under the
command of the highly popular and successful General Lord Wolseley,
and including Captain Herbert Kitchener, arrived at Khartoum two days
too late to save the city or Gordon, whose severed head had been stuck in
the fork of a tree outside The Mahdi's tent. However, it is not Gordon's
head with which this piece is concerned.

By 1898, the Mahdists had made little progress north. The Mahdi was
long since dead, and his body was resting in an elaborate tomb in Khartoum. Meanwhile, Captain Kitchener had become Major General Sir
Herbert Kitchener, Sirdar of the Egyptian Army and Commander-in-Chief
of an Anglo-Egyptian army of 26,000 men, including the young Lieutenant Winston S Churchill attached to the 21st Lancers. This force headed
up the Nile, hell-bent on avenging General Gordon, and committed to the
restoration of the Egyptian (for which read British) rule of law in the Sudan.

On 2nd September 1898, Kitchener's force locked horns with the
Dervishes outside the town of Omdurman, and long before nightfall had
swept the Mahdists out of Khartoum. During the battle, Kitchener's gun
boats had used the prominent dome of The Mahdi's tomb for target practice. After the battle, Kitchener had the building completely destroyed
by Gordon of Khartoum's nephew, Major W S 'Monkey' Gordon. The
sarcophagus containing the Mahdi's mortal remains was dismantled
and thrown in the Nile, along with the late fundamentalist's bones. As
the Sirdar would later explain, this was done to 'leave nothing for the
Mahdi's followers to rally around'. But the Mahdi's 'large and shapely'
skull was presented to Kitchener, who suggested sending it to the Royal
College of Surgeons in London, where he thought, wrongly, that
Napoleon's intestines resided.

When the story of The Mahdi's head got out, the British press worked
itself into a cynical froth of righteous indignation, awkward questions
were asked in Parliament, and even Queen Victoria said that she was not
amused and that 'removing the Mahdi's skull was too much like the
Middle Ages'.

To add to the kerfuffle, Winston Churchill wrote in *The River War*, his
controversial account of the campaign, that he was scandalized by the
barbarous manner in which Kitchener had carried off the Mahdi's head
in 'a kerosene can as a trophy'. By the order of Sir Evelyn Baring, the
British Agent and Consul General in Cairo, Kitchener was obliged to

Major General Sir Herbert
Kitchener

The Queen's Own Cameron Highlanders shooting trophies: panels from the Mahdi's tomb, Omdurman

write an apologetic letter to the Queen, and the head was secretly buried in a Muslim cemetery at Wadi Halfa.

Panels from the Mahdi's Tomb

Meanwhile, no fuss at all was made about the wanton destruction of the Mahdi's elaborate tomb, which was not rebuilt until 1947. Nor were any concerns raised about the treatment of the tomb's decorations and embellishments, or an assortment of Dervish weapons, armour, flags, and other battlefield memorabilia, which found their way into various royal, regimental and private collections.

The spoils of war from the battlefield include a fine set of Sudanese quilted armour, now held at the Royal Armouries in Leeds, and said to have been 'taken from the Mahdi's tent' by Major George Rae. However, this provenance cannot be correct, as not only was The Mahdi resting – at least for the time being – in his tomb, but his successor, the Khalifa Abdullah al Taishi, who did have a tent on the field of battle at Omdurman, was seen to dismantle it the night before his defeat. He did this when the British gunboats on the Nile raked the Dervish encampment with powerful spot lamps, and the Khalifa thought they were deliberately targeting him and his tent.

Spoils from the Mahdi's tomb itself include a large brass finial from the top of the dome, now in the Royal Collection and currently on loan to the Royal Engineers' Museum in Chatham, and a brick from the building, which was used as a doorstop in an Irish country house, until it was offered for sale in 2015, with a pre-sale estimate of 200-300 Euros

Several panels were also taken from the wooden tabernacle within the tomb by Lieutenant (later Brigadier General) Rudolph Ladeveze Adlercron, an Irishman serving with The Queen's Own Cameron Highlanders. These panels are all double-sided, with a yellow Islamic geometric device or decoration on the obverse, and verses from the Koran on the reverse, written in classical Arabic script. One pair is held in the collection of The Highlanders' Museum in Inverness, and a second pair is owned by General Sir Jeremy Mackenzie, an officer of The Queen's Own Highlanders and Regimental Colonel of The Highlanders from 1994 to 2001.

The history of the acquisition of these spoils is described on the frame of one of the panels held by The Highlanders' Museum: 'This panel was taken from the Tabernacle in the Mahdi's tomb at Omdurman on the night following the Battle by Lieut R L Adlercron, 1st Battn: 79th Queen's Own Cameron Highlanders, who presented it to the 1st battn: as an officers shooting shield in 1911.'

Additional information is provided by General Mackenzie:

When the Camerons amalgamated with the Seaforth Highlanders in 1961, it was decided to give two of the framed panels to the regimental museum and award the rest as prizes for the Champion Officer Shot, in the annual shooting competitions we held on the ranges. Having been brought up in Africa, where I did a lot of shooting, I managed to win three of these contests. I later decided to return one of my three trophies to the Regiment, because the panels are an important part of our history. My suggestion was that, rather than giving it away, the Regiment should make it the trophy in future, but mount it on a plinth with a silver plate, and then inscribe the name of each Champion Officer Shot on the plate and keep it with the Mess silver. I also gave them the money to buy the plinth.

The two panels which General Mackenzie retained are about the size of a mobile telephone. They are mounted in engraved silver frames supported on silver sphinx feet (the symbol of the Egyptian Campaign), and topped with the Victorian-era badge of The Queen's Own Cameron Highlanders, which – along with the hallmarks – dates them as pre-1901.

The panels held in The Highlanders' Museum are larger in size, but are otherwise identical to General Mackenzie's and date from the same period, although the frames are of wood inlaid with silver rather than solid silver. One of these panels, with the device on the obverse, was (as was later the case with General Mackenzie's panels) a regimental shooting prize. It was last awarded in 1950, before the amalgamation of the Cameron and Seaforth Highlanders. The silver inlays on the frame of this panel include the Victorian-era badge of The Queen's Own Cameron Highlanders, the name of the winners from 1911 to 1950, and the plaque describing the acquisition of this spoil of war. On the other frame, which surrounds text from the Koran, there are two silver inlays missing; the extant silver inlays are depictions in low relief of the Mahdi and his tomb.

Regimental lore asserts that all of the panels taken from the Mahdi's tomb date from the era of the Prophet Mohammad and were originally mounted on stone slabs, from which they were removed before the slabs were thrown by the Highlanders into the Nile. Given their condition, and their provenance, it is far more likely that the panels were made when the Mahdi's tomb was built, following his death in 1885, the date attribution being assumed on account of the Koranic inscriptions. As for the stone slabs, that part of the story is also apocryphal, given the inscription on the wood-and-inlaid-silver-framed shooting prize, as transcribed above.

CHAPTER 25

THIRD ANGLO-BURMESE WAR (1885)

On the Road to & from Mandalay

A carved & gilded wooden bee (Mandalay, 1885)

Lying in a safe in an English country house, far from its original palatial home in the foetid mangrove swamps of Burma, is a carved and gilded wooden bee, approximately seven inches long. Although of no particular merit as a piece of wood carving, this crudely fashioned object is nonetheless of considerable value, as was attested to when it buzzed briefly onto the *Antiques Road Show* many years ago. For, like so many other spoils of war, the bee's actual value – then estimated at a sweet six-figure sum – arises from its provenance, and not from its intrinsic worth.

Bee finial from King Thibaw Min's Bee Throne

Although the assembly of the British Indian Empire was largely completed by 1850, it took a few more decades to add the jewels of some outlying territories on the sub-continent to the Indian Crown Imperial. The largest of these was Burma, the incremental conquest of which started with the First Anglo-Burmese War of 1824 to 1826. It concluded

Surrender of the Burmese Army

in 1885 with the Third Anglo-Burmese War, at the end of which the 133-year-old Konbaung Dynasty was finally toppled by the bayonets of the Hampshire Regiment. Its remaining territory in Upper Burma was brought under the rule of the Raj, and the seven-year reign of the twenty-six-year-old King Thibaw Min came to an abrupt end.

It must be rather a blow to be the last of a dynasty, even one as relatively *arriviste* as that of the Konbaungs. And doubly so when your kingdom is subsumed into that of an alien conqueror, who turfs you out of

King Thibaw Min with Queen Supayalat and Princess Supayaji

your palace and sends you to some far-away God-forsaken spot, to eke out the rest of your days on a pittance of a state pension. But that was the fate of Thibaw Min, who was obliged to exchange his pampered life of deference and courtly splendour – and there was no lack of either at the Burmese Court – for the existence of an exile, lodged in a brick-built bungalow on the west coast of India. Not surprisingly, the ex-King rarely left the confines of his new, rather modest home, and went to join his ancestors in 1916 at the comparatively early age of fifty-seven. This was not at all the end that Thibaw Min had determined upon in 1878, when aged nineteen he stepped over a hundred bloody corpses of his nearest and dearest relations and onto the Burmese throne, the youthful beneficiary of a palace coup, cold-bloodedly plotted and executed by his mother-in-law, Queen Hsinbyumashin.

Almost from the outset, Thibaw Min was determined to recover Lower Burma from the British, and in pursuit of that noble aim, made friendly overtures to the French. This was unquestionably a mistake, which he compounded by imposing a completely unwarranted fine of £230,000 (2020: £29 million) on a British firm, the Bombay Burmah Trading Corporation, followed by a failed attempt to humiliate a British diplomatic delegation by ordering its members to remove their shoes in his presence, something which the British resolutely refused to do.

The Great Shoe Question, as it came to be known, was followed in 1885 by a Royal Proclamation, in which King Thibaw Min commanded his subjects to liberate that part of Burma which was no longer under his royal sway. For the government of British India, the overtures to the French – to say nothing of the Great Shoe Question – had been bad enough, but the proclamation was the final straw. Major General Harry Prendergast VC, a hero of the Indian Mutiny of 1857, was ordered to lead an Expeditionary Force of 9,000 men to complete the conquest of Burma that had started in 1824, a feat which he accomplished in under a month with negligible casualties.

However, it was not just King Thibaw Min's rice fields which were seized by Prendergast and his Anglo-Indian Force. The contents of the King's palaces were also confiscated, and piles of jewellery, silks, gold, and priceless objects were shipped off to Britain, where they were parcelled out to members of the Royal Family and the government. Meanwhile, in Mandalay a Prize Committee was set-up to auction off what remained, including the King's Bee or Bhamara Throne from the Glass Palace. This short-legged platform, covered with an ornate carpet, was made of gilded caraway wood, and so called because it was embellished with thirty-six carved and gilded bees. Ironically, these insects were supposed to symbolise Thibaw Min's wisdom, which unfortunately for him had not extended to his dealings with the British.

Presumably the Prize Committee determined that no one would be interested in bidding for a complete throne, and so the bees decorating it were auctioned off separately. The carcass of the bee-less throne, along with six of the seven others which remained in Burma, were destroyed in a bombing raid during the Second World War. The only survivor, the vast Lion Throne, is now on display at the National Museum in Yangon (Rangoon), the capital of Myanmar (Burma). The whereabouts of only four of the carvings from the Bhamara Throne are now known: two are in the Victoria & Albert Museum; one is in the Pitt-Rivers Museum in Oxford; and the fourth is in the country house safe. The story of how it came to rest there is rather different to that of other spoils of war.

The original purchaser of the bee is unknown, as is its history between 1885 and 1923. However, from the known facts which follow, it is reasonable to assume that this particular bee remained in Burma after the Mandalay Prize Auction, probably in the collection of a British colonial official. In January 1923, Sir Harcourt Butler was appointed Governor of Burma. He made his way to take up his appointment in the company of, amongst others, Lieutenant Colonel John Mackenzie, who had the distinction of having organised the Delhi Durbar of 1911, was

Comptroller of the Household for three Viceroys of India between 1907 and 1921, and then Military Secretary to the Governor of Bengal from 1922 to 1927. Whilst in Rangoon with Sir Harcourt, Colonel Mackenzie was given the bee, although why and by whom is not recorded, and it has remained in the ownership of his descendants ever since. The fact that Colonel Mackenzie did not actually purchase the bee does not invalidate its provenance, which has been described as 'impeccable' by the Victoria & Albert Museum.

A Buddhist Shrine
The post-acquisition history of a large Buddhist shrine, now in the Victoria & Albert Museum in London, is for the most part better known. Carved in teak, and covered with gilded lacquer inlaid with semi-precious stones and pieces of mirror, the nineteenth-century shrine is nine feet and four inches (285.7cms) in height. Featuring the figure of the Buddha Shakyamuni, it includes a manuscript chest, offertory vessels, and the Buddha's chief disciples kneeling on couches. The form of the shrine mirrors that of Burmese royal thrones of the period, thereby linking the Buddha's spiritual monarchy with the semi-divine nature of Burma's kings.

This particular shrine was taken from one of the royal palaces at Mandalay in 1885 by Lieutenant Colonel Frederick Duncan Raikes, who was born in India, educated at the Royal Military College Sandhurst, and joined the Indian Army in 1868. From 1875 onwards, he was frequently involved in quelling hostilities in Burma, and was later a Commissioner there. Although it is not recorded that Raikes acquired the shrine at the Prize Auction, it is almost certain that he did, as there was no random looting at Mandalay, and the shrine was far too large to be sneaked out of the palace.

In 1906 Raikes donated the shrine to the Bristol City Museum & Art Gallery, who for reasons unknown deaccessioned it in 1966. It was subsequently bought by the Victoria & Albert Museum from Oriental Antiques Ltd in 1969 for £6,000

A Buddhist shrine from King Thibaw Min's palace

(2020: £97,000). As Thibaw Min's palace was destroyed by bombing during the Second World War, the shrine is one of the few large wooden objects to have survived from his court.

A Betel Box

An altogether more complex and potentially controversial history surrounds a Burmese betel box, also now held by the Victoria & Albert Museum. The gold box is in the form of a *hintha*, a mythical Burmese bird, and is outlined with bands of rubies and imitation emeralds. It was part of the royal regalia of King Thibaw Min, and was made to hold betel leaves, a mildly narcotic chewing quid, which was commonly used by every household in Burmese society.

Betel Box from Burmese Royal Regalia

The Mandalay Regalia consisted of 167 gold and gem-studded items, ranging from weapons to cutlery, and jewellery to footwear. Excluded from the Prize Auction, the entire collection was requisitioned as indemnity at the end of the Third Anglo-Burmese War and sent to England, where it was deposited at the Victoria & Albert Museum in 1886. Following Burmese independence in 1948, the government of Burma made repeated requests for the return of the Mandalay Regalia. Finally, in 1964, the new Labour government led by Harold Wilson, which favoured a policy of rapprochement, returned the regalia 'in the interests of promoting closer relations between Britain and Burma'.

This arbitrary decision caused a rumpus in the House of Commons, with John Tilney, the Conservative Member of Parliament for Liverpool Wavertree, demanding to know 'by what authority Her Majesty's government have decided to return the Mandalay Regalia to Burma'. Adding in for good measure a hope that 'the regalia will not go the way of the Abyssinian crown', he also asked what the government's attitude would be 'to a request from, say, Ghana, to return the golden ornaments of the Ashantehene [sic], or a request from Egypt for the return of the Rosetta Stone?' Harold Wilson, the ever slippery Prime Minister, replied that Tilney's supplementary question was 'hypothetical' and then added, in what every museum in the United Kingdom must hope is never cited as a valid reason for the repatriation of spoils of war: 'The regalia in question was taken by military force ... [and] it should be returned'.

In a surprise move, the Burmese leader General Ne Win donated the gold *hintha* betel box back to the museum, as 'a gift from the Government and people of Burma in generous recognition of the Victoria & Albert

Museum's safekeeping of the Burmese royal regalia from 1886 to 1964'. This object therefore represents possibly the only spoil of war to be repatriated to its original country, and then in turn given back to the nation that took it as a spoil.

Carved Head of King Thibaw Min

King Thibaw Min's head
Although the carving from King Thibaw Min's Bee Throne was bought through the Prize Auction that followed his downfall, the acquisitions of a wooden model of his head and an engraved portrait of the unfortunate monarch were almost certainly not, given the texts attached to these items. Now held at the Royal Hampshire Regiment Museum in Winchester, the label accompanying the head reads:

> The last King of Burma. He was captured by the British army in 1885, The Hampshire Regiment took part in this Campaign. This head carved from teak by The Chief priest on The King's staff was a true likeness of the man. Presented by Major G R Macnab, late The Gordon Highlanders, to the Officers of The Royal Hampshire Regiment for their museum. The donor was in the position to know what an excellent likeness the carving was of the late King. He saw him personally while in captivity in Ceylon in 1890 and in Egypt, where he died still in captivity. He was a Buddhist – as shown by the knot of hair on top of the head.

Without wishing to cast aspersions on Major Macnab's assertions, it is worth noting that King Thibaw Min was only twenty-six when he was dethroned, and this carved head is of a much older man. Furthermore, the ex-king never lived in Ceylon or Egypt, and was exiled to Ratnagiri on the west coast of India, where he died aged fifty-seven.

Displayed alongside Thibaw Min's head is the faded and framed engraving of the deposed Burmese ruler, which was presented to the Officers Mess of the Royal Hampshire Regiment by General Sir Richard Haking, Colonel of the Regiment from 1924 to 1945. He had served as a Lieutenant in the Burma campaign, and added the following note to the mount:

> This portrait of the Old King of Burmah was picked up in the Palace at Mandalay by my native servant, the morning after I had taken King Thebaw [*sic*] prisoner, and was used by my servant as a tray to bring me my tea.
> The Palace, Mandalay, 30th Nov 1885

One wonders if this servant also brought the King's wooden head on a plate to the Colonel.

The Nga Mauk ruby

Although King Thibaw Min lost his country, his multiple thrones, and most of his possessions at the conclusion of the Third Anglo-Burmese War, he was allowed to keep certain items of value, including his pregnant wife's diamond necklace and an eighty-carat cabochon ruby ring known as the Nga Mauk.

The Marquess of Dufferin, Viceroy of India

Officially part of the royal regalia, this stone was said to have mythic powers, including that of healing and wealth creation. However, shortly before the ex-King was forced to mount the bullock cart taking him and his family to a steamer and permanent exile in India, Colonel Edward Sladen, the Chief Political Officer assigned to Prendergast's Expeditionary Force, relieved him of a quantity of items, including the ruby ring, which Sladen slipped into his pocket.

Accounts differ as to how and why the ex-King surrendered the ring and the other artefacts. According to the historian M B Synge, writing in 1911, he feared for his life:

> A guard of British soldiers was drawn up; they presented arms on the appearance of the royal prisoners. As their bayonets flashed in the sunlight, the king fell on his knees in abject terror. 'They will kill me,' he cried wildly. 'Save my life.' His queen was braver. She strode on erect – her little child clinging to her dress – fierce and dauntless to the last.

Thibaw Min would later claim that he asked the Colonel to take these items into temporary safe-keeping during the journey to India, and that Sladen deliberately did not return them. Whatever the truth of the matter, from 29th November 1885 onwards, the Nga Mauk disappeared. But that was by no means the end of the matter.

In June the following year, Thibaw Min wrote to the Viceroy of India, the Earl (later Marquess) of Dufferin, requesting the return of the possessions he had given to Sladen. Along with the letter he attached an inventory, said to have been compiled by his former Treasurer, which included '1 ruby ring known by the name of Nga Mauk'. The Viceroy ordered an investigation into the whereabouts of the jewel. In a letter written to Dufferin, and still on file in the British Library, Sladen somewhat suspiciously obfuscated the events of the day. More incriminating still is Sladen's contemporaneous diary, in which an entry relating to the ring and the other items has been redacted, presumably by the man himself at the time of the Viceroy's investigation. In any event, Dufferin was obliged to write back to the ex-King, saying in effect that the Nga Mauk could not be found. Undeterred, Thibaw Min and his successors continued to bombard the authorities in British India with demands for its return. When they received no satisfaction from that quarter, they switched their fire onto King George V and his successors, including the present Queen. But all to no avail.

At which point the conspiracy theorists stepped in, led most recently in 2017 by the film director, Alex Bescoby, working with Thibaw Min's great-grandson, the seventy-year-old U Soe Win. These men and their conspiracy theory predecessors, who included Thibaw Min's youngest daughter and U Soe Win's uncle, Taw Phaya Galae (otherwise known as the Red Prince on account of his fervent embrace of Communism), posit two theories.

The first is that Sladen presented the Nga Mauk to Queen Victoria, for which he received a knighthood, and that the Queen Empress then either assigned it to the Crown Jewels or had it set in a bracelet, which she later bequeathed to her daughter, Princess Louise, Duchess of Argyll. The second theory is that Sladen kept the jewel for himself.

There are multiple problems with the royal acquisition. Whilst it is true that Sladen was awarded a knighthood in Gladstone's Resignation Honours List of 1886, for 'special service in Burma', this is not proof that it was conferred at the behest of Queen Victoria in return for Thibaw Min's ruby. Had this been the case, Sladen, who had a long and distinguished career in the service of the Crown Imperial (rather than the Queen Empress herself), would have been made a Knight Commander of the Royal Victorian Order, an award reserved 'for distinguished personal service to the Monarch', rather than a Knight Bachelor as was the case.

There is then the fact that no such jewel is to be found amongst the Crown Jewels. The possibility, advanced by the current conspiracy theorists, that the Nga Mauk was divided into four faceted stones, which were then set in the *crosses-pattée* on the Imperial State Crown of India, is highly unlikely. While it is true that the rubies in this crown, made for King George V to wear at the Coronation Durbar of 1911, are of Burmese origin, so too are almost all rubies of any quality, and there is 'no archival documentation to indicate their origin'. Besides which, no jeweller would divide an eighty-carat stone into lesser jewels, unless it was too large to use, such as the Cullinan Diamond, or its composition was deeply flawed and merited such treatment, which does not appear to have been the case with the Nga Mauk.

The proposition that the ruby was reset in a bracelet for Queen Victoria, left to Princess Louise in the old Queen's Will, and then subsequently mislaid or hidden by the Dukes of Argyll, is ruled out by the facts. The Royal Collection Trust have stated authoritatively that Princess Louise's bangle was made from a seventy-five-carat ruby presented to her mother by Burmese Ambassadors on behalf of the King of Burma. This delegation visited Queen Victoria in 1872, six years *before* Thibaw Min ascended the bloody Burmese throne. After 1872 there were no Burmese ambassadorial delegations to London, nor would there have been any following Thibaw Min's deposal in 1885, as Burma was thereafter absorbed into the British Empire, and had neither King nor royal Ambassadors. Besides which, if the stone had been presented to Queen Victoria in 1872, it couldn't have been taken by Sladen in 1885. Clearly, Princess Louise's bracelet was made from a different Burmese ruby.

Which leaves the non-royal theory that Sladen pocketed the stone. Of the two, this is the more convincing, particularly given Sladen's redacted diary and his prevaricating letter to the Viceroy, both of which look as though he was covering his tracks. If that were not enough, there is an additional fact about Sladen which was not disclosed by Bescoby, who perhaps for the sake of a good story for television preferred to wave a vaguely accusing finger at Britain's Royal Family. On his death at his house in fashionable Lowndes Square in 1890, Colonel Sir Edward Sladen, who was a poorly-paid career imperial servant and himself the son of an underpaid colonial doctor, left an intestate estate of £18,019.19s.2d (2020: £2,270,000).

Sladen's fortune, when added to the documentation outlined above, provides strong circumstantial evidence that the Colonel kept the Nga Mauk. When it became a subject of imperial controversy, he sold it quietly to avoid embarrassment, and banked the proceeds.

CHAPTER 26

BOXER REBELLION & SIEGE OF PEKING (1899–1901)

Treasures from Peter Jones in Peking

A cloisonné opium dish & a cloisonné incense burner (Peking, 1900)

Forty years after the sacking of the Old Summer Palace in Peking in 1860, the British army was back in China. However, the events that led-up to the second emptying of the Summer Palace were not related to the opium trade. Instead they concerned the aggressively hostile behaviour towards Europeans and Christians of a militant Chinese sect known as the Boxers. To further complicate matters, the Boxers were aided, abetted and encouraged by the Chinese Imperial government, with whom the rebels were – somewhat bizarrely – in open conflict.

The Boxers, so called because they referred to themselves as 'The Righteous Fists of Harmony', were a populist movement which had tapped into the Chinese peasants' fear that Christian missionaries and their converts would expropriate their land. The rebellion started in northern China in 1898, with the stated aim of crushing Christianity and driving foreigners out of China. From the outset, the Imperial government's attitude to the Boxers was ambivalent. While fearing the mayhem created by the Boxers, and their wholesale murder of more than 100,000 Chinese Christians, the Empress Dowager Cixi – a former Imperial concubine and the self-appointed Regent of China – was still rankling from the consequences of the Second Opium War forty years previously. Her Ministers in the Imperial government reasoned that, while the Boxers undoubtedly posed a threat to the stability of the Imperial throne, it should be possible to use them as arm's length proxies to evict the Treaty Powers from China, namely Austria-Hungary, France, Germany, Italy, Japan, Russia, the United Kingdom and the United States of America. Once that job was done, they would then crush the rebellion. It was to prove a serious and costly miscalculation.

Empress Dowager Cixi

Relief of the Legation Quarter, Peking

216

As a direct consequence of the atrocities by the Boxers against Europeans in early 1900, the Treaty Powers commenced a build-up of armed forces on the Chinese coast at Taku. This force, led by the British Major General Alfred Gaselee, included the 2nd Battalion of The Royal Welsh Fusiliers,[1] and the US Marine Corps. Initially, the strategic objective was not the toppling of the Imperial regime, but the restoration of the *status quo ante* in China, in order that the valuable trading concessions and the tax advantages enjoyed by the Treaty Powers were not disrupted. The allies also feared that these benefits might be reversed, should the Boxer Rebellion result in a change of government to one less compliant than the decadent rule of the Qing dynasty.

1. Now part of the Royal Welsh

By early June the Boxer fighters, convinced they were invulnerable to foreign weapons, had converged on Peking with the slogan: 'Support the Qing government and exterminate the foreigners.' The brutal assassination by the rebels of the German Minister, Freiherr (Baron) Clemens von Ketteler on 20th June 1900, triggered the crisis that followed. To some extent, Baron von Ketteler was the architect of his own demise. Earlier in the month, he and a party of German soldiers had arrested and then inexplicably executed a Boxer boy, making him a marked man. When the Empress Dowager heard that the Treaty Powers were on the Chinese mainland in large numbers, she issued an order on 19th June stating that all diplomats and foreigners in the Legation should leave within twenty-four hours, under escort of the Chinese Army. The diplomats, not trusting the Army, resolved to stay put; and it was when von Ketteler went to inform the Imperial Court of this decision that he was killed.

Colonel Sir Claude MacDonald

Alarmed by the Boxers' threat of extermination, the foreign nationals and Chinese Christians in Peking also sought refuge in the Legation Quarter, where the diplomats were already holed up. Before long, they were besieged by the Boxers and the Imperial Army. However, despite the deployment of her troops, the Empress Dowager – known by the British as 'the old Buddha' – still prevaricated. But when she received reports that the eight Treaty Powers were marching from Taku on Peking to lift the siege, she finally announced her support for the Boxers, and on 21st June declared war on the foreigners.

The ensuing siege of the foreign Legations lasted for fifty-five days, with 473 foreign civilians, 409 soldiers and sailors, and about 3,000 Chinese Christians penned into the compound. The Legation staff and military guards, under command of the British Minister to China, Colonel Sir Claude MacDonald, defended the area with small arms and three machine guns. They also created a cannon from disparate parts, and nicknamed it the 'International Gun', because the barrel was British, the carriage Italian, the shells Russian, and the crew American. It was only on 14th August that the relieving British troops finally broke into the Legation Quarter through the sewers, to be greeted by the ladies of the Diplomatic Corps in evening dress, offering them glasses of champagne.

Cloisonné dish

The temporary occupation of Peking followed, along with an officially sanctioned orgy of looting, most notably of the New Summer Palace. Each nationality, with the exception of the British, accused the others of being the worst looters, as an American missionary wrote home: 'The conduct of the Russian soldiers is atrocious, the French are not much better, and the Japanese are looting and burning without mercy'. The British, however, set up a Prize Committee, and then held five days of afternoon Prize Auctions at the British Legation (except Sunday, of course), at which tens of thousands of items were sold. The cash proceeds were then shared out amongst the troops by the Prize Committee.

Cloisonné incense burner

One of those to attend the Prize Auctions was a US Marine Corps officer who acquired, amongst other things, a cloisonné opium tray and a small cloisonné incense burner. He later presented these items to Captain W G Vyvyan of the Royal Welsh Fusiliers, with whose unit the US Marines had developed a close bond since setting out together from Hong Kong. These spoils of war were later donated by the original recipient's grandson, Lieutenant Colonel J G Vyvyan, to the Royal Welsh Fusiliers' museum in Caernarvon Castle, where they joined a fur-lined Mandarin's jacket, an Imperial Chinese fish-tail banner, and a Boxer drum.

Boxer drum

Many of the purchasers sent their loot to the coast as fast as they could. Herbert Squiers, the First Secretary at the US Legation in Peking, shipped home an entire trainload of Chinese porcelain, which he had acquired for a song at the Prize Auctions and elsewhere, sometimes under dubious circumstances, so it was whispered. Once back in the United States, Squiers initially offered to loan his collection to the Metropolitan Museum in New York. However, the museum was nervous about accepting it in light of the allegations, and it was eventually loaned in 1907 to the Smithsonian Institute, who had no such scruples and held the collection until 1908. Following Squiers' death in 1911, the entire collection was sold at a New York auction in April 1912, and realised US$48,000 (2020: £1.6 million).

Lady MacDonald's tea pot (Peking, 1900)

While Herbert Squiers filled up a train with his loot, the redoubtable Lady MacDonald, wife of the British Minister, Colonel Sir Claude, was heard to remark that she had 'hardly started to pack', after filling eighty-seven packing cases with auction items. No pieces from Lady MacDonald's haul were loaned to museums and few have since come onto the market, although an eighteenth-century bronze teapot made an appearance on the *Antiques Roadshow* in 2016. Valued only in the low tens of thousands of pounds, the teapot's provenance was established by a handwritten label affixed to the underside of the lid, stating it was from Her Ladyship's collection.

It would appear that items in the Royal Welsh Fusiliers Museum at Caernarvon Castle are probably only the tip of a Welsh iceberg, as evidenced by an officer of the Regiment, the author and poet Robert Graves, who noted in his autobiography that before the First World War the Officers Mess table of his regiment was 'enriched by spoils of the Summer Palace Peking 1900'. In a poem about a stormy relationship, entitled the *Hung Wu Vase*, he wrote:

> With women like Marie no holds are barred.
> How do they get the gall? How can they do it?
>
> She stormed out, slamming the hall door so hard
> That a vase on a gilt shelf above – you knew it,
> Loot from the Summer Palace at Pekin
> And worth the entire contents of my flat -
> Toppled and fell ...
> I poured myself a straight gin,
> Downing it at a gulp. 'So that was that!'

Whether or not Graves was using poetic licence, the Officers Mess of the Fusiliers' successor Regiment, the Royal Welsh, no longer has any Imperial Chinese artefacts. Furthermore, the Welshmen's American friend cannot have been much of a connoisseur, for the cloisonné pieces he donated to Captain Vyvyan are not now thought to be of any great value, although their provenance gives them a worth somewhat in excess of their intrinsic market value.

above, left to right

Sikhs in the Peking sewer

Major (later Lieutenant
General Sir) Thomas Scott

Major Scott meets Sir Claude
MacDonald, Peking, 1900

Home decorations (Peking, 1900)

Major (later Lieutenant General Sir) Thomas Scott commanded a
Company of the 4th Regiment of Infantry (Punjab Frontier Force) in the
relief of the Legation Quarter. It was he and his Punjabis who were the
first to emerge from the Peking sewers into the British Legation garden,
an event that was prominently portrayed in *The Illustrated London News*.
Scott acquired a substantial collection from the New Summer Palace at
the Prize Auction, including delicate ivory fans, a set of twenty-one
miniature carved elephants, a large red ivory chess piece, pierced-work
boxes, embroidered silk panels and bell pulls, a pair of curtains (since
lost), and a Mandarin's coat. These items, none of which are of any great
value according to a Christie's expert, remain in the various homes of
Scott's descendants, where they are occasionally shown to dinner guests
as some of the relics of Empire. Doubtless there are thousands of other
New Summer Palace spoils of war still in private collections, held by the
descendants of the Peking Legation liberators.

Finally, on the subjects of quality and value, it is interesting to note that
items from the New Summer Palace are generally of much poorer quality
than those taken from the Old Summer Palace, one of which – a rare
bronze teapot dating from 1000 BC – recently sold at auction for
£410,000. There is a plausible reason for this: the Old Summer Palace
was developed over a period of 150 years, and furnished with priceless
artefacts, some of which were more than two thousand years old, by a
succession of Emperors who were not constrained by an empty Treasury.

To build and furnish the New Summer Palace in a mere eleven years, between 1884 and 1895, the Empress Dowager not only had to raid the Chinese Navy's budget, but probably had to furnish her new quarters from Peking's equivalent of Peter Jones.

above, left to right

Fan bought at the British Legation Auction

Ivory elephants bought at the British Legation Auction

Silk bell-pull bought at the British Legation Auction

The medics' clock (Peking, 1900)

There are of course exceptions to this generalisation about quality and value. The Empress Dowager almost certainly transferred one or more clocks from the substantial collection held in the Forbidden City to her New Summer Palace. This may account for an outstanding eighteenth-century musical clock of English manufacture that was acquired at the British Legation Prize Auction in 1900 and later presented to the Royal Army Medical Corps (RAMC).

Unlike other New Summer Palace spoils held in military and private collections, this clock is of great quality and probably of considerable value. In a thesis published in 2015, Dr Paul Bevan argued that it may be a pair to one of the two Chinese clocks in the National Trust's collection at Anglesey Abbey. These were made by John Mottram, and in all probability also have a New Summer Palace provenance. However, Chinese clocks' expert Richard Higgins states that clocks made for the Chinese market were rarely created in pairs, and an anecdotal description of the RAMC's clock does not match either clock at Anglesey Abbey.

In any event, in the late-eighteenth and up to the mid-nineteenth century, the East India Company bought many such clocks in London to oil the wheels of their trade negotiations with Chinese officials, from harbour masters up to the Emperor himself. Many of the Emperors were avid collectors. Despite the depredation of their collections in 1860 and 1900, more than 2,500 English-made clocks – presented to or acquired by

One of the thousands of elaborate clocks in the Forbidden City, Beijing

Imperial Chinese clock by Henry Bovell at Anglesey Abbey, believed to be similar to the RAMC clock © *National Trust*

Chinese Emperors – still exist in the collections of the Clock Museum at the Forbidden City, Beijing, and the National Palace Museum in Taiwan.

Most of these clocks, particularly those that were taken from China in 1860 and 1900, are very valuable. In recent years, several examples similar to the one owned by the RAMC have sold at auctions around the globe for sums in excess of £2 million. This probably explains why theirs is not on public display, and the Corps is coy about acknowledging its existence. Or perhaps they, unlike the National Trust, are needlessly worried that the Chinese will demand its return?

Whatever the reason, the New Summer Palace provenance of the RAMC's clock is well-documented. The horological antiquarian Ian White, in his *English Clocks for the Eastern Market*, wrote that it was:

> … taken from Peking in the aftermath of the Western relief of the siege of the foreign legations in 1900… by Lt-Col. W. J. R. Rainsford and Major J. J. C. Watson of the Royal Army Medical Corps sometime in 1901 [*sic*] and presented by them to the Royal Army Medical Corps, in whose possession it remains.

Similarly, Major General Sir Courtenay Clarke Manifold recorded, in his privately published autobiography, *The 'All Blaze' of Life*:

> Colonel Rainsford of the Royal Army Medical Corps, on seeing some lacquer screens [at the auction viewing] that he admired, put his card on them to indicate that they were reserved for him. The General on later seeing them declared that they would make a suitable present from him to the Queen, and removed Rainsford's card, replacing it with his own. Rainsford then selected a clock …

There will almost certainly also be paperwork in the RAMC's archives confirming the clock's provenance and its gift to the Corps. Meanwhile, the clock was said to be 'undergoing restoration' in 2015, after which it was to be returned to the RAMC's Headquarters in the former Staff College building at Camberley. Presumably, it remains there, a spoil of war hidden from public gaze, unlike its siblings at Anglesey Abbey.

CHAPTER 27

SECOND BOER WAR (1899–1902)

Slim Pickings

Any British soldier who expected that the second war with the Boers would produce spoils of war similar to those from other nineteenth-century colonial wars in Africa would have been very disappointed. The Low Church, republican Boer farmers did not believe in well-decorated presidential palaces or antique-furnished homesteads. So, at the end of the conflict there were no Prize Auctions, merely a desire on the part of the British Army to get home as fast as a troop ship could carry them and their horses.

The origins of the first conflict of the modern age of warfare were relatively straightforward. The discovery beneath the Boer farmlands of diamonds in 1866 and gold in 1886 led to an influx of non-Boer miners and speculators. Known as *uitlanders* (foreigners), they were mainly men from Britain in search of wealth and employment. From that flowed two consequences. First, the generation of huge wealth for some of the miners, most notably Cecil Rhodes, his business partner Alfred Beit, and their rival, the ex-music-hall performer and professional boxer, Barney Barnato. Second, the determination on the part of the Boer governments to tax the *uitlanders*, without giving them any parliamentary representation.

Boers besieging Mafeking

General Sir Redvers Buller VC

This latter issue led directly to the badly planned, ineptly executed, and unsuccessful Jameson Raid launched on 29th December 1895, which attempted to seize political and military control of the Transvaal from the Boers. Backed by Rhodes and Beit, Leander Starr Jameson, a British colonial politician, assembled a private army of about 500 men (including three serving officers of the Household Cavalry), and marched towards the border of the Transvaal. The aim of this aggressive move was to promote a military reaction against the *uitlanders* in the Boer state, and then use that as an excuse to invade and annex the territory. When the Boer uprising failed to materialise, Jameson invaded anyway, was quickly defeated by the Boers, and was then arrested. Ironically, the Raid's farcical failure pushed the two Boer republics into a military alliance and a major re-armaments programme, actions which were in turn matched by the British with a military build-up in the Cape. The end result was bound to be war, which was declared by the Boers on 11th October 1899.

In lightening pre-emptive strikes, the highly mobile farmers crossed the border and quickly bottled up the principal British garrisons at Ladysmith, Kimberley and Mafeking. Relief forces were assembled under the command of the brave but notoriously bibulous General Sir Redvers Buller VC, who was described by a contemporary as 'an admirable Captain, an adequate Major, a barely satisfactory Colonel and a disastrous General'. Self-evidently not a student of military history, Buller split his forces into three columns, each tasked with relieving a British garrison. As inevitably as night follows day, given the historically-proven consequences of dividing a military force, disaster followed, including the capture of Winston Churchill, who was in South Africa as a reporter for the *Daily Mail* and the *Morning Post*.

In what came to be known as 'Black Week' (10th-15th December 1899), Buller's three relief columns were heavily defeated at the Battles of Stormberg, Magersfontein and Collenso. The Boers had quickly learnt the art of constructing entrenched defensive positions, protected by wire and enfiladed fire. If Black Week was not bad enough, the British suffered a further humiliating defeat at the Battle of Spion Kop on 23rd to 24th January 1900. With Buller and his commanders issuing disastrously contradictory orders, 350 British soldiers were killed and nearly 1,000 wounded. Although not recalled from South Africa, the boozy General was then replaced as Commander-in-Chief by Field Marshal Lord Roberts VC.

Field Marshal Lord Roberts VC

With Roberts in charge, Buller was directed to concentrate all his forces in a single thrust. As a result, while Roberts forced a Boer Army to surrender after the Battle of Paardeberg on 18th to 27th February, Buller was able to relieve Ladysmith – and to a limited extent his reputation – on 28th February. In March, newly-arrived British troops led by Roberts captured the Orange Free State capital, Bloemfontein. In May they relieved Mafeking, and then went on to capture Johannesburg. This was followed by the seizure of the Transvaal capital Pretoria in early-June. Meanwhile Churchill had re-joined the Colours, having escaped from a Boer prison camp at the end of December 1899, and was one of the first men into Pretoria. In October 1900, President Kruger fled the African continent with the help of Queen Wilhelmina of the Netherlands, who in defiance of the British blockade sent a Dutch warship to rescue him and the remnants of his Transvaal government.

Once the British had taken control of both the Orange Free State and the Transvaal, the conflict should have come to an end. However, the Boer farmers did not give up easily and adopted highly effective guerrilla tactics. Following British media and political uproar at their continued activities, a scapegoat was sought, and Buller was publicly and somewhat late in the day sacked in October 1901, presumably *pour encourager les autres*. Buller, with his partially-restored reputation once more in tatters, retired in a considerable grump to his family seat in Devon and its well-stocked cellar. The war dragged on for another seven months, finally ending on 31st May 1902, after the brutal repression of the Boers' guerrilla support-network by the new Commander-in-Chief, General Lord Kitchener.

Queen Wilhelmina of the Netherlands

The Fighting General's Table

One of the spoils of war from this highly controversial period is a dining table, now in The Green Howards Museum in Richmond, North Yorkshire. It formerly belonged to one of the Boers' most successful guerrilla leaders, General Christiaan de Wet, known as The Fighting General. De Wet's farmstead was destroyed as part of Kitchener's scorched earth policy, which was designed to cower the Boers into submission. Most unusually for a spoil of war, there exists a first-hand account of its acquisition by an officer in the 3rd (Militia) Battalion, The Princess of Wales's Own (Yorkshire) Regiment:

> The other day about 500 of us went out to the De Wet's farmhouse, or rather what remained of it, for the walls only are standing, and commenced digging

above, left to right

Boer Flag, Johannesburg

Boer Drum, Johannesburg

all over for buried ammunition but we found nothing. His farm has been burned and his household goods scattered. In our Mess hut is De Wet's table, and we eat our daily rations with our legs stretched under his own mahogany, or what answers to the name in this country.

The details of the table's two-year journey to England is recorded on a brass plaque affixed to it.

General Cronje's revolver (Paardeberg, 1900)
Elsewhere there were very slim pickings in terms of spoils or trophies. Boer General Piet Cronje's five-chamber Colt .45 revolver was surrendered by him to an unknown soldier, following the defeat of the Boers at the Battle of Paardeberg. It is now in the collection of historical firearms at the Royal Military Academy Sandhurst, to which it was donated by the descendants of Dr James Dunlop of Glasgow, an Army surgeon, who had been given it by one of his patients in South Africa.

A Boer Flag & Drum (Johannesburg, 1900)
The 2nd Battalion of the Cheshire Regiment managed to acquire a Boer drum and a flag, captured when Johannesburg fell in May 1900. The drum, which was thereafter paraded at the front of the Battalion, was lost in France during the retreat to Dunkirk in 1940. Miraculously, it was found by an officer of the Regiment after the Normandy Landings in 1944, still in the same village where it had been abandoned. It is now in a locked display case in the Cheshire Military Museum in Chester.

General Piet Cronje

226

President Kruger's pipe & a Danish volunteers' pennant (near Pretoria, 1900)
The 2nd Battalion of the King's Own Shropshire Light Infantry acquired a pipe, the bowl of which is carved in the shape of a man's head, which bears a striking likeness to its original owner, President of the Transvaal, 'Oom Paul' Kruger. It was found in an abandoned tent, along with a pennant belonging to Danish volunteers fighting with the Boers. The date and location of these acquisitions are not recorded, but were presumably sometime and somewhere after the fall of Pretoria, and before Kruger fled with the aid of Queen Wilhelmina. Both the pipe and the banner are now in the Shropshire Regimental Museum in Shrewsbury.

President Kruger, also known as Oom Paul

Whilst on the subject of the Dutch sovereign and the Danish pennant, it is worth noting that continental Europe was generally hostile to the British during the Second Boer War. Kaiser Wilhelm II of Germany, who features later in this book, was the most outspoken continental critic of Britain's involvement and a verbose supporter of the Boers; although bizarrely he would later claim that the British only won the war because of the battle plan he had sent Lord Roberts.

CHAPTER 28

FIRST WORLD WAR
(1914–1918)

Souveniers from the Mud & the Sand

On 28th June 1914, the heir to the Austro-Hungarian Empire, Archduke Franz-Ferdinand and his morganatic wife Sophie, Duchess of Hohenberg, were assassinated in Sarajevo by a Serbian student. At the time, no one thought that within two months the United Kingdom, France, Italy, Russia, Germany, Austria-Hungary and the Ottoman Empire would be locked in a conflict that would drag on for four years, cost the lives of seventeen million men, and topple the Emperors of Russia, Germany and Austria-Hungary, along with the Ottoman Sultan.

From this conflict alone, there are enough spoils of war in Britain's military and private collections to fill a substantial museum and several books. German, Austro-Hungarian and Ottoman helmets, cavalry pennants, shell cases, weapons, tanks, musical instruments, and much else besides proliferate in museum display cases from Inverness to Plymouth. The small selection which follows has been chosen because

Archduke Franz Ferdinand, assassinated in Sarajevo, 1914

Kaiser Wilhelm II of Germany and Emperor Franz-Joseph of Austria-Hungary

the items are distinctly different from the mass of detritus acquired on the battlefields of the First World War, a calamitous conflict the point of which is still a subject of intense academic debate.

Robert Graves' ball of chalk (Bezantin, 1916)

The poet and author, Robert Graves, was not averse to acquiring loot, as attested to by his poem on the *Hung Wu Vase* (*see* p.219), and a rather curious lump of chalk, on which is carved a small, brick wall, the dates '1914–1916', three flags and an Iron Cross. In his autobiography, *Goodbye to All That*, Graves wrote:

Robert Graves

> I picked up a souvenir [on 18th July 1916]. A German gun-team had been shelled as it was galloping out of Bezantin towards Martinpuich. The horses and driver had been killed. At the back of the limber were the gunners' treasures. Among them was a large lump of chalk wrapped up in a piece of cloth. I sent it as a present to Dr Dunn. I'm glad to say that he and it survived the war; he is in practice in Glasgow, and the lump of chalk is under a glass case in his consulting room.

Robert Graves' ball of chalk

Captain C J Dunn was the Medical Officer of the 2nd Battalion of the Royal Welch Fusiliers. He later presented the curious trophy to the Regiment's museum in Caernarvon Castle, where it can be seen to this day.

Lawrence of Arabia and the Hejaz Railway station bell (Hejaz, 1917–18)

By 1916 the First World War had degenerated into static trench warfare in Europe and stalemate in the Middle East, where the war in Mesopotamia was bogged down at Kut. British troops had been evacuated from the Dardanelles fiasco, and the western side of the Sinai Peninsula was the Ottoman 4th Army's rather permeable front line with Britain's quaintly named Egyptian Expeditionary Force.

However, on or around 8th June 1916, the precise date remains unclear, the situation in the Middle East changed forever, when Grand Sharif Hussein, the guardian of the holy city of Mecca and a descendant of the Prophet Mohammad, entered into a military alliance with the British and French governments. In return for his help, Hussein demanded British support for the creation of a single, independent and unified Arab state, stretching from Aleppo in Syria to Aden in Yemen.

Grand Sharif Hussein bin Ali

General Sir Edmund Allenby

Lawrence of Arabia

Over the next twenty-eight months, the Sherif's initially ill-equipped conventional forces, in close cooperation with the Egyptian Expeditionary Force and with the benefit of British training and weapons, waged war against the Ottoman 4th Army. Meanwhile, Hussein's sons, notably Prince Faisal, instituted a highly effective guerrilla war campaign, with British assistance in the form of advisers, Rolls-Royce armoured cars, and various aeroplanes. It focussed on the Hejaz Railway, the Ottomans' principal north-south line of communication.

By the end of September 1918, the Ottoman front line had been pushed back to Damascus. When the war ended in the Middle East the following month, the Ottoman *vilayets* (provinces) of Mosul, Baghdad and Basra in modern-day Iraq had been captured by British and Indian troops, under the command of Lieutenant General Sir Frederick Maude. Meanwhile, the combined forces of General Sir Edmund Allenby's Egyptian Expeditionary Force and Sherif Hussein's Arab Army had ousted the Ottoman-German forces from the *vilayets* of Aleppo, Beirut, Syria, the Hejaz, and the independent *sanjaqs* (counties) of Lebanon and Jerusalem, while simultaneously neutralising them in Arabia and the Yemen.

Those are the bare facts of the British victory in the Middle East and the contribution to it of the Arab Revolt. Later, however, these facts were to be overshadowed, and in some respects overturned, by accounts of the activities of a shy and enigmatic Classics scholar, archaeologist, author, intelligence officer, and self-confessed masochist, Thomas Edward Lawrence, one of the British military advisers to Prince Faisal, and the man known to history as Lawrence of Arabia.

Lawrence and Prince Faisal initiated and led the brilliant guerrilla-style campaign against the Hejaz Railway. The former's military exploits in the desert were largely unrecognised at the time by anyone outside the immediate theatre of operations. However, after the war his raids and tales of derring-do were mercilessly puffed, to the detriment of the facts, by the American journalist-turned-showman, Lowell Thomas. Lawrence further enhanced his own repetition with his book *Seven Pillars of Wisdom* (1926), his much-publicised retreat into anonymity, his habit of then frequently reversing into the limelight, and his death following a motorbike accident in 1935. His funeral in Dorset was attended by, amongst others, Florence Hardy, widow of the novelist Thomas, E M Forster, Siegfried Sassoon, and Winston Churchill, who cried openly by the graveside. Twenty-seven years later, in 1962, the Lawrence myth was set in concrete by David Lean's film, *Lawrence of Arabia*. As a result, it is

sometimes difficult to separate fact from fiction, as the story of the Deraa Station bell well illustrates.

Deraa Station on the Hejaz Railway

The Hejaz Railway, built before the First World War with German help and money from an Islamic trust, facilitated the annual pilgrimage of the faithful to Mecca. It also had the secular benefit of enabling the Ottomans to control their territories in Syria and the Hejaz by linking their military garrisons, and thus obviating the necessity for them to occupy the whole of the vast region. The railway stretched from Damascus to Medina, a distance of approximately 800 miles; along its narrow-gauge track were more than eighty stations, including Mezerib, Tel Shahm and Deraa. From June 1916 to October 1918, Damascus in the north was isolated from the Ottomans' Hejaz garrisons in the south, thanks to the constant destruction of stations, track and trains by Faisal's Arab irregulars under Lawrence's leadership. This was a vital tactic in Allenby's strategic plan to roll the Ottoman forces back from the Suez Canal to Constantinople.

In the course of these operations, Lawrence acquired various spoils of war, although he later gave most of them away to his friends. Apparently included in his haul of loot was a station bell from the Hejaz Railway, for on 23rd October 1920 a delivery note from the Arab Bureau in Cairo was sent to Lawrence. Now in the Bodleian Library in Oxford, it states: 'I beg to inform you that I am dispatching by parcel post in a wooden box the station bell of Deraa, which I understand is your property'.

So far so good, except that Lawrence never mentioned acquiring the Deraa Station Bell in *Seven Pillars of Wisdom*. To further complicate matters, there exists a photograph of the bell still hanging at the station.[1] Two further issues arise. First, a Hejaz Railway station bell belonging to Lawrence was until recently on loan to the Tank Museum at Bovington, and was included in a temporary Lawrence exhibition at the Imperial War Museum in 2005. For the exhibition, this bell was catalogued as coming from Mezerib Station, where it was 'acquired by Lawrence on 16th September 1918'. It has since disappeared without trace and there is no photograph of it on file. Second, in Chapter XCIV of *Seven Pillars of Wisdom*, Lawrence wrote about an attack on the railway station at Tel Shahm, on or around 19th April 1918:

> We cranked up our Rolls tenders; the Arabs leaped on to their camels; Peake's now-bold men broke into a run, and the force converged wildly upon the station. Our car won; and I gained the station bell, a dignified piece of Damascus brass-work. The next man took the ticket punch and the third the office stamp, while the bewildered Turks stared at us, with a growing indignation that their importance should be merely secondary.

So, perhaps the Arab Bureau, the Tank Museum at Bovington, and the Imperial War Museum were all in error, and the bell did not come from either Deraa or Mezerib, but from Tel Shahm as Lawrence stated. This is confirmed by Robert Graves, who wrote in *Goodbye to All That* that when Lawrence was a Fellow of All Souls College at Oxford after the war, he kept a bell in his rooms which was taken from Tel Shahm.

Lawrence was a well-known practical joker and a skilled pre-war Oxford undergraduate roof-climber. In a second reference to the Tel Shahm bell in his autobiography, Graves recorded that Lawrence had managed to fly a red Hejaz Railway flag from a pinnacle of the tower at All Souls, and that:

> …one afternoon he rang the station bell from his window into the Quadrangle. 'Good God,' I said, 'you'll wake the whole College!'

> 'It needs waking up.'

1. *See* www.nabataea.net, a website dedicated to the Hejaz Railway

All Souls, Oxford

232

With the disappearance of the Tank Museum's bell, which may be the one that awoke the Fellows of All Souls, and the apparent non-existence of any other Lawrence-associated Hejaz Railway bells, it is a matter of individual choice – as with so much else pertaining to Lawrence – in deciding where the truth lies.

German trench wallpaper (Estrées, 1917)
Some of the most abiding images of the First World War, perpetuated by film and television, are the trenches: waterlogged and rat-infested channels cut through the fields of Flanders, and fenced-in with coils of barbed wire. Within these trenches were hovel-like shelters, in which the soldiers ate, slept, and waited for death or injury, in conditions that would have been condemned anywhere else as unfit for human habitation. Outside, as the rain poured down, mud-caked Tommies rested on their rifles and smoked, knee-deep in mire, while waiting for the whistle blast that would order them to scramble up ladders and go over the top to eternity. Such were the British trenches of 1914–1918.

German trench wallpaper

However, on the other side of no man's land, no such slum tenement conditions prevailed. The German trenches were solidly built, well-drained, and reinforced against even the heaviest artillery bombardment, as the British found to their cost during the Battle of the Somme between 1st July and 18th November 1916. While not exactly home from home, the

A German trench

German trenches were considerably more comfortable and secure than their British equivalents. The reason for this lay in the fundamentally different approach to the conduct of the war by the British and German High Commands.

Throughout the whole of the war on the Western Front, the British remained convinced that the task in hand was to push the Germans back to their frontier. For the British Commanders-in-Chief, Field Marshal Sir John French and later Field Marshal Sir Douglas Haig (who were both cavalrymen by training and experience), the war was about *movement*, as it had been in 1914, and would be again in 1918 once the tank got into its stride. To build a semi-permanent defensive structure was completely contrary to their thinking. The Germans, on the other hand, saw the trench system as a strategic fortification, designed to protect the territory that they had already acquired, and from which to break out to seize more.

It was therefore unthinkable that a British trench could be furnished with creature comforts and wallpapered like the nursery at home. However, for the Germans this was an entirely natural state of affairs, as shown by a scrap of pink floral wallpaper now held in the Imperial War Museum in London. According to a hand-written note in one corner, it was: 'Taken from wall of Boche Dug Out near Ectrées' by a British soldier on 6th February 1917. The wallpaper is backed with a page from a German newspaper dated 30th July 1915.

The Blue Boy, RAF Club, Piccadilly

The Boy in Blue (Château de Fouilloy, 1918)

In a corner of the Churchill Bar at the Royal Air Force Club in Piccadilly is a mid-nineteenth-century, French School painting of a young boy dressed in white trousers, with a white collar fringing a pale blue blouse. The child is holding a small posy of flowers in his left hand, and is probably a member of the de Berry family, the *seigneurs* of Upper and Lower Fouilloy, from whose château the painting was removed in 1918.

At first sight, it is a wholly unremarkable painting of the sort that might achieve a hammer price at auction of a few hundred pounds. However, on further inspection the diligent observer will see that the *Blue Boy*'s blouse is adorned with pilot's wings, above three British First World War campaign medal ribbons; more remarkable still, he wears a khaki officer's hat, which bears the badge of the Royal Air Force. In addition, a tiny white-coated terrier can be seen in the lower left corner of the canvas.

These adornments are clearly an over-paint. But how did they come to be there? And how did the painting end up in the Royal Air Force Club?

The Royal Air Force (RAF) was founded on 1st April 1918. This new arm of Britain's armed services was formed by merging the Army's Royal Flying Corps (RFC) and the Royal Naval Air Service, and initially wore a khaki uniform. At the time, it was the largest air force in the world.

Shortly before the RAF unfurled its wings, the Germans launched a major offensive on the Western Front, designed to roll back the British and French front lines, and end the war before the United States Army could fully deploy. The Spring Offensive of 1918, also known as the Ludendorff Offensive, started on 21st March, but by late-April it had petered out, largely because the Germans were unable to supply their advancing troops fast enough. Although a significant amount of territory had been gained, including the Château de Fouilloy which had been the headquarters of the RFC's V Brigade, the Germans failed to make their hoped-for breakthrough. On 21st August the Allies launched the Second Battle of the Somme, and by 2nd September the German front line had been rolled back to the Hindenburg Line, from where they had set out in March. Two months later the First World War was over.

As the British troops pushed the Germans back in the last great battle of the war, the Château de Fouilloy once again became V Brigade's HQ. It is not clear from the records of the Royal Air Force Club whether the *Blue Boy* was removed from the château during the Spring Offensive or after its recapture. What is certain is that the added adornments to the young de Berry, including the khaki cap, must have been made after the RAF's formation in April 1918, and before it adopted its signature blue-grey uniform on 15th September 1919. Whatever the precise dates of the picture's acquisition by the RAF or the over-painting, it was presented to the Royal Air Force Club in 1922, to adorn the walls of its new premises on Piccadilly. It thereby became the first painting in the Club's collection.

This just leaves the mystery of the terrier in the bottom left-hand corner of the painting. One possible explanation is that the dog was the mascot of either V Brigade or of one of its Squadrons. The adoption of animal mascots by Britain's armed services has been wide-spread since times immemorial (*see* p.248). It is a habit from which the RFC (and its successor the RAF) were not exempt, and which included the adoption by RFC units of a fox, which was frequently taken into combat and was said to enjoy flying, as well as an eagle and a goat. Alternatively, the terrier may have been the RAF artist's pet or an in-joke of the type beloved by servicemen, the explanation of which has been lost in the mists of time. What is certain is that it was not a Squadron badge.

Kaiser Wilhelm II at the Church of the Redeemer, Jerusalem, 31st October 1898

Imperial German graffiti at the Temple of Apollo (Baalbek, 1918) & the Kaiser's Bronze Wreath (Damascus, 1918)

In 1898 Kaiser Wilhelm II of Germany made a much-publicised and lavishly planned forty-six-day private visit to the Ottoman Empire, which started at Constantinople (now Istanbul) and included Jerusalem, the Holy Sites and Damascus. Although described by the media as a personal pilgrimage, the Kaiser was accompanied by his wife and a huge Imperial entourage. The retinue for this *private* tour included twelve cooks, sixty waiters, ten guides, and twelve dragomen, in addition to the Kaiser's Ottoman hosts and guards, all of whom required 230 tents, 130 coaches, twelve baggage wagons, 1,395 horses, and 600 drovers. Bizarrely, or perhaps as a tribute to his English grandmother Queen Victoria, all the travel arrangements were made by Thomas Cook in London.

The main reason for this grand tour-masquerading-as-a-pilgrimage was the Kaiser's attendance at the solemn consecration of the new Lutheran Church of the Redeemer in Jerusalem on 31st October. The real reasons were to further strengthen the German influence and military-economic ties with the Sublime Porte, and to sow the seeds for a future German-financed *jihad*. Despite the Kaiser's preference for English travel agencies, the aim of this holy war was to drive his Britannic cousins out of the Middle East. Fanciful though this last proposition may sound, it was not only the core proposition of John Buchan's First World War thriller, *Greenmantle*, but a well-documented fact.

Kaiser Wilhelm II heads a parade into Jerusalem

While in Damascus, the Kaiser issued a Proclamation on 8th November 1898 in which he stated, in German and Arabic, that he was the 'Protector of Muslims everywhere'. Somewhat curiously, given the publicised reason for his earlier presence in Jerusalem, the Kaiser also confided in a letter to Tsar Nicholas II of Russia (and to others verbally – it was soon the talk of the bazaars) that he was considering converting to Islam. This typically daft plan to use militant Islam as a means of displacing the

British was re-activated thirty years later by Adolf Hitler. Fortunately, on both occasions the plan failed, despite the fact that when the Ottoman Empire entered the First World War in November 1914, Sultan Abdul Hamid II, in his role as Caliph, issued a *fatwah* within their Declaration of War, which stated that it was the sacred duty of all Muslims to kill infidels – except those of German, Austrian or Hungarian extraction.

Ottoman Sultan Abdul Hamid II

During his visit the Kaiser bombastically rode into Jerusalem in full dress uniform, at the head of a military cavalcade, passing under two specially constructed triumphal arches. One arch was paid for by the Ottoman government and the other was funded by, of all people, Jerusalem's Jewish community. In December 1917, following the British capture of Jerusalem, the more religiously-sensitive and better-read General Sir Edmund Allenby deliberately entered the Holy City unarmed and on foot. However, despite the Kaiser's insensitive behaviour, a number of tangible outcomes resulted from his visit in 1898. The most obvious military outcome was German assistance with the construction of the Hejaz Railway from 1900, the initiation of the Berlin-to-Baghdad railway in 1903, and the increasing presence of German advisers, instructors and weaponry in the Ottoman Army.

Royal Engineers remove the Kaiser's plaque from the Temple of Apollo, Baalbek

In addition, there were two significant cultural results of the German Imperial Presence in Syria. The first was the Kaiser's decision, following a visit to Baalbek on 10th November 1898, to fund four years of excavations at the ancient Roman site. This Imperial generosity was not allowed to pass unmarked, and a ten-foot-high stone inscription was later affixed above the main portico of the Temple of Apollo, recording the Kaiser's gracious and benevolent sponsorship of the excavations. In 1918 a team of Royal Engineers unceremoniously removed this plaque, an event which was recorded in a watercolour by the official war artist, James McBey, now in the Imperial War Museum, London. The present whereabouts of this unusual spoil of war is unknown; it was probably broken on removal, or later destroyed as being too large to transport back to the Royal Engineers' home base in Chatham.

A more lasting spoil of war originated from the Kaiser's visit to Damascus, prior to his departure from Syria on 12th November, followed five days later by a triumphal

Saladin's tomb, Damascus

The Kaiser's bronze wreath
© *Imperial War Museum*

military procession in Berlin fit only for a conquering hero. Given the Kaiser's self-identification with strong and successful military leaders, and his desire to associate himself with the warlike traditions of Islam, it was inevitable that once in Damascus he would visit the carved wooden sarcophagus of Salah ah-Din Yusuf bin Ayyub, known to Europeans as Saladin. It was probably also predictable that he would pay for the restoration of the mausoleum which housed the tomb, in the grounds of the Umayyad Mosque. Not content with restoring the fabric and decoration of the mausoleum, the Kaiser had pre-ordered the construction of a second sarcophagus in inlaid marble, on which he placed a gilded bronze wreath during his reverential visit. History does not record if the Kaiser intended that Saladin's remains should be transferred from their original resting place to the new tomb, and in the event that has never happened.

However, the Kaiser's intentions regarding the wreath were clear from the embellishments and inscriptions on it, which are in a mixture of Roman, Arabic and Kurdish script, Saladin being a Kurd rather than an Arab. At the top of the wreath, below the Kaiser's personal cypher topped by the Prussian crown, hangs the chain and badge of the Order of the Black Eagle, Prussia's equivalent of the Order of the Garter. The purpose of the wreath was thereby to invest the long-deceased Muslim Saladin with the German Empire's highest decoration, blithely ignoring the facts that it was a Christian Order of Chivalry, the Kaiser's crown was embellished with crosses, and the Black Eagle's badge displayed a Maltese cross.

Not surprisingly, as early as 1916 Prince Faisal told T E Lawrence that one of the first duties he would perform on capturing Damascus – then a distant dream – would be to cleanse Saladin's tomb by removing the wreath, encrusted as it was with Christian symbology. Immediately after the capture of Damascus on 1st October 1918, Prince Faisal and Lawrence visited Saladin's tomb and duly removed the offending tribute. Shortly afterwards, Lawrence left the Middle East, travelling back to England with the trophy – a gift from Prince Faisal – in his luggage. On 8th November, he in turn donated it to the Imperial War Museum, along with a hand-written and signed certificate which, in typically puckish Lawrence-style, stated:

> This is to certify that the Kaiser's wreath from Saladin's tomb in Damascus was removed by me, as Saladin no longer needed it, at Damascus on 1.10.18. Signed T E Lawrence, Lt Col, 2 Polstead Road, Oxford. 8.11.18

Prince Faisal

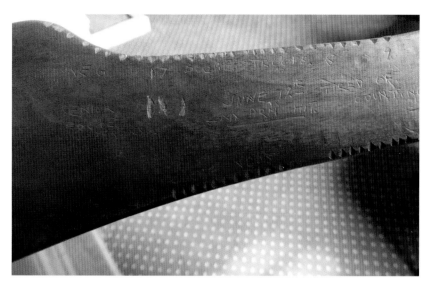

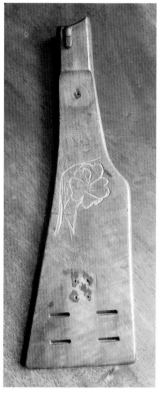

Luger pistol butt

Obverse of the Luger pistol butt, with carvings

A Luger Pistol butt (Provenance uncertain)

In addition to a nineteenth-century Chinese or Burmese altar currently being used as an entrance hall table (*see* p.192), there is a slim piece of nondescript wood lying on an anteroom side table in the 160th (Welsh) Brigade's Officers Mess at The Barracks in Brecon. No one currently serving in the Brigade Headquarters knows where this unlabelled and somewhat unloved artefact came from, how it was acquired, or what its former function was. Indeed, it is a small miracle that it was not chucked onto the anteroom fire, in the halcyon days before the fire place was blocked up during a Ministry of Defence economy drive, or tossed into a wastepaper basket. However, a close inspection of this unprepossessing object reveals that it is a most unusual spoil of war from the 1914–1918 conflict in France, and provides a brief and somewhat laconic history of its later use.

The identification of the piece lies in its shape and the presence at the narrow end of a metal fixing. Too slim to be the butt of an infantry rifle, it is in fact the detachable extension of a First World War-period, German long-barrelled Luger pistol, model P08 (an abbreviation of Pistol Para-bellum 1908), a weapon that was issued to Imperial German artillery units. The wooden extension, which slid onto the base of the handle of the pistol, had various leather straps now missing, although their location slots remain. They allowed the weapon to be used, in conjunction with an additional 'snail-drum' magazine that replaced the conventional magazine, as a sub-machine gun. While serving with the 21st Lancers at the Battle of

239

Omdurman in 1898, Winston Churchill had armed himself with a similar pistol made by Mauser, the wooden holster of which doubled up as a rifle butt. In the case of the Luger, the temporary extension had no such secondary function. Interestingly, a complete P08 pistol with its butt extension was acquired during the First World War by the Devonshire Regiment. Unknown to the officers of the 160th (Welsh) Brigade, it is now in a display cabinet at The Keep Military Museum in Dorchester, Dorset.

The history of the unprepossessing spoil of war in Brecon can be found on its surface. The crest stamped into the wood is a Guelphic crown over the letter 'S'. The Guelphic crown was used by the German Kingdom of Saxony, and the stamp mark is probably the Saxon equivalent of the British WD arrowhead establishing it as government property. Further marks post-date the object's manufacture and issue, and include a crudely carved flower (possibly a poppy) on one side and a series of notches or gadrooning on the top and bottom edges of the flip side. These embellishments take on an altogether more sinister significance when, in an oblique light, it is possible to detect scratched words and dates in English: 'June 6 Boche troops 17, Senior Boche officers 3, Boche NCOs 11. June 8 – 9 Boche troops 13.'

These tallies of hits on the enemy match exactly the number of notches on the edges. Had the owner been an early fan of the Western film genre, in which the cowboys notch their pistol butts every time they fell a Native American? The final message smacks strongly of the well-known graveyard humour of the British soldier: 'June 12 Arm hit – Tired of counting.' So not only is the object a Luger accessory, but it is also a score card for the British Tommy who had acquired it. Although there is no year inscribed, given that the P08 was issued to German artillery units, it is reasonable to assume that it was acquired in the more fluid battles of 1918 that followed the German Spring Offensive, rather than in the earlier years of static trench warfare, when the artillery was positioned well behind the front lines. But whenever and however it was acquired, it must rank as the most neglected spoil of war in this book.

CHAPTER 29

SECOND WORLD WAR
(1939–1945)

Wreckage of the Third Reich

The Dry Roger (Germany, 1945)

Placed on a side table in the anteroom of the Officers House of the House-hold Cavalry Regiment at Bulford Camp in Wiltshire is a twenty-four-inch-high wooden statue, which has been a treasured possession of The Life Guards since 1945.

In the years that followed the Nazi Party's rise to power in Germany in 1932, much of Europe was subjected to unprecedented aggression, repression, terror, tyranny, and the industrialised extermination of assorted groups by Hitler and his criminal cronies. No less sinister, but rather less violent, was the Third Reich's suppression of 'decadent' art, including works by the Impressionists and the Cubists. On viewing Van Gogh's

Adolf Hitler in Paris, 1940

241

The Life Guards' *Dry Roger*

Lebensborn centre, Ordensburg Vogelsang

1. In 1939 the Household Cavalry (formed in 1660) comprised The Life Guards, a 1922 amalgamation of the 1st and 2nd Regiments of Life Guards, and the Royal Horse Guards (The Blues), which had been elevated to the status of Household Cavalry in 1820. In 1969, The Blues were amalgamated with a Line Cavalry Regiment, the 1st Dragoons (The Royals); the new Regiment so formed retained its status as Household Cavalry

The Sower, Hitler famously opined that: 'Anyone who sees and paints a sky green and pastures blue ought to be sterilised'. In the place of such works, the Nazis promoted figurative art, the purpose of which was to glorify the regime and promote its so-called values and objectives.

One of those objectives was the breeding of blond-haired, blue-eyed 'Aryan' children, using the voluntary insemination of 'racially pure and healthy' young women by members of the *Schutzstaffel* (protection squadron), better known as the SS. In order to facilitate this, the SS established the *Lebensborn* (fount of life) programme, building breeding centres in Germany, and later in some of the countries occupied by the forces of the Third Reich.

One such centre in Germany was created within the Ordensburg Vogelsang, a large purpose-built SS military, educational and cultural centre, in the Eifel region of North Rhine-Westfalia. This stone-built complex, most of which still stands today, was clearly designed to last a thousand years. Not only adorned with the regime's symbols, such as the ubiquitous swastika, it was also decorated with heroic depictions (in marble, stone and mosaic) of the master race, stripped for action and ready for reproduction, the latter doubtless in a bid to encourage the camp's occupants to focus on their duties under the *Lebensborn* programme.

Prominent amongst the artists sanctioned and commissioned to produce the Nazis' iconography and soft-core pornography were Arno Breker and the aptly named Willy Meller. Almost ninety percent of Breker's work on German public buildings was destroyed in 1945. However, at Vogelsang (and elsewhere) much of Meller's work survives, although in a modified form after the Allied forces shot off the genitalia on many of his statues in the shady glades and bowers at the camp.

One of the Allied units engaged in the invasion of Germany and the desecration of its erotic art was the 1st Household Cavalry Regiment (1HCR). At the beginning of World War II, the two Regiments of the Household Cavalry,[1] were stationed with their horses in London and Windsor. However, in 1940 the Regiments were temporarily combined for the duration of the war into 1HCR, predominantly made up of Life Guards, which was sent as part of the 1st Cavalry Division to Palestine, and the 2nd Household Cavalry Regiment (2HCR), mostly comprising The Blues, which was based in London and Windsor.

By 1941 it was clear that a Cavalry Division on horses in Palestine was about as useful to the war effort as a longbow. Consequently, 1HCR was obliged to hand over its horses to the Regimental Depot and shoot all

animals over the age of fifteen, to the considerable dismay of all ranks. Once remounted on an assorted collection of ancient lorries and motorised trucks (including a Haifa taxi), they trundled north to rescue a besieged RAF garrison at Habbaniya in Iraq. Eventually, after a brief incursion into Persia, where the Regiment was the first Allied unit to shake hands with the Russians, 1HCR was equipped with armoured cars and deployed in the North African campaign, and then in the invasion of Italy. In October 1944, the Regiment returned to England, only to be redeployed in March 1945 as part of the Guards Armoured Division for the invasion of Germany.

Regimental lore is not clear as to how 1HCR acquired a wooden maquette for a life size (or larger) statue of a naked man and woman. Probably by either Meller or Breker, and certainly in their style, the couple are locked in an embrace that was clearly going to lead to at least one more Aryan baby for the *Lebensborn* programme. Regimental opinion is also divided as to whether the acquisition was made in Goslar or Wolfenbüttel. However, the *Dry Roger*, as the statue was immediately christened by louche Life Guards, has been proudly and prominently displayed in the Regiment's Officers House since 1945. In the years following the war, the mildly-erotic statue travelled with The Life Guards from Belfast to Singapore via Palestine, where it was not improved by immersion in a bath, and to Cyprus where the lady's toes were chipped. At various times, enterprising officers with an eye for anatomical detail have attempted to add some genital embellishments in cork, but despite all this the *Dry Roger* has survived virtually in its original state.

above, left to right

German statues of idealised manhood, defaced by US troops

German idealised man & horse

German idealised man, neutered by US troops

Typical Third Reich era statue by Willi Meller

Hitler's Table (Bad Godesberg, 1938 & 1945)

Whilst, within its borders, the leaders of the Third Reich were doing everything they could to get its Aryan citizens in the mood for breeding the Master Race, in foreign affairs they were doing their best to deceive Germany's neighbours as to their expansionist intentions. Almost as soon as the Nazi Party gained power, Hitler gave the order for Germany to rearm, albeit secretly and in breach of the Versailles Treaty, and withdrew the country from the League of Nations. This was followed by the German military re-occupation of the Rhineland in 1936, again in defiance of the Treaty of Versailles. Britain, France and the USA did nothing. Emboldened by this passivity, in 1938 the German Army marched into Austria, and Hitler declared that it was now part of the Greater German Reich. The British, the French and the Americans, using the excuse that it was really none of their business, still did nothing, beyond verbal protests.

It was only when it became clear that the next country to be invaded was Czechoslovakia that the British Prime Minister, Neville Chamberlain, and his equally weak French counterpart, President Edouard Deladier, finally commenced an extended run of shuttle diplomacy, designed to avert war. Following on from an initial meeting at the Führer's mountain retreat at Berchtesgaden in the Bavarian Alps, the second of these ultimately futile negotiations was held between 22nd and 24th September 1938 in the German spa town of Bad Godesberg. It was no accident of planning that this was the German Chancellor's holiday resort of choice or that the Rheinhotel Dreesen was his favourite hotel, recommended to him by his deputy Rudolf Hess, who had been educated in Bad Godesberg. Hitler

Adof Hitler & Neville Chamberlain at Bad Godesberg

stayed at the Rheinhotel Dreesen over seventy times, and it was from there that he planned the murderous purge of the *Sturmabteilung* (SA) leaders in 1934, known as the 'Night of the Long Knives'.

At 1.30 am on the final day of their conference, Hitler and Chamberlain signed the Godesberg Memorandum, which sanctioned the occupation of the Sudetenland area of Czechoslovakia by German troops and stipulated the holding of a plebiscite to determine its future nationality. Chamberlain agreed to take these terms to the Czechoslovak government, but its terms were repudiated almost immediately by the British, French and Czech governments. The crisis escalated and Chamberlain made a final dash to Munich on 29th September, in a last-ditch attempt to avoid war. He returned to Heston Aerodrome the following morning, brandishing the so-called Munich Agreement, which he waved over his head as he addressed the media with these words:

> The settlement of the Czechoslovakian problem, which has now been achieved is, in my view, only the prelude to a larger settlement in which all Europe may find peace. This morning I had another talk with the German Chancellor, Herr Hitler, and here is the paper which bears his name upon it as well as mine. Some of you, perhaps, have already heard what it contains but I would just like to read it to you: '... We regard the agreement signed last night and the Anglo-German Naval Agreement as symbolic of the desire of our two peoples never to go to war with one another again.'

Later that day he stood outside 10 Downing Street and famously stated:

> My good friends, for the second time in our history, a British Prime Minister has returned from Germany bringing peace with honour. I believe it is peace for our time. We thank you from the bottom of our hearts. Go home and get a nice quiet sleep.

Eleven months and three days later Britain was at war with Germany. So much for the history.

Unknown to almost everyone outside the Household Division, there is a curious relic of the meeting in Bad Godesberg at Horse Guards in London. Used today as a desk by the Chief of Staff, London District, it is an elaborate, reproduction Louis XV *bureau plat*. It was over this piece of furniture that the Godesberg Memorandum was discussed in Room 106, the so-called *Führersuite*. Part of a set of fake Louis XV furnishings that

The Bad Godesberg Desk at
Horse Guards, London

was specially ordered and installed ahead of the meeting, on the orders of the German Foreign Ministry, the provenance of the desk is definitively established by a silver plaque screwed to the writing surface: 'Neville Chamberlain and Adolf Hitler talked across this table at their meeting at Bad Godesberg in September 1938.'

Sadly, for urban myths and Guards folklore, for many years those that had not read the plaque – or misunderstood it – incorrectly described the desk as the table on which the Munich Agreement was signed.

That aside, there is still the question as to how the desk came to be a prized possession of the Household Division and one of the spoils of the Second World War. Colonel Hugh Boddington, late of the Grenadier Guards and a recent Chief of Staff London District, records:

> The following is an extract from a letter to Brigadier Wilkinson DSO, Commanding 4th Infantry Brigade, dated 23rd May 1949:
>
> The story I was told of the table in your room is that when 5 Guards Armoured Brigade was at Bad Godesberg in 1945 Brigade HQ was in the hotel where Hitler stayed when he met Chamberlain. The Brigadier used Hitler's room as his office and used this table across which Chamberlain talked.
>
> When 5 Guards Armoured Brigade left Bad Godesberg they took the desk with them. Subsequently it was used by the Commanders of 4th Guards Brigade, 4th Guards Brigade Group and 4th Guards Armoured Brigade at Hubbelrath, Iserlohn and Munster respectively until the Brigade was disbanded on 1st October 1976. In 1977 the desk was sent to Horse Guards for the office of the Chief of Staff London District.

And there it remains to the present day.

The Rafwaffe
At about the darkest moment of the Second World War in 1941, the Royal Air Force established No. 1426 (Enemy Aircraft) Flight RAF, a formation equipped with German aeroplanes captured, looted or otherwise 'acquired' from the *Luftwaffe* (German Air Force). The Flight was created to evaluate enemy aircraft and to demonstrate their characteristics to

Allied personnel, thereby exposing them to 'the appearance, performance, and even the sound' of hostile aeroplanes under operational conditions. Needless to say, No. 1426 Flight was quickly nicknamed the 'Rafwaffe'.

Established on 21st November 1941 at RAF Duxford, the Rafwaffe was initially staffed with maintenance test pilots from No. 41 Group. Between them, they had less than a hundred hours of flying experience on enemy aircraft. Initially, there were three planes in the Flight: a Heinkel He 111 bomber, shot down in Scotland in February 1940; a Messerschmitt Bf 109, the single-engine fighter that was Fighter Command's main opposition during the Battle of Britain, captured during the Battle of France in 1940; and a Junkers Ju 88A-5 bomber, a surprise acquisition made when its inept Luftwaffe pilot made a night-time landing at RAF Chivenor in the belief – so he said – that it was an airfield in France.

Messerschmitt Bf110 in RAF livery

The Rafwaffe's first enemy aircraft recognition tour at British airfields commenced in mid-February 1942 and lasted for two weeks. It was swiftly followed by a demonstration for the Army at Travellers Hill, and some sound recordings for the RAF Film Unit. This was the Rafwaffe's first, but by no means last, exposure to the glamourous world of the movies.

Poster for *In Which We Serve*

Further tours were made in successive months, during one of which the Rafwaffe's Ju 88 was photographed by the Two Cities Film Company, for use in Noël Coward's morale-boosting film, *In Which We Serve*. Based on the early-wartime activities of Captain Lord Louis Mountbatten, the young David Lean cut his teeth as the film's assistant director.

This was by no means the end of the Rafwaffe's roles on the silver screen. Towards the end of 1942, Metro Goldwyn Mayer photographed the Ju 88 and Me 110 for use in the film *The Adventures of Tartu*, a now completely forgotten patriotic piece of spy-thriller hokum, starring the British matinée idol, Robert Donat. Further stardom came in April 1943 when the Rafwaffe's Ju 88 was flown for a documentary, *The Re-Discovery of Britain*, made by the Crown Film Unit, and the following month when the Ju 88 and He 111 were flown for the Army Film Production Unit, which was making a film about Lieutenant General

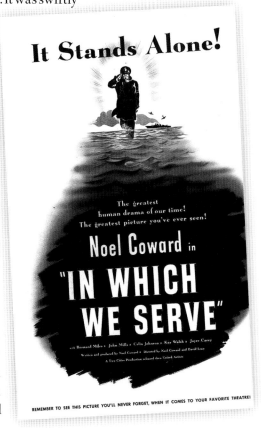

It Stands Alone!

The greatest human drama of our time! The greatest picture you've ever seen!

Noel Coward in

"IN WHICH WE SERVE"

with Bernard Miles · John Mills · Celia Johnson · Kay Walsh · Joyce Carey
Written and produced by Noel Coward · Directed by Noel Coward and David Lean
A Two Cities Production released thru United Artists

REMEMBER TO SEE THIS PICTURE YOU'LL NEVER FORGET, WHEN IT COMES TO YOUR FAVORITE THEATRE!

Bernard Montgomery's successful campaign in North Africa against Field Marshal Erwin Rommel.

The Rafwaffe's role as movie stars was interrupted on 27th May, when the Flight was inspected by King George VI and Queen Elizabeth at RAF Digby, but not for long. On 7th July, the Rafwaffe's Ju 88 and He 111 were flown to USAAF Polebrook to enable the 'king' of Hollywood, Captain Clark Gable, to make an instructional film for US Army Air Force air gunners. However, rubbing shoulders with British and American royalty could not last forever, and the Flight came down to earth with a bump when it received a visit from Verity Films Ltd, who needed to take some interior shots of the He 111 for the instructional film *Movement by M.T.*, about which nothing is now known.

The Rafwaffe was back in front of the cameras on 15th February 1944, when six newspaper reporters, two Paramount film cameramen, and three Movietone Newsreel men visited the Flight and spent hours with the enemy aircraft. Five days later a film crew from the Nettlefold film unit arrived to shoot footage for use in the film *Fighter Room*. In July, the Me 109G was flown for some ground-to-air shots for the RAF Film Production Unit, and in the same month the Ju 88 was flown for the Realist Film Unit, who were making a film called *Tinker Tailor*.

Like all established film stars, the Rafwaffe also performed for charity, when they flew their Ju 88, FW 190 and Me 110 to Hatfield for nine days of display flying in September, organised by DeHavilland in aid of the RAF Benevolent Fund. Back on the red carpet, this was followed in November with a second booking by Two Cities Film Company, although the shoot was cancelled because of bad weather. In the event, this was the Rafwaffe's last chance to appear in front of the camera. With the Allies advancing across Europe and the end of the war in sight, No. 1426 (EAC) Flight RAF was disbanded on 17th January 1945. However, one of these large spoils of war, a Messerschmitt Bf 109E, can still be seen at the Royal Air Force Museum in London, along with three other German aeroplanes surrendered at the end of the European war in May 1945. The latter, which did *not* fly with the Rafwaffe, are a Messerschmitt Bf110 6G, surrendered in Denmark, and a Junkers JU 87G-2 and a Heinkel He 111, both captured in Germany.

Fritz the Wehrmacht pet (Normandy, June 1944)

The British Army's habit of acquiring mascots, giving them a rank, and even putting them on the payroll is a deep-rooted one that bewilders friends and foes alike. Military animals fall into two categories: mascots are held on the unit's strength and are funded by the Ministry of Defence; pets are held off the strength, and their costs are the responsibility of the unit. Some of the earliest regimental animals recorded belonged to the Regiments that now form the Household Division (The Guards). They include *Duke*, a Newfoundland dog who attached himself to The Blues during the Peninsular War. *Duke* was used by the Regiment during the

Fritz, pet dog of 1st Bn Royal Hampshire Regiment

advance through Spain to flush out rats from deserted farmhouses, prior to the ruins being occupied as bivouacs. Somewhat unkindly, given his ratting duties, the dog was repeatedly traded-in with locals in return for free wine. Nonetheless, *Duke* always managed to re-join his comrades and returned with the Regiment to England. His portrait still hangs in the Officers House of the Household Cavalry Regiment. Another Blues dog, *Spot*, was present at the Battle of Waterloo; he was also memorialised, in a painting by William Henry Davis, executed on 5th November 1816.

More unusual for a Guards animal was *Jacob*, a goose belonging to the 2nd Battalion, Coldstream Regiment of Foot Guards. *Jacob*'s adoption as an unofficial mascot by the Regiment occurred in 1839, during the 2nd Battalion's tour of duty in Quebec as part of a British force deployed to supress a French-Canadian insurrection. A Coldstream Guardsman, Private John Kemp, was on sentry duty when he saw a goose being chased by a fox and decided to save the bird. He dispatched the fox with some quick bayonet work, and the goose attached itself to the sentry box in gratitude, and would keep the sentry-of-the-moment company. That, however, was by no means the end of the story. That winter, with snow thick on the ground, *Jacob*'s saviour was on sentry duty when a group of men armed with knives tried to sneak up on him in the dark, their footsteps muffled by the snow. *Jacob* spotted what was going on and flew at the men, flapping his wings and honking loudly. Alerted by the goose, the sentry shot one attacker, bayonetted another, and with *Jacob*'s help held the rest at bay until reinforcements appeared on the scene and arrested those left standing. In gratitude, the officers of the Regiment bought *Jacob* a brass gorget and a Good Conduct ring. *Jacob* wore both for the rest of his life. At the end of the Battalion's tour of duty in North America,

Jacob the goose

Philip the bear

the Coldstream Regiment of Foot Guards took the goose back to London, where undismayed by his new surroundings and wearing his gorget and Good Conduct ring, *Jacob* duly took post by the sentry box outside Portman Street Barracks and accompanied the Battalion on Queen's Guard. When informed of the story, members of the Royal Family, the Duke of Wellington, and others flocked to see the goose. *Jacob* met an untimely death under the wheels of a delivery cart whilst on duty in Croydon in 1846, but his head, gorget and ring are preserved in the Guards Museum, London. He has also been the subject of a biography, and his likeness has been cast in bronze and silver.

Other than a small collection of photographs and an eyewitness letter, little is now known about a brown bear called *Philip*, who belonged to Captain Sir Herbert Naylor-Leyland of the 2nd Life Guards. *Philip* was not a regimental mascot, but must have had the status of a regimental pet, for he was housed with the Regiment and had a 2nd Life Guard soldier, Corporal Bert Grainger, to look after him. The pair would often give wrestling displays. When war broke out in 1914, *Philip* was dispatched to London Zoo.

Meanwhile, not to be outdone by their regimental rivals, the 1st Life Guards had a stuffed bear in the entrance hall of the Officers House at Regent's Park Barracks, and The Blues had a live bear with its own handler at Combermere Barracks in Windsor. But the three bears were not by any means the full extent of the Household Cavalry's official pets in the mid-to late-nineteenth century. These included a monkey called *Jack*, who held the rank of Corporal of Horse and wore a specially made Life Guard tunic.

With the outbreak of hostilities in August 1914, it was not long before the 2nd Battalion Scots Guards had acquired a pair of pets in France in the shape of two milking cows, which were quickly named *Bella* and *Bertha*. Originally acquired to provide the Officers Mess with fresh milk, the two cows quickly became a wartime enterprise, with a Scots Guardsman appointed as official cowman. During the winter months the cows were kept under cover behind the Front Line, where their feed was treated as an Officers Mess overhead, and in the summer they were allowed to graze. Their milk, on which the Medical Officer had first call, was transported to the Scots Guards' trenches in a car that had once belonged to a Life Guards officer and for reasons unknown was called *Michael*; the two milkers' annual calves were bartered on the military black market for, on one occasion, a new set of tyres and two hundred gallons of petrol for *Michael*.

Having been marched with the Battalion to Cologne at the end of the war, *Bella* and *Bertha* were shipped back to England as 'officers' chargers'. Stabled first in Windsor and then at Hyde Park Barracks, where they grazed in Hyde Park, the two cows took part in the first stage of the Guards Division's Victory March through London in 1919, and incredible though it may now seem actually Ranked Past King George V and Queen Mary at Buckingham Palace. *Bella* and *Bertha* ended their days in retirement at Blythswood in Renfrewshire, as befitted probably the most practical pets ever adopted by a Guards Regiment. Their memory lingers on in the shape of two bovine silver statuettes and a silver-mounted cloven-hoofed snuff box currently located in the Officers Mess of The Queen's Guard at St James's Palace.

Bella and *Bertha* the milking cows

Elsewhere in the British Army, more conventional animals serving as mascots or pets include the drum horse of The Queen's Royal Hussars, whose predecessor unit, The Kings Own Regiment of Dragoons, captured a pair of French silver kettledrums in 1743, which The Queen's Royal Hussars still carry on parade, despite no longer being a horsed unit (*see* pp.27–8). The Royal Scots Dragoon Guards, another mechanised Line Cavalry Regiment, also have a drum horse, which has its own rank and ration book.

Somewhat smaller in scale are the Shetland pony mascots of the Parachute Regiment and The Royal Regiment of Scotland (a tradition taken over from the Argyll & Sutherland Highlanders), all of whom hold the rank of Lance Corporal. *Lance Corporal Cruachan II* of the Argyll & Sutherland Highlanders was presented to the Regiment in 1952, and became infamous for his stubborn temperament and fondness for beer, particularly Guinness. On more than one occasion, he was punished for drunken behaviour while on duty, by being locked up in the stables with his handler, known as the Pony Major. On one royal parade he bit the flowers the Queen was holding and her glove. On another, just as Her Majesty was about to arrive, *Cruachan* spotted a police horse, which happened to be in season, and bolted towards the mare, dragging the Pony Major with him. As they shot past the Regiment's Commanding Officer, he yelled at two nearby Military Policemen: 'Arrest that pony AT ONCE!' The policemen and the Pony Major then literally carried the still tumescent *Cruachan* back into line in front of the Regiment and held him down, just as the Queen's car came around the corner. She had in fact seen the whole debacle and had asked her driver to pause, remarking with a smile as she disembarked: 'I gather you were having a few problems with *Corporal Cruachan*'.

The latest *Lance Corporal Cruachan*

Then there are the rank-less Irish wolfhounds of the Royal Irish Regiment and the Irish Guards. Not to be outdone on the canine front, the Leicestershire Regiment had a lurcher bitch as a Company mascot in 1917. By contrast, the three Battalions of the Royal Welsh each have a Kashmir goat, which are held on the Battalions' strength as though they were operational soldiers; accordingly, when a Royal Welsh goat is promoted to Lance Corporal, it becomes a member of the Corporals Mess and must be accorded all the privileges of its rank.

Back in England, the Mercian Regiment has a Swaledale Ram, with the rank of Lance Corporal, but without the privileges of its Welsh cousins. However, the animal which holds the title of the most exotic regimental mascot must be accorded to the successive Indian Black Buck antelopes of the Royal Regiment of Fusiliers, almost all of them known as *Corporal Bobby*. At the end of the Second World War, the 2nd Battalion liberated one from Hamburg zoo, which then accompanied the Fusiliers on their tour of Egypt and Palestine. The unofficial mascots of the 1st Battalion the Yorkshire Regiment (Prince of Wales's Own) are two ferrets named *Imphal* and *Quebec*.

Returning to what should be the saner reaches of the canine world, the 3rd Battalion of the Mercian Regiment (Staffords) has proudly paraded a Staffordshire Bull Terrier since 1882, and the present Staffie, *Lance Corporal Watchman V*, was inducted in 2010, promoted to Sergeant in 2015, and to Colour Sergeant in 2017. However, unlike his wolfhound cousins, *Watchman V* is classified as a pet, rather than an official mascot.

Not so *Fritz*, a German-owned Pyrenean Mountain dog, who became a spoil of war at the end of the Second World War, and the mascot of 1st Battalion, Hampshire Regiment.[2] The circumstances of Fritz's acquisition are laconically recorded in an un-dated letter from Major M J Jeffrey, Commanding the Regimental Depot, to various Officers Commanding other Hampshire Regiment units:

2. From 1946, the Royal Hampshire Regiment and now the Princess of Wales's Royal Regiment

When the 1st Bn. landed in Normandy on D-Day, one of the objectives was Armanches [*sic*]. The attack on this village was led by Captain C. Thomas DSO and in the course of the action he captured a German officer with his St. Bernard [*sic*] dog. This dog was sent back to England and, on arrival at a British port, was to have been destroyed if no one would guarantee the payments of its quarantine fees. This was done by a young Wren Rating. Captain Thomas is now back in Scotland wounded and has contacted the editor of the Sunday Pictorial, who states that, providing the sum of £18 can be provided [to repay Leading Wren Elgar], he will arrange that the dog is released to the Regiment as a regimental pet.

I have consulted several serving and retired officers here and they are of the opinion that it would be very much appreciated if the dog could be obtained for the 1st Bn. As the matter is rather urgent, and the 1st Bn. are being kept rather busy, I wonder whether you would consider the gift of £5 each from your P.R.I. Funds for this purpose. I very much regret that I cannot do so, as, being in an American occupied barracks, I do not get any rebate but I am perfectly willing to look after the animal until after the war. Will you therefore give this your consideration and let me have your reply as soon as possible so that I can inform Captain Thomas whether to proceed or not.

The money was forthcoming and *Fritz* became not only the mascot, but the treasured pet of the Hampshires until his death in 1949. According to the Royal Hampshires website, *Fritz* was initially a reluctant recruit, causing considerable damage to his kennel in an effort to escape. However, he soon settled down and, thanks to his training as an attack dog, was willing to take orders from his new owners, even though none of them spoke German.

Finally, to prove that mania for pets and mascots is not confined to the Army, No 6 Squadron Royal Air Force, known as the Flying Tin Openers, had a tortoise mascot (name unknown) emblazoned with the Squadron badge, which sneaked onto Flight Lieutenant Philip Nelson's Canberra bomber in Bengazi, in the days when King Idris ruled Libya and the RAF still had a base there. The tortoise managed to survive the flight to the Squadron's station at Akrotiri in Cyprus, despite being without oxygen at 40,000 feet, and landed in a perkier condition than it had been prior to take off.

Fifty years earlier, on 14th March 1915, a pig was spotted swimming frantically in the Pacific Ocean. It was recovered by sailors from HMS *Glasgow*, one of the warships which had just blown up the porker's previous home, the German cruiser SMS *Dresden*. Named *Tirpitz*, the pig became the ship's mascot, until he was retired to the Whale Island Gunnery School in Portsmouth. *Tirpitz* lived at the Gunnery School for some time until he was auctioned for charity, as pork. He raised the enormous sum of £1,785 (2020: £99,000) for the Red Cross. When he died, his head was stuffed, and can now be seen at the Imperial War Museum in London.

Tirpitz the pig

Tirpitz in Tromsø Fjord, Norway

The Tirpitz bulkhead (Tromso, November 1944)

When the Second World War broke out in 1939, the two ships most feared by the British were the battleships *Bismarck* and *Tirpitz*, both the pride of the German Navy. On 24th May 1941, *Bismarck* sank the British battleship, HMS *Hood*, which was believed to be unsinkable. In retaliation, Prime Minister Winston Churchill famously issued his order to the Royal Navy to 'Sink the *Bismarck*', which after several naval mishaps was achieved three days later on 27th May. Lest a similar fate befall *Tirpitz*, Hitler ordered that she be hidden in the fjords of Norway, where she remained a significant threat to the vital Arctic Convoy routes to Soviet Russia. The *Tirpitz* was attacked many times, including once by British midget submarines in 1943, but although severely damaged, she remained afloat. Lieutenant (later Commander) Donald Cameron and Lieutenant (later Rear Admiral) Godfrey Place, the commanders of submersibles X6 and X7, were both awarded the Victoria Cross for this action. Finally, in 1944 it was decided to sink the ship using 12,000lb Tallboy bombs

The upturned hull of *Tirpitz* after the RAF raid

designed by Barnes Wallis, the genius responsible for the Wellington bomber and the bouncing bombs used in the Dambusters Raid.

On 12th November 1944, in the final of three attacks by the RAF, Lancaster bombers from IX and 617 Squadrons flew from RAF Lossiemouth to destroy the ship. *Tirpitz* was hit by only two out of the twenty-nine Tallboys dropped, but nonetheless capsized in the shallows of Tromsø fjord. The final and decisive bomb – and this is important to the story which follows – was delivered by IX Squadron.

In 1947, a Norwegian company was salvaging the *Tirpitz* for scrap, when the salvage workers discovered that the German crew had painted a representation of the ship on one of the propeller shaft bulkheads. This bulkhead, weighing over 100 kilos and measuring 1,200 × 1,000mm, had just been removed from the ship when by chance a former member of IX Squadron called 'Jeep' Jenson visited Tromsø, heard about the bulkhead, and told the local authorities that if it ever became available it would be much appreciated by IX Squadron.

The bulkhead from *Tirpitz*

The Mayor of Tromsø duly passed the story to the Norwegian government, and in November 1949 the bulkhead was presented to the Royal Air Force and put on display at RAF Binbrook, where both IX and 617 Squadrons were then based. This turned out to be a very unfortunate coincidence, for soon after the trophy arrived at the RAF station, IX Squadron removed it from Station Headquarters and placed it in their own Squadron building. In due course, 617 Squadron responded by raiding IX Squadron and moving the bulkhead to a wall in their building.

The raids and counter-raids of the last remaining piece of the *Tirpitz* became an ongoing battle between the two Squadrons, occasionally at the taxpayers' expense. This was definitely the case when IX Squadron, while stationed in Cyprus in 1971 and temporarily without its *Tirpitz* souvenir, sent a Vulcan bomber to 617 Squadron's base at RAF Waddington. On landing, the IX Squadron crew removed the bulkhead, loaded it into the back of a commercial van, and had it driven to RAF Wittering. Although the IX Squadron Vulcan was searched before take-off by members of 617 Squadron, of course nothing was found. Then, just after take-off for Cyprus, the IX Squadron Captain declared an in-flight emergency and diverted the Vulcan to RAF Wittering. Here the recently arrived van pulled up next to the Vulcan bomb bay and the bulkhead was quickly transferred. Several hours later it arrived in Cyprus.

Eventually a truce was called in 1981 by both Squadrons and the bulkhead was moved to the Royal Air Force Museum in London. But that was by no means the end of the story. The following year, when IX Squadron learned that the bulkhead was lying on the floor in the Bomber Command Room at the RAF Museum, they immediately sent a team to recover it, prior to putting it on display at RAF Honington. From there in 1986 it moved with the Squadron to RAF Bruggen in Germany.

However, despite the *Tirpitz* bulkhead having spent nine unbroken years with its rivals, 617 Squadron's interest had not waned. While they were on exercise in Holland in 1991, a team of aircrew disguised as navvies broke into the IX Squadron crew room, removed the bulkhead, loaded it into a van, and then drove it to RAF Marham, where it was concreted into their crew room floor.

That should have been the end of the tit-for-tat raids, but the following year IX Squadron were engaged on Tornado trials with 617 Squadron. Although the IX Squadron crews were followed everywhere by their rivals, a member of IX Squadron managed to memorise the entry code to the 617 Squadron Headquarters, and was able to take some pictures of the bulkhead mounting. Back at RAF Bruggen, a plan was devised to recover the much-prized piece of the *Tirpitz*. Although the use of dynamite was seriously considered, in the end power tools were hired – but to no avail. After eight hours work under the cover of darkness, the bulkhead remained secure in its concrete bed. Indeed, when 617 Squadron were later moved to RAF Lossiemouth, it reputedly took four workmen several days to extricate the bulkhead from the floor. Aware of the likely attempts by IX Squadron to remove it from its new home in Scotland, 617 Squadron secured the last bit of the *Tirpitz* with steel bolts and welded nuts, and then installed an elaborate security system as further protection.

Finally, in 2001 it was agreed by both Squadrons that the *Tirpitz* bulkhead should return to the RAF Museum in London, so that it could be seen by the general public. On 8th November 2002, it was formally handed back to the museum for display.

Heinrich Himmler

Himmler's Compass (Meinstedt, 1945)
Although Hitler's Nazi Party was totally devoid of what any reasonably sane person would call a moral compass, it is ironic that one of the arch villains of the regime, the bespectacled Heinrich Himmler, Reichsführer of the SS, was captured with a compass in his pocket by British soldiers serving with the Royal Artillery. The five men involved were Lance Sergeants Patrick Mannion and William Morris, and Gunners Michael Fahy, John Fletcher and George Snee. An account of the event was later scribbled on a buff luggage label, and attached to the instrument:

> This compass was carried by HIMMLER – Head of the Nazi SS – at the time he
> was captured by the Regiment I was commanding – 73 Anti-Tank Regiment

Himmler's compass

RA – Monday evening May 21st 1945. He was arrested at a small hamlet called Meinstadt near Seedorf, North of Zeven, with two other SS officers, all disguised. Himmler had a black patch on one eye, but was wearing a military macintosh. He said he was recently discharged from hospital, having had severe ulcers. He had some 'medicine drops in a tube' which he said he had to take daily. These drops later turned out to be cyanide – with which he committed suicide on the Wednesday of the same week! A G Proudlock.

The body of Heinrich Himmler

Curiously, this story contradicts the version in Peter Longerich's biography of Himmler, published by Oxford University Press in 2012, which states that Himmler was detained at a checkpoint by former Soviet prisoners of war. However, this myth has since been debunked by a BBC North West Inside Out investigation, broadcast on 24th October 2016, and the true facts are also recorded in a permanent display at the Imperial War Museum.

Following his capture and the loss of his compass, Himmler, who at that point was unrecognised, was sent for interrogation, and later committed suicide by taking cyanide while being examined by a doctor at the headquarters of the Second British Army in Lüneburg. Himmler died unmourned and was hastily buried in an unmarked grave. His compass remained in the possession of the Proudlock family until it was loaned to Firepower – The Royal Artillery Museum, where its luminous dial was discovered to be so radioactive that, for the safety of the public and museum staff, it had to be stored in a lead-lined box. The museum was closed in 2016 and its collections are currently in store. At the time of going to print, it is intended that they will be redisplayed in a new Salisbury Plain Heritage Centre in Wiltshire, due to be opened in 2020.

Hitler's Desks & Cutlery (Berlin, 1945)

When Adolf Hitler stepped into the Reich Chancellery in Berlin on 30th January 1933, as the newly-elected Chancellor of Germany, he declared that the building was fit only for a soap company. However, it took him until January 1938 to give his favourite architect, Albert Speer, *carte blanche* and a blank cheque to build a new Reich Chancellery, as part of a masterplan for a rebuilt capital fit for the new German Reich.

Twelve months and ninety million Reichsmarks later

Hitler seated on one of his desks

Entry to the new Reich
Chancellery, Berlin

(2020: £49.5 million), the new Chancellery building had an imposing entrance, flanked by two nude bronze statues by Arno Breker, a hall that was double the length of the Hall of Mirrors at Versailles, seventeen-foot-high doors, and vast reception rooms. The offices – Hitler's was a mere 4,300 sq ft – were ready for occupation, although some of the decorations, were still undelivered two years later, including Hitler's personal office furniture and desk.

There are at least three desks still in existence which are known to have been used by Adolf Hitler. One, now in Berlin's Deutsches Historisches Museum, is a grand *bureau plat* designed by Albert Speer for Hitler's official office in the new Reich Chancellery. He used this room for entertaining official visitors, but seldom worked in it, until it became briefly the central war planning room in 1944. This desk was presumably moved to safe storage when the Battle of Berlin commenced.

Another is a small, plain kneehole desk of late-nineteenth-century design, which according to an illustrated article published in the *Daily Mail* on 1st June 2014, was taken by the Americans from Hitler's private quarters in the Berlin Chancellery. However, the maker's label on the back of the desk – clearly visible in a photograph in the *Daily Mail* article – establishes that the desk was made by M. Ballin of Promenadeplatz, Munich, and was supplied to Herr A Hitler of Flat 2, 16 Prinzregentenplatz, Munich, on 2nd November 1929, three years before Hitler was elected Reich Chancellor.

Given that Hitler's Munich flat remained fully furnished until the end of the war, when the Americans commandeered it as the headquarters of their Sector, there can be little doubt that this Munich-made desk never left that city. Following its use as an American headquarters, the fully-furnished Prinzregentenplatz flat was comprehensively looted by them.

Quite what happened next is a matter of conjecture. According to the *Daily Mail* article, the desk was in an American soldiers' rest home 'in Berlin' from 1957 to 1996, was then returned to the German government in 2000, now resides in a government storeroom in Weissensee near Berlin, and will 'never be sold' despite being worth hundreds of thousands of dollars. However, the same desk (as evidenced conclusively by photographs) was sold for a mere US$29,000 in 2018 by Milestones Auction of Willoughby, Ohio, USA. The desk was catalogued as having been a gift to Hitler from Princess Elsa Cantacuzene of Romania, who had married the German publisher Hugo Bruckmann in 1898, and became an early Nazi supporter; the catalogue also stated that the desk had been taken from Hitler's flat in Munich by American soldiers. By way of contrast, Paul Fraser Collectibles note that the desk on which the Munich Agreement was signed, sold in 2011 for US$423,000.

The third desk to be considered here is a large plain, art deco-style, mahogany-veneered kneehole desk with locking doors. It is in The Keep Military Museum in Dorchester, along with a letter establishing its provenance:

Hitler's last desk from the Führerbunker

Land Commissioner's Office

Dusseldorf

BAOR 4

Hitler's Writing Table

In September, 1945 the Russian Army started to remove the furniture from Hitler's Chancellory [*sic*] in the Russian Sector of Berlin. The Russian officer responsible for this work offered me a wooden writing table which he told me he had taken from Hitler's offices in the Chancellory. (Those who visited the Chancellory in those days will remember that the whole place was in a state of great confusion, with a large amount of furniture, some of it badly damaged, scattered in all directions).

On the following day the table the Russian officer had shown me was delivered to me at my residence in Kladow by the Russian army.

I have since utilised this table in my study, and now have great pleasure in presenting it to the Museum of my old Regiment.

W H A Bishop

Major General (Retd)

Commissioner

North Rhine Westphalia

22nd March, 1950

This would seem to be conclusive, particularly as sheets of Hitler's personal writing paper and a Christmas card signed by the Führer and dated 1943 still remain within its drawers. Or could the provenance be a Soviet lie? For General Bishop's gift to the Dorset museum is self-evidently *not* the desk from the Führer's grand office in the Reich

Chancellery, nor is it the Munich desk acquired by Hitler in 1929. It could of course have come from Hitler's private apartment in the old Reich Chancellery, except that there exists a Heinrich Hoffman photograph of that desk in 1934, and it is nothing like the one given by the Soviets to General Bishop.[3] Besides which, the Reich Chancellery had been reduced to a hollow ruin by air raids and artillery fire before the Russians ever got to it. Andrei Gromyko, a Soviet diplomat who visited the Reich Chancellery complex a few weeks after the fighting had ceased, described the scene:

3. This photograph can be found at *www.historyextra.com/period/second-world-war/where-did-hitler-live*

> We reached it not without difficulties. Ruined edifices, formless heaps of metal and ferro-concrete encumbered the way. To the very entrance of the Chancellery, the car could not approach. We had to reach it by foot … only walls remained, riddled by countless shrapnel, yawning by big shot-holes from shells. Ceilings survived only partly. Windows loomed black by emptiness.

Winston Churchill sits on a damaged chair from the Führerbunker, surrounded by British & Soviet officers

The one remaining office location from which the desk could have been taken is the Führerbunker, located beneath the old Reich Chancellery garden. By the time it was captured by the Soviets, this underground command centre was in disarray, but it was *not* bomb or shell damaged. As General Bishop's gift shows only minor damage to the base, and given that the Soviet officer had no need to lie, probably did not have a perfect command of English, and would almost certainly have referred to the Führerbunker as the Chancellery (albeit an underground part of it), the probability is that this is Hitler's last desk from his underground office in the Führerbunker.

Another trophy from the bunker was a set of Adolf Hitler's personal cutlery, which was liberated by the celebrated BBC war correspondent, Richard Dimbleby. Unfortunately, according to Dimbleby's son, Jonathan, these relics of the innermost circle of the Third Reich have since been mislaid, although he was keen to point out that they were never used by the Dimbleby family. However, this assertion is somewhat at odds with his father's account on the BBC's *Desert Island Discs* in 1958, when he said that if he ever entertained an awkward guest to dinner, he would ensure that their place was set with the Fuhrer's knife, fork and spoon.

The Spoils of Berchtesgaden (Bavarian Alps, 1945)

High up in the Bavarian Alps, set on a rocky pinnacle, is the remains of the Berghof, Hitler's weekend retreat, which he had built in 1935. Designed in the brutalist-modernist style so beloved of the Führer, the extant photographs show a grandiose and rather uncomfortable-looking house, with high ceilings and spectacular views. Here Hitler relaxed with his Alsatian dog *Blondi*, and his putative mistress and future wife Eva Braun, surrounded by fawning colleagues.

Braun was a naïve and highly-strung Bavarian *mädchen*, model and photographer, who came into Hitler's life after his previous companion, his half-niece Geli Raubal, had committed suicide in 1931. From then on, Braun was Hitler's companion, kept out of sight of all but his inner circle of cronies. She and Hitler killed themselves (and *Blondi*) in the Führer-bunker on 30th April 1945 after just forty hours of marriage. This was not Eva Braun's first suicide attempt; she having tried twice before. The Hon Unity Mitford, who was similarly smitten with Hitler, also unsuccessfully tried to kill herself in 1939.

Five days before Hitler's death, the Berghof and its surrounding Waffen-SS installations were the target of a British bombing raid. The following day the Bavarian buildings were torched by the SS, a few hours before the remains were ransacked by advancing US Army soldiers. One of the Americans, whose name has subsequently been forgotten, found in one of the Berghof's wrecked bunkers an opal cluster ring surrounded by rubies, a bright red lipstick in an 'EB' monogrammed silver container, and a pair of lilac-coloured silk knickers, trimmed with lace and white satin ribbon and embroidered with the initials 'EB'.

above, left to right

The Great Hall at the Berghof

Eva Braun at the Berghof, with Hitler and *Blondi*

Lee Miller, war correspondent

Grand Admiral Karl Doenitz

4. Now part of The Rifles

There can be no doubt that these items belonged to Eva Braun, although whether Hitler ever saw the knickers in place, or had to wipe the lipstick off his face, is a matter still being debated by historians, some of whom believe that while Miss Braun was undoubtedly besotted with the German dictator and willingly shared his fate, it is unlikely that she ever shared his bed. Whatever the truth of their relationship, the opal ring undoubtedly brought its original wearer bad luck. This was a fate not shared by a later owner, who sold it at auction in 2016 for £1,250, along with the lipstick which sold for £360. The frilly knickers, said in the auction catalogue to be clean and in good condition, were knocked down for £2,900, more than seven times the auction estimate.

Other items belonging to Eva Braun were removed from Hitler's Munich flat by Lee Miller, the only female American war photographer. Miller was with the lead US troops in Bavaria and was the first photographer into Dachau concentration camp, an experience that scarred her for life. She spent that night in the Prinzregentplatz apartment, where she was famously photographed naked in Hitler's bath, with her boots still covered in the filth of Dachau deliberately positioned on the bath mat in the foreground. Following her death in 1977, Miller's Nazi loot was bequeathed to a museum.

Grand Admiral Dönitz's Baton (Flensburg, 1945)

One of the most striking exhibits in the Shropshire Regimental Museum in Shrewsbury is the baton, or *Admiralstab*, of Grand Admiral Karl Dönitz, the last President of Nazi Germany. Dönitz was arrested in Flensburg on 23rd May 1945 by men of the RAF Regiment, and then handed over to the 4th (Territorial) Battalion of the King's Shropshire Light Infantry (KSLI).[4] The RAF Regiment Heritage Centre at RAF Honington still has the Grand Admiral's *Kriegsmarine* (German Navy) flag, taken during the arrest.

Dönitz's baton, which weighs about two pounds, is made of a hollow tube of silver covered in navy blue velvet, and is decorated with the eagle and swastika symbol of the Third Reich, navy fouled anchors, and Iron Crosses, all made of gold. The octagonal gold caps at either end are decorated in silver and platinum, with the badge of the German submarine service embossed on the top and a swastika on the base.

Grand Admiral Dönitz was a career submariner who had served in U-boats during the First World War. From 1st October 1939, he was the commander of the German U-boat fleet, which wreaked terrible damage on the British convoys sailing to and from North America. In recognition of this, and as an unshakeably loyal Nazi, Dönitz was appointed Commander-in-Chief of the German Navy on 30th January 1943, and was simultaneously promoted to Grand Admiral and given his baton by Adolf Hitler.

A Nazi Admiralstab depicted on a Grand Admiral's flag

Dönitz continued in this naval role until Hitler's suicide in 1945. In his will, the Führer named Dönitz as his chosen successor as President, and Joseph Goebbels as Chancellor. Amazingly, there was stiff competition for these roles from other self-deluded senior members of Hitler's murderous mob, most notably Reich Marshal Hermann Göring and Martin Bormann, Hitler's private secretary. As Germany imploded, the Grand Admiral, who was motivated by the imperative to save his countrymen from the Russian advance, immediately adopted the role bequeathed to him by the deceased Führer, and established a skeleton Nazi government in Flensburg on the German-Danish border. It was here that he was taken into custody twenty-three days later by the Shropshire lads, who found in his baggage his Grand Admiral's baton. This in due course ended up on the desk of the KSLI's Brigade Commander, Brigadier (later Major General) 'Jack' Churcher, of the 159th Infantry Brigade.

In 1964 Churcher donated the baton to the KSLI's regimental museum in Shrewsbury. In the meantime, Dönitz had been put on trial at Nuremburg, and was found guilty on two counts of planning, initiating and waging wars of aggression, and committing crimes against the laws of war; he was acquitted of conspiracy to commit crimes against humanity. At the insistence of the Soviet government (the Allies would have set him free), he was sentenced to ten years' imprisonment in Spandau Prison, from where he was released on 1st October 1956. In this he was luckier than his Chancellor and the other would-be contenders for the top Nazi jobs, who all committed suicide. Josef Goebbels and his wife killed themselves in the Führerbunker, she having previously drugged and then poisoned their six children; Martin Bormann bit on a cyanide capsule to avoid being

The arrest of Grand Admiral Doenitz

The Shropshire Regimental
Museum

5. The various batons of Admiral
Dönitz are extensively covered at
www.wcstumpmilitaria.blogspot.co.uk

captured by the Russians; and Hermann
Göring also used cyanide to avoid the
hangman on the eve of his execution.

The ex-Grand Admiral lived in retirement for the next twenty-four years, dying
on Christmas Eve 1980 aged eighty-nine.
In his will, and despite the fact that he had
been relieved of his baton in 1945, Dönitz
bequeathed his *Admiralstab* to a German
naval veterans' organisation, the *Deutsche
Marinebund*, with instructions that it be
displayed in the German submarine ser-
vice's Laboe Naval Memorial and Museum near Kiel. According to an
assistant at the Shropshire Regimental Museum, and with remarkable
chutzpah given all the circumstances, the veteran German submariners
promptly demanded the return of the baton. They did so on the grounds
that it was the personal possession of the late Grand Admiral, and
therefore could not be deemed a spoil of war. After consulting with their
lawyers, who ruled that the baton was a legitimate spoil of war, the
Shropshire Regimental Museum replied with a firm *nein*, and there the
matter was allowed to rest.

However, there remains a slight complication with regard to Dönitz's
wand of office now in the Shrewsbury museum, for it is not the only one
in existence. Without going into the various claims and counterclaims by
the owners of other so-called Dönitz batons, it would seem that the one
acquired by the KSLI was actually the *second* baton paid for and
presented to the Grand Admiral by Hitler, the first having been rejected
by Dönitz because it was not embossed with the badge of his beloved
submarine service.[5]

It is testimony to Dönitz's standing with Hitler – and possibly a
contributing factor to Hitler's testamentary nomination of the Grand
Admiral as President – that the submariner could have looked this
particularly short-fused and utterly ruthless gift horse in the mouth and
lived to tell the tale. Anyway, notwithstanding the existence of any other
real or fake *Admiralstab*, there can be no doubt that the one in Shrewsbury was that used by Dönitz, and even more convincingly it is the one
that his ageing ex-matelot heirs wanted back.

Spoils from the Land of the Rising Sun

A Japanese regimental flag, an officer's sword, and an imperial sword hilt (Burma, 1945)

Despite the Allies' European triumphs in late-1944 and early-1945, the war in the Far East continued to rage for several more months. By February 1945, Lieutenant General Sir William Slim and the British 14th Army were making successful advances against the Japanese in central Burma. At the same time, a combined American and Chinese force was pressing forward from the north-east; and the 15th Corps, under Lieutenant General Sir Philip Christison, was harassing the enemy on the south-western coastal strip known as the Arakan. The operations of the latter were intended to keep the Japanese forces there occupied, prevent them from joining the main battle in central Burma, and secure parts of the Mandalay to Rangoon road as a supply route for the 14th Army when it reached the lower reaches of the Irrawaddy River.

The Allied offensive in the Arakan began in December 1944. By the end of January 1945, Christison's troops – the 25th and 26th Indian Divisions, 81st and 82nd West African Divisions, 3 Commando Brigade and 50 Indian Tank Brigade – had captured much of the coastal strip. Cutting their enemy's escape route to the north, they scattered the Japanese into the hills, leaving behind over a thousand dead and vast quantities of guns and equipment.

Lieutenant General Sir William Slim

In support of this offensive, the 22nd (East African) Brigade, which included the 3rd Battalion Northern Rhodesian Regiment under the command of Lieutenant Colonel J W E Mackenzie, arrived in Burma in December 1944. Initially, the East Africans were given the subsidiary task of guarding the 25th Indian Division's lines of communication, and in February 1945 mopping-up small groups of Japanese who had dispersed into corners of the coastal island of Ramree, which had been initially invaded by the 26th Indian Division in January.

Hunting the Japanese in thick jungle and swamp was a dangerous and difficult task, and unlike anything the 22nd (EA) Brigade had undertaken during training. However, the patrolling provided valuable experience for the combat to come. In mid-March 1945, they were ordered to sail from Ramree to the mainland, to help with the clearance of sections of the Mandalay to Rangoon road. On landing, the 22nd (EA) Brigade were ordered south to join the 4th Indian Brigade, who were attacking Taungup, a vital 110-mile-long pass over the mountain range from the coastal strip to the Irrawaddy valley. The move involved a 127-mile march, through Japanese-occupied jungle and bamboo forests, with many hills and two major *chaungs* to cross, and all to be achieved in ten days. By leap-frogging over each other, the three Regiments of the 22nd (EA) – the 1st King's African Rifles, 1st Rhodesian African Rifles, and the 3rd Northern Rhodesian Regiment – completed their epic advance.

In April, the Brigade's first task was to attack the northern flank of a Japanese force covering the Taungup pass. One of the first and most successful actions was undertaken on 11th to 12th April by the Northern Rhodesian Regiment, under Lieutenant Colonel Mackenzie, when they conducted a deep outflanking move against the Japanese lines of communication and their line of retreat. This was achieved by using an elephant track, while carrying just four days' rations, four mortars, two No. 22 wireless sets and charging engines, and with only a troop of medium artillery in support.

Earlier in the month, one of the Brigade's patrols caught some Japanese eating their lunch, captured their regimental flag, killed three of the enemy and wounded another three before withdrawing. The Japanese, thrown into total confusion, continued to fire, mainly at each other, for another half an hour.

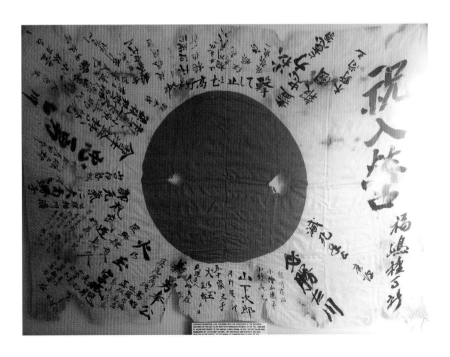

Japanese Regimental Flag, Burma, 1945

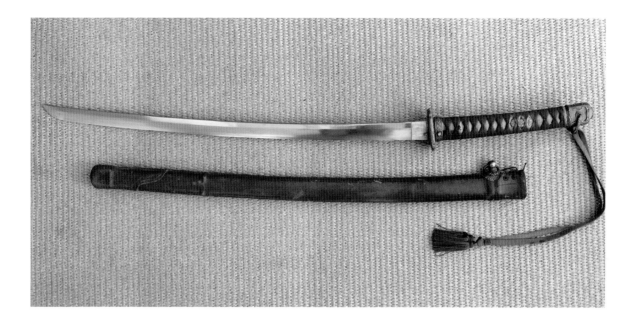

Towards the end of April, the 22nd (EA) Brigade faced stiffening resistance as they approached the final, strongly-defended Japanese positions. Named by the British 'Berger' and 'Valerie', these were situated on the razor-edged peak of a precipitous feature rising to 900 feet and covered in dense bamboo. On 26th April, following an airstrike and an artillery bombardment, the Rhodesian African Regiment and the King's African Rifles attacked and drove the Japanese from both positions. Meanwhile the Northern Rhodesian Rifles maintained their pressure on the Japanese rear flank.

Plans for further major attacks on adjoining positions at the beginning of May were cancelled, when it was found that the Japanese had abandoned them, after firing all the artillery they were unable to remove from their ammunition dumps. Shortly afterwards, the 22nd (EA) Brigade was ordered to regroup on the Taungup Pass. With heavy monsoon rains rapidly destroying all the tracks, artillery could no longer be brought forward, and it was impossible to maintain the Brigade in action any longer on air support. However, Lieutenant Colonel Mackenzie and his Northern Rhodesian Regiment pursued the Japanese for another fifty miles down the pass, capturing vast quantities of equipment, including an old British 25-pounder gun.

Perhaps fortunately for his descendants, Lieutenant Colonel Mackenzie returned the enormous 25-pounder gun he had liberated from the Japanese to the British Army. However, at the end of the Second World War, he

Japanese officer's sword, Burma, 1945

Japanese officer's sword hilt, Burma, 1945

went back to his home in East Africa with three spoils of war from his fighting in Burma.

One was the Japanese flag, signed by all the officers of their Regiment; the second was a fine officer's sword, compete with its leather sheath; and the third was the hilt from a Japanese sword, one of many issued to the officers by the Emperor, all of which were unique and so personalised their weapons.

Lieutenant Colonel Mackenzie's achievements with the 3rd Northern Rhodesian Regiment in the Second World War were recognised in March 1947, when – perhaps to his surprise – the insignia of the Distinguished Service Order was posted to him in Nairobi by Air Mail from the War Office in London. The Warrant for the medal followed by Registered Post in May, although the appointment had been published in the London Gazette in June 1946.

CHAPTER 30

MALAYAN EMERGENCY (1948–1960)

Cap in Hand

A Communist insurgent's Cap (Malaya, 1950–51)

The Malayan Emergency was one of a number of post-Second World War conflicts intended to suppress the rise of Communism in South-East Asia. It was fought largely in jungle terrain between soldiers of the British Commonwealth and the Malayan National Liberation Army (MNLA), the military wing of the Malayan Communist Party. The fighting pre- and post-dated the independence of Malaya from Britain in 1957.

In the early part of 1948, the MNLA established a series of jungle bases in central Malaya and began attacking British colonial government targets and Commonwealth military installations, while also terrorising workers in the country's strategically important rubber plantations. To combat

Wounded insurgent being held and questioned after his capture, 1952

269

the MNLA, the British formed rapid-response units, which were deployed on a series of 'search-and-destroy' missions.

In October 1950, Captain Michael Wyndham of The Life Guards (the last in a long line of Wyndhams who had served in the Household Cavalry and the Foot Guards since 1660) was seconded to one such unit formed by officers and men of Sir Winston Churchill's former Regiment, the 4th Queen's Own Hussars.[1]

1. Amalgamated with the 8th King's Royal Irish Hussars in 1958 to form The Queen's Royal Irish Hussars. This Regiment was amalgamated in 1993 with The Queen's Own Hussars to form The Queen's Royal Hussars

Out on patrol in the jungle with his soldiers, Wyndham was hacking through the dense vegetation with his machete, when suddenly – no more than three feet in front of him – there appeared a small man, dressed in a shabby, grey-blue Mao suit and a cap adorned with a red Communist star. When recalling this encounter, Wyndham would always say, in a laconic tone of voice: 'He made the mistake of trying to raise his gun to his shoulder; I pulled out my pistol and shot from the hip. I won!' Having dispatched the Communist insurgent, Captain Wyndham removed the man's cap and kept it as a souvenir.

Meanwhile, back in England, Air Chief Marshal Sir William Elliott had been appointed Chairman of the British Joint Services Mission at the Pentagon in Washington DC. A long-standing friend of Wyndham's father, Colonel Hon Humphrey Wyndham (a former Commanding Officer of The Life Guards), Elliott announced that he wanted the young Life Guard as his ADC. 'You can't have him', his Staff replied. 'Why not?' said the Air Chief Marshal. 'We don't know where he is,' was the answer.

Tich

Hugh Cubitt

Tony Bethell

Captain Michael Wyndham
LG, *back left*

Eventually, it was discovered that Wyndham was deep in the Malayan jungle, a search was instigated, and he was extracted and returned immediately to the UK. He spent the journey in a state of considerable anxiety, as those sent to find him had no idea why he was being recalled, and he therefore assumed that he had committed some unknown crime and was in terrible trouble.

Greatly relieved to discover that the reason for his extraction was a posting to Washington, the twenty-two-year-old bachelor soon found himself much in demand in the US capital as an escort for unaccompanied females on the diplomatic circuit. However, the Americans at the Pentagon were perpetually confused by Wyndham's Service Dress uniform of breeches, boots, spurs, Sam Browne belt, and the three brass Garter stars of a Life

Guards Captain on his shoulders, assuming him to be – despite his evident youth – a 3-star General from some unspecified South American country. His spurs also made their mark. A secretary in the Pentagon, when writing handover notes for her successor, said:

> Captain Wyndham is the one who continuously needs to rest his legs – on the desk. Do not object to this, but if you would be so kind as to note each morning whether he is or is not in possession of his spurs, you will be doing Captain Wyndham, The Life Guards, and the Pentagon Stationery Office a great service. The spurs are apparently necessary to prevent his feet from sliding off the desk.

And what of Wyndham's spoil of war from the Malayan Emergency? Before leaving for the United States, he gave the cap with its red star to his four-year-old nephew, David Cobbold, who took it with him to school. Unsurprisingly, it was much admired by all the other boys, and treated with as much reverence as an Abyssinian crown.

CHAPTER 31

INDONESIA-MALAYSIA CONFRONTATION (1963–1966)

A Headhunter's Trophy
The skull of a Chinaman (Sarawak, c. 1857 & 1966)
In a storage box in the reserve collection of The Highlanders' Museum at Fort George, Inverness, resides a smoke-stained human skull. The story of how it came to be there is related by General Sir Jeremy Mackenzie:

> From 1964 to 1966, I was attached to 22 SAS in Borneo where units of the British Army, along with other Commonwealth troops, were involved in an

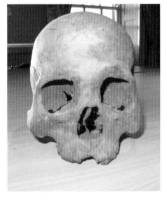

Skull of a Chinaman

Borneo head hunters

undeclared war, euphemistically referred to as a 'confrontation', with Indonesia. This confrontation had arisen because of President Sukarno's ambition to create a Greater Indonesia through the acquisition of Sabah, Sarawak and Brunei.

Sukarno's version of events was that the creation of the Federation of Malaysia in 1963, through the British-led amalgamation of Singapore, North Borneo, Brunei, Sarawak and the states of the Malayan peninsula, was a direct threat to the sovereignty of Indonesia and the actual *causus belli*. Whatever the reason, British Forces – and the Special Air Service (SAS) in particular – were deployed in considerable numbers in one of the British Empire's last acts of gunboat diplomacy. General Mackenzie continues:

Brigadier (later General Sir) Jeremy Mackenzie in the jungle

> As my previous job had been training Indian Army paramilitaries, I had the responsibility of teaching local tribesmen to operate deep in the jungle behind the Indonesians, particularly along the rivers which were the Indonesian Army's principle lines of communication. The tribesmen under our command were primitive peoples, Muruts in my case, who had only recently given up being head-hunters. Evidence of their headhunting activities was very much on display in their communal longhouses, where the skulls of their victims were hung in wicker baskets around the rooves' supporting poles; as trophies of battle, they were afforded considerable respect.

The Muruts (the word means 'hill people') still flourish today along the Sapulut and Padas Rivers, and the border areas of Sarawak. They were the last of the tribes in the region to give up headhunting, which was an important part of their culture. For example, a tribesman could only get married once he had presented his prospective in-laws with at least one enemy head. General Mackenzie, again:

> At the end of my tour with the Muruts, to my considerable surprise I was presented with one of these skulls which, so I was told by my pupils, was that of a Chinaman killed by their forebears in 1857, when they were under the command of another Briton, James Brooke (known to history as the White Rajah of Sarawak), whose self-appointed task had been to supress piracy in the region. The skull was, therefore, not only an appropriate gift but, because these trophies were highly valued by the tribe, it was also a significant albeit rather grisly one.

Rajah Brooke was one of the great swashbuckling figures of the mid-nineteenth century, who embodied all the virtues supposed to typify the builders of 'the Empire upon which the sun never set'. Handsome and dashing, Brooke was the second son of Thomas Brooke, an East India Company judge and his second wife, Anna Maria Stuart, the daughter of the 9th Lord Blantyre and his mistress, Harriet Teasdale. Raised in India until the age of twelve, he boarded briefly at Norwich Grammar School, before running away. When his parents returned to live in Bath, he acquired a private tutor. During a brief period soldiering in Burma, he was wounded in one lung, although the oft-repeated assertion that he lost his testicles as well is not true. Brooke then turned to commerce but was unsuccessful. The fortuitous inheritance of £30,000 in 1835 (2020: £3.7 million) allowed him to purchase a 142-ton schooner, with which he began a mission to eliminate piracy in the South China Seas. This resulted in 1842 with Brooke being ceded sovereignty of Sarawak in perpetuity. Probably homosexual, Brooke had no children and was succeeded as the White Rajah by his sister's second son, Sir Charles Brooke. General Mackenzie ends his story:

Sir James Brooke, the White Rajah of Sarawak

In due course, I returned to the UK with the decapitated remains of the Chinaman. At Heathrow, I had considerable difficulty persuading HM Customs & Excise that I was not an accomplice in some horrific murder. Eventually they let it through, without either raising duty on my gift or placing me in the hands of the police, and I deposited the skull with my mother at our family home in Dorset.

To say that my mother was less than delighted with this gruesome trophy would be a considerable understatement. She was even less than impressed when I explained that, according to the Murut tradition, every six months the skull had to be smoked and then walked around the boundary of the house, so that the spirit attached to the skull could observe any additions to the property and thereby not become restless. I also warned her that, according to the Muruts, if these procedures were not followed the spirit in the skull would break up the house.

Unfortunately, my mother did not observe the Murut traditions and, instead, consigned my Chinese spirit to the attic. She soon wished that she hadn't: without any reason, pictures fell from the walls, a glass decanter – a family heirloom of great antiquity – shattered, as did a large Chinese vase. At this point my mother decided that enough was enough, and I was instructed by her to send the skull to The Highlanders' Museum at Fort George. This I did, along with clear instructions that it should be taken round the museum before being placed in a display cabinet.

Despite this warning, the skull was consigned first to a storage box and then, in 1978, it was placed on display along with other souvenirs of the Borneo campaign. It wasn't long before inexplicable injuries to the museum's staff and property started to occur and the Chinaman's head was returned to its box. When I heard of these mishaps I was in Hong Kong, but nonetheless I told the Curator to do as I had earlier instructed my mother to do and all would be well. So, one bleak winter's evening the skull was duly walked around Fort George – since when there have been no problems.

The skull can be viewed, by those brave enough to risk it, by applying to the Curator of The Highlanders' Museum, Fort George, Inverness.

CHAPTER 32

THE TROUBLES, ULSTER (1968–1998)

The Colonel's Tipple
A bottle of IRA poteen (RAF Long Kesh, near Lisburn, 1970)

The Life Guards is the most senior Regiment of the British Army. It is also the most often re-roled of any British Regiment, having since its formation prior to 1660 fought as ship-borne marines, horsed-infantry, dismounted infantry, camel-borne infantry, cycle-borne infantry, Land Rover-borne infantry, heavy cavalry, in tanks, helicopters and armoured cars, and as a truck-borne heavy machine gun Regiment and a tractor-towed siege artillery Battery. As further evidence of its multi-tasking capability, the antecedent formations of The Life Guards had also – albeit in the sectarian days of the late-seventeenth century – included a Scottish Troop, a Catholic Troop, and a Dutch Troop.

Major (later Brigadier Sir) Arthur Gooch and soldiers of The Life Guards confront rioters in Belfast

Trooper Hadfield and Lance Corporal of Horse Savage of The Life Guards, Belfast

It is not therefore surprising that 'B' Squadron of The Life Guards (in which the author was at the time a Troop Leader) was the first armoured car unit to be posted to Northern Ireland in August 1969, as part of Op BANNER. This was an operation to provide military support for the Northern Ireland garrison, in the face of the violent Protestant backlash, which followed the Catholic civil rights protests and the minor Stormont parliamentary reforms of 1968. It was the start of a succession of tours of duty for The Life Guards in Northern Ireland, which continued virtually unbroken until 1982.

From early-1969 until mid-1971 the Regiment was commanded by Lieutenant Colonel Desmond Langley, later Major General Sir Desmond Langley and the Governor of Bermuda. An amiable but highly professional officer with a carefully controlled stammer, like many of his colleagues Langley enjoyed the comfort of a drink, providing it was taken in moderation.

Although he was not in Northern Ireland in 1969, Langley found himself there in 1970. A larger formation of Life Guards, including Regimental Headquarters (RHQ) and HQ Squadron, was sent to the Province in armoured cars for the second time, although the vehicles had long-since shown themselves to be completely unusable in urban riot situations. Based at a Nissen-hutted, Second World War RAF station called Long Kesh, which was later rebuilt as the notorious Maze Prison, RHQ had to

Colonel (later Major General Sir) Desmond Langley

content itself with deploying its armoured car-equipped Troops to support the Royal Ulster Constabulary (RUC), and the recently-formed Ulster Defence Regiment (UDR), with armoured vehicle patrols along the porous Ulster-Eire border between Newry and Crossmaglen.

In the course of these military activities, Langley became friendly with his opposite numbers in the RUC and UDR, one of whom presented The Life Guards' Commanding Officer with a spoil of war which had been acquired during a police raid on a suspected IRA house. Although the raid had not produced any Catholic terrorists, weapons or bombs, it had resulted in the police uncovering an illegal whisky still. The spoil of war was a green glass medicine bottle of poteen, the bootlegged and home-distilled potato spirit reputed to be as alcoholically powerful – and as dangerous – as absinthe.

Rather than send the poteen back to the Regiment's museum, then located in Windsor, Colonel Langley decided to try it for himself. He found that neat, poteen was completely undrinkable. He then experimented by diluting the potato spirit with a variety of different mixers. At last he found a combination that was palatable. 'You know,' Langley said before lunch one day, 'it's really not that b-bad if you d-dilute it with a splash of t-tonic water.'

CHAPTER 33

FALKLANDS WAR (1982)

To the Victor the Spoils

An Argentinian Army Artillery Laser Rangefinder (Port Stanley, 1982)

The British government often likes to boast that, while Britain's Army is small, it is the best equipped and trained in the world. The truth of the first of these claims rarely bears close inspection, as emerged during the Falklands War in 1982.

Since time immemorial, artillery has zeroed in on its targets using a technique known as 'bracketing'. This involves estimating the range to the target and firing a shell. If it falls short, the range is increased so that the second shell falls beyond the target (or *vice versa* if the first shell falls long). The range is then reduced by fifty percent of the difference, and the third shell should then fall slap on top of its intended victim. In the late 1970s, a Norwegian firm called Simrad perfected an electronic device which used a laser beam to determine the precise range to the target, thereby eliminating the need for bracketing. Being squeamish about defence exporting, the Norwegian government licensed the technology to an international defence electronics company called Avimo Ltd, which was based at Taunton in Somerset.

The sales team at Avimo quickly found a ready market for these artillery laser rangefinders in armies around the world, including that of Argentina. However, they were rebuffed by the UK's Ministry of Defence, who thought that bracketing was more cost effective – and more manly – than the purchase of expensive laser rangefinders. So, when the British Task Force set sail to recapture the Falkland Islands on 5th April 1982, its artillery was equipped with nothing better than the bracketing technique.

The Yomper, Falklands War Memorial, Royal Marines Museum, Portsmouth

Argentinian POWs awaiting
repatriation

This deficiency notwithstanding, the Task Force triumphed, and by
14th June 1,313 Argentinians were prisoners-of-war, along with considerable quantities of their arms, ammunition and military equipment.
Amongst the captured swag was a quantity of artillery laser rangefinders,
which the men of 29 Commando Regiment Royal Artillery duly acquired
as legitimate spoils of war. However, many of these laser rangefinders
had been damaged during the conflict and were inoperable. In an attempt

to rectify the damage, the Gunners opened up the equipment. Much to their surprise they found the maker's label
inside the steel cases: Avimo Ltd.

Once safely back in England, a letter was duly sent by the
Royal Artillery to Avimo, requesting an estimate for the
repair of the equipment. By return the Gunners received a
letter from Avimo's chairman, the future Chief of Defence
Procurement and Lord Mayor of London, Peter Levene
(later Lord Levene of Portsoken KBE), offering to repair
the lasers at no cost. These ex-Argentinian laser rangefinders remained in unofficial service with the Royal
Artillery, until some years later the Ministry of Defence –
in its wisdom – decided to procure its own stock.

Avimo's LP3

ABOUT THE AUTHOR

Educated at Oxford University and the Royal Military Academy Sandhurst, Christopher Joll was commissioned into The Life Guards in 1968, served four tours of duty in Northern Ireland, and in 1975 left the Army to go into business.

At the turn of the Millennium, after twenty-five years in the City, industry, and latterly running the UK's leading commercial real estate public relations consultancy, Christopher decided to concentrate on devising, writing and directing major and national events for charities. Among a long list, these included the Household Cavalry Pageant on Horse Guards Parade, the British Military Tournament at Earls Court, the Gurkha 200 Pageant at the Royal Hospital Chelsea, and *The Great War Symphony* at the Royal Albert Hall, for which he researched and edited a sixty-minute film of Imperial War Museum archival material.

At the same time, Christopher embarked on writing books, articles and reviews. These have included *Uniquely British: A Year in the Life of the Household Cavalry*, the best-selling illustrated book with a foreword by HM The Queen, and *The Drum Horse in the Fountain: Tales of the Heroes & Rogues in the Guards*. Since 1st April 2013, every six months Christopher has published successive books in an ongoing series of nineteenth- and twentieth-century military-historical 'faction' stories, collectively known as *The Speedicut Saga*, which have been featured in *The Times* and have been recommended by Stephen Fry.

Christopher is also a regular podcaster and lecturer, and is an adviser on militaria for Cheffins, the Cambridge-based auctioneers. Awarded the Army Museums Ogilby Trust Prize in 1968, he is a trustee of the Museum of the Year Prize, for which in 2019 he wrote and directed a series of short films about commercially innovative British museums (*Thinking Outside the Box*). One of the founder donors of the Household Cavalry Museum at Horse Guards, London, in 2017 Christopher was appointed the Regimental Historian of the Household Cavalry.

APPENDICES

1. *Styles, titles, honorifics & regimental names*

As a general rule, I have used the ranks and titles of those mentioned which they held at the time of the events described in the text. So, Field Marshal the Earl Haig, as he was from 1919, is styled as General Sir Douglas Haig, which was his rank and title when he is mentioned in connection with trench warfare. Similarly, Field Marshal Duke of Wellington is variously styled in the text as Colonel Hon Arthur Wellesley, Lieutenant General Sir Arthur Wellesley, General Viscount Wellington and General Marquess of Wellington, as appropriate to the battle or campaign under consideration.

When the description of a spoil of war covers an extended period – such as Lawrence of Arabia's Hejaz Railway bell – I have tended to omit any mention of the person's ascending and/or descending rank as to do so would unnecessarily clutter the text. For the record, T E Lawrence started the First World War as a Lieutenant and ended the war as a Colonel; in 1922, he became an Aircraftsman in the Royal Air Force, then a Private in the Royal Tank Corps, followed by the re-adoption of his RAF rank; he died a civilian.

The matter of including honorific post-nominals also created problems of clarity, as particularly in the nineteenth century the number of honours bestowed on an individual frequently increased in number, or changed with promotion within an Order, as a campaign progressed. In the end, and with the single exception of the Victoria Cross (VC), I decided to exclude them altogether, for which I apologise to the shades of departed Knights Grand Cross, Knights Commander, Knights Companion, Knights Bachelor, Commanders, Companions, Officers, Lieutenants and Members of Britain's myriad Orders of Chivalry.

As the result of military reforms, role re-designation and/ or amalgamations, almost every Regiment in the British Army has changed its name in the course of its history, often more than once. In the Line Infantry, the original designation was 'Regiment of Foot' until the Childers Reforms of 1881, when

Regiments were given county affiliations, and then more recently national identification. So, the 24th Regiment of Foot, raised in 1689, became the South Wales Borderers in 1881, then the Royal Regiment of Wales, and is now part of the Royal Welsh. The names of Line Cavalry Regiments are even more complex. To give but one example: Humphrey Gore's Regiment of Dragoons, raised in 1715, became – in succession through re-designation and later through amalgamation – Cobham's Regiment of Dragoons, the 10th Regiment of Dragoons, the 10th (Prince of Wales's Own) Regiment of (Light) Dragoons, the 10th (Prince of Wales's Own) Regiment of (Light) Dragoons (Hussars), the 10th (The Prince of Wales's Own) Royal Hussars, the 10th Royal Hussars (Prince of Wales's Own), The Royal Hussars (Prince of Wales's Own), and is currently The King's Royal Hussars. Given that most of the readers of this book will not be military identity wonks, I have used the regimental titles borne during the events described and then, in footnotes, noted some of their evolution to their present titles.

2. *Principal British Campaigns 1337–2014*

Campaigns included in this volume are in *italics*

1337–1453	*Hundred Years' War*
1585–1604	Anglo-Spanish War
1627–1629	Anglo-French War
1642–1651	*English Civil War*
1652–1654	First Anglo-Dutch War
1665–1667	Second Anglo-Dutch War
1672–1674	Third Anglo-Dutch War
1688–1697	Nine Years' War
1689–1690	First Jacobite Rising
1701–1714	War of the Spanish Succession
1715–1716	Second Jacobite Rising
1740–1748	*War of the Austrian Succession*
1745–1746	Third Jacobite Rising
1746–1748	First Carnatic War (India)

1749–1754	Second Carnatic War (India)
1756–1763	*Seven Years' War*
1756–1763	Third (and final) Carnatic War
1767–1769	First Anglo-Mysore War (India)
1775–1782	First Anglo-Maratha War (India)
1775–1783	*American War of Independence*
1778–1783	*Anglo-French War*
1780–1784	Fourth (and final) Anglo-Dutch War
1780–1784	Second Anglo-Mysore War (India)
1790–1792	Third Anglo-Mysore War (India)
1792–1802	*French Revolutionary Wars*
1798–1799	*Fourth (and final) Anglo-Mysore War (India)*
1803–1805	Second Anglo-Maratha War (India)
1803–1806	*War of the Third Coalition*
1804–1810	*The West Indies Campaign*
1807–1814	Gunboat War (Denmark–Norway)
1807–1812	Anglo-Russian War
1807–1814	*Peninsular War (Spain)*
1812–1815	*War of 1812 (USA)*
1813–1814	War of the Sixth Coalition
1815	*The Hundred Days (Belgium)*
1817–1818	Third Anglo-Maratha War (India)
1823–1831	*First Anglo-Ashanti War (West Africa)*
1824–1826	First Anglo-Burmese War
1839–1842	First Anglo-Afghan War
1839–1842	First Opium War (China)
1843	*Sindh Campaign (NW India)*
1845–1846	First Anglo-Sikh War (NW India)
1848–1849	Second (and final) Anglo-Sikh War (NW India)
1850–1864	Taiping Rebellion (China)
1852–1853	Second Anglo-Burmese War
1853–1856	*Crimean War*
1856–1857	Anglo-Persian War
1857–1858	*Indian Mutiny*
1856–1860	*Second (and final) Opium War (China)*
1863–1864	Second Anglo-Ashanti War (West Africa)
1867–1868	*Abyssinia Expedition*
1873–1874	*Third Anglo-Ashanti War (West Africa)*
1878–1880	Second Anglo-Afghan War
1879	*Anglo-Zulu War*
1879–1882	*Urabi Revolt (Egypt)*
1880–1881	First Boer War (South Africa)
1881–1899	*Mahdist War (Sudan)*
1885	*Third (and final) Anglo-Burmese War*
1895–1896	Fourth Anglo-Ashanti War (West Africa)
1897	Benin Expedition (West Africa)
1899–1901	*Boxer Rebellion & Siege of Peking Legations (China)*
1899–1902	*Second (and final) Boer War (South Africa)*
1900	Fifth (and final) Anglo-Ashanti War (West Africa)
1914–1918	*First World War*
1916–1918	*Arab Revolt*
1917–1922	Russian Civil War
1919	Third Anglo-Afghan War
1939–1945	*Second World War*
1948–1960	*Malayan Emergency*
1950–1953	Korean War
1952–1960	Mao–Mao Uprising (Kenya)
1955–1959	Cyprus Emergency
1956–1957	*Suez Crisis*
1963–1966	*Indonesia–Malaysia Confrontation*
1963–1967	Aden Emergency
1968–1998	*The Troubles (Northern Ireland)*
1982	*Falklands War*
1990–1991	Gulf War
1998–1999	Kosovo War
2001–2014	War in Afghanistan (Fourth Anglo-Afghan War)
2003–2011	Iraq War

3. *Prize law, prize money & prize auctions*

Many of the items included in this book were acquired through the internationally accepted and legally sanctioned system, developed from the seventeenth century onwards, under which spoils of war were monetized and the proceeds distributed to the victorious combatants. Given the nature and size of the items captured, the methodology used differed between the Royal Navy and the Army.

In the case of the Royal Navy, where the items concerned were usually ships and their cargoes, the system was governed by Prize Law and regulated by the Admiralty-run Prize Courts. Although the implementation of Prize Law depended on circumstances, the following general principle operated. In the wake of the capture of an enemy vessel, a Prize Crew would sail it to the nearest British-controlled port, where an Admiralty Prize Court would be convened. It was the job of the Prize Court to establish British legal title to the ship and its cargo, and then dispose of it, either by sale to a third-party or through acquisition by the Admiralty. Either way, the value of the prize was established and the cash proceeds, known as Prize Money, were distributed by rank to the crew that captured the vessel.

Individual Prize Money for a single captured ship could amount to as much as twenty times an ordinary seaman's annual pay, and was in consequence a very important incentive, particularly when more than one ship was captured during a campaign. In the case of the senior ranks, vast fortunes were accumulated by some, resulting in the acquisition of large estates and the construction of substantial houses. The allocation of Prize Money was not, however, without controversy, and the decision of Prize Courts was often challenged, resulting in hearings that could last for years.

One particular case hinged on whether or not Vice Admiral Thomas Griffin, Commander-in-Chief of the East Indies Station, was entitled to Prize Money. On 30th April 1748, off Cape Comorin, HMS *Medway's Prize*, part of Admiral Griffin's Squadron, captured the *Santa Catherina*. This was a French-owned but Portuguese-crewed merchantman, leased to Armenian merchants trading between the Persian Gulf and India. According to the records now held at the National Maritime Museum, the *Santa Catherina* had a cargo of fifty chests of silver *zolotas*, fruit, dates, almonds, wine and rosewater, and was on a voyage from Basra to Calcutta when captured. In the middle of that year Griffin was replaced as Commander-in-Chief by Vice Admiral Edward Boscawen, and at the start of 1749 Griffin sailed for England. In his absence *en route* to England, the *Santa Catherina* and its cargo were sold by a Vice Admiralty Court in India. Because he was no longer 'in post', Admiral Griffin was not on the list for the distribution of the very substantial Prize Money. Griffin challenged the decision in the Admiralty Court in London, and after a case which lasted four years, the Court found against him.

For the Army, the system was somewhat different, more immediate and less protracted. At the close of a successful battle or a campaign, the General Officer-in-Command would appoint from his Staff one or more Prize Agents who would form a Prize Committee. The Committee's job was to cen-tralise the spoils, which could include captured or abandoned cannons, horses, arms, armour, vehicles, stores, coinage and artefacts. A Prize Auction, or series of auctions, was then convened *in situ*, and – as with the Royal Navy – the cash proceeds would be distributed according to rank. On rare occasions, such as after the Battle of Waterloo in 1815, the Army's Prize Money was funded by an indemnity levied by the victor on the vanquished, as well as by the sale of captured items.

Although Prize Money for the Army generally amounted to substantially less than that which could be earned in the Royal Navy, nonetheless some campaigns generated sufficient funds to enrich senior officers. Following the Battle of Waterloo, the Prize Money pot amounted to £978,850 (2020: £85,614,691)*. This was divided into sixteen equal shares of £61,178 (2020: £5,350,907) of which the Duke of Wellington received one share. For the rest of the British Army at Waterloo the following Prize Money tariff applied:

Private soldiers	£2.11.4	(2020: £220)
Sergeants	£19.4.4	(2020: £1,600)
Subalterns	£34.14.9	(2020: £3,000)
Captains	£90.7.3	(2020: £7,900)
Field Officers	£433.2.4	(2020: £38,000)
General Officers	£1,274.10.10	(2020: £112,000)

More often, the sums earned were only sufficient to pay off a Mess bill or commission commemorative objects.

In one important respect, however, the Army's Prize Auctions differed from the Admiralty's Prize Courts, for they afforded the victorious combatants, providing they were discerning and had enough loose change, the opportunity to acquire objects of high intrinsic value for very little money. As the following pages show, this was particularly true after the fall of Seringapatam in 1799, the sacking of the Summer Palace in Peking in 1860, and the fall of Magdala in 1868. Some of the objects acquired by private individuals at these and other Prize Auctions have provided their heirs and successors in the twentieth and twenty-first centuries with enormous rewards.

---

* To find the approximate 2020 values, I have used the Bank of England's inflation calculator, see *www.bankofengland.co.uk/monetary-policy/inflation/inflation-calculator.*

4. Sources and locations

Hundred Years' War (1337–1453)
Joan of Arc's ring Sources: Timeline Auctions; www.bbc.co.uk/news/ world-europe-35728604 (accessed October 2019); Location: Grand Parc du Fou, Les Epesses, France.

English Civil War (1642–1651)
The right forearm of a Royalist Sources: Charles Dalton, The Scots Army 1661–1688, (Edinburgh, 1909); John Buchan, Montrose: A History, (Edinburgh, 1928); Location: Unknown.

War of The Austrian Succession (1740–1748)
Two pairs of French kettledrums Sources: Regimental histories; Location: The Queen's Royal Hussars (The Queen's Own & Royal Irish); The Museum of The Royal Dragoon Guards, York.

Seven Years' War (1756–1763)
The Nawab of Bengal's jade flask and other fabulous spoils of war Sources: Christie's, London; Location: The Al Thani Collection Foundation.

American War of Independence (1775–1783)
The Honourable Artillery Company [HAC]'s American trophy Sources: Archives of the HAC, London; Location: Armoury House, HAC, London. *Standard of the 2nd Regiment of Continental Light Dragoons & Colour of the 3rd Virginia Infantry Regiment* Sources: Sotheby's, New York; Museum of Colonial Williamsburg, Virginia. Location: Private collection in the United States of America. *Lieutenant General Earl Cornwallis's sword* Source: Antiques Road Show; Location: Private collection.

Anglo-French War (1778–1783)
The upper-deck guns of the French warship Protée Sources: avid Rutland and Emma Ellis, Resolution, (2017); Location: Belvoir Castle, Rutland. *The chapel bell of the French warship Ville de Paris* Sources: Records of Shropshire Regimental Museum, Shrewsbury; Location: Shropshire Regimental Museum, Shrewsbury.

French Revolutionary Wars (1792–1802)
A section of the main mast of the French flagship L'Orient Sources: Robert Southey, The Life of Horatio, Lord Nelson, (1822); Tom Pocock, Horatio Nelson (1987); Location: The Crypt, St Paul's Cathedral, London. *The Rosetta Stone* Sources: R.T. Wilson, History of the British Expedition to Egypt, (1803); Robert Solé, Dominique Valbelle and W.V. Davies, The Rosetta Stone, (2006); Archives de la Guerre, Paris; Location: British Museum, London. *Two French Republican Colours* Sources: Captain John Ford, *Flag Book*, Royal Hospital Chelsea, London; Location: No longer in existence. *The Turkish Gun* Sources: Sir Frederick Maurice, The History of the Scots Guards, (1934); Location: Horse Guards Parade, London.

Fourth Anglo-Mysore War (1798–1799)
A pair of cannons and a mortar Sources: National Trust; Location: Powis Castle, Wales; and currently in store, pending move to a new Royal Artillery Museum at Larkhill on Salisbury Plain. *Tipu's Ring* Sources: Christie's, London; Location: Private collection in India *Tipu's Bedroom Sword* Sources: DNW Auctions, London; Location: Private collection in India. *Tipu's Tiger* Sources: *www.vam.ac.uk/articles/ tipustiger* (accessed October 2019); Location: Victoria & Albert Museum, London. *Tipu's Throne* Sources: Bonham's, London; National Gallery of Scotland; The Times of India; Asiatic Annual Register (1800); Locations Royal Collection Trust, Windsor Castle, Berkshire; Powis. Castle, Wales; The Al Thani Collection Foundation *Tipu's Tent* Sources: *www.nationaltrust collections.org.uk object/1180731; www.national galleries.org.exhibition/ tiger-and-thistle-tipu-sultan-and-scots-india ; www.collections. britishart.yale.edu/vufind/Record/2054875* (all accessed October 2019); Location: Powis Castle, Wales.

War of the Third Coalition (1805)
A French musket ball Sources: Royal Collection Trust (RCIN 61158); IMDb; Tom Pocock, Horatio Nelson, (1987); Location: Royal Collection Trust, Windsor Castle, Berkshire. *Nelson's State Funeral Carriage* Source: Tom Pocock, *Horatio Nelson*, (1987) Location: National Maritime Museum, London.

West Indies Campaign (1804–1810)

Eagles of the French 82nd and 26th Regiments Sources: Records of Royal Welch Fusiliers Museum and Royal Fusiliers Museum; Captain John Ford, *Flag Book*, Royal Hospital Chelsea, London Locations: Royal Welch Fusiliers Museum, Caernarvon Castle, Wales; Fusiliers Museum, Tower of London; Royal Hospital Chelsea, London. *Eagle of the French 66th Regiment* Sources: Regimental histories of the 1st, 15th, 19th, 25th, 63rd and 90th Regiments of Foot; Captain John Ford, *Flag Book*, Royal Hospital Chelsea, London; Location: Royal Hospital Chelsea, London.

Peninsular War (1807–1814)

The lost Eagles of the French 24th and 96th Regiments Sources: www.worcestershireregiment.com (accessed October 2019); United Services Journal (1830); Location: Unknown. *The 'Cuckoo' Eagle of the French 8th Regiment* Sources: Regimental histories of the Royal Irish Fusiliers; Captain John Ford, *Flag Book*, Royal Hospital Chelsea, London; *Belfast Newsletter*; Location: Royal Irish Fusiliers Museum, Armagh, Northern Ireland. *The watery Eagle of the French 39th Regiment* Source: Captain John Ford, *Flag Book*, Royal Hospital Chelsea, London; Location: Royal Hospital Chelsea, London. *The Eagle of the French 62nd Regiment* Source: Regimental histories of the Essex Regiment; Location: Essex Regiment Museum, Chelmsford. *The Eagle & 'Jingling Johnny' of the French 101st Regiment* Sources: Regimental histories of the Connaught Rangers; Royal Military School of Music, Kneller Hall, Twickenham; Locations: National Army Museum, London; Museum of Army Music, Royal Military School of Music, Kneller Hall, Twickenham. *The Eagle of the French 22nd Regiment* Sources: Captain John Ford, *Flag Book*, Royal Hospital Chelsea, London; *The Soldier's Companion or Martial Recorder*, (1824); Location: Lancashire Infantry Museum, Fulwood Barracks, Preston. *Other Peninsular War Eagles* Sources: Edward Fraser, *The Soldiers whom Wellington Led: Deeds of Daring, Chivalry & Renown*, (1913); Luis Sorando Muzás (tr. Caroline Miley), *Trophies taken by the British from the Napoleonic Army during the War of Spanish Independence (Peninsula War) 1808–1814*; Location: Royal Hospital Chelsea, London. *The Prince Regent's Bomb*

Source: Household Division records; various regimental histories; Location: Horse Guards Parade, London. *The King of Spain's Pictures and Joseph Bonaparte's Sword* Sources: Julius Bryant, *Apsley House: The Wellington Collection*, (2015); Lord Egremont, *Wyndham and Children First*, (1969); Locations: Apsley House, London; unknown. *An Imperial Pisspot and a Water Tumbler* Sources: Regimental histories; Location: The King's Royal Hussars, Tidworth; The Royal Military Academy Sandhurst, Camberley. *Bonaparte's Silver Tumbler* Source: Sir Anthony Weldon Bt; Location: Private collection. *Marshal Jourdan's Baton* Source: Royal Collection Trust (RCIN 61176); Location: Windsor Castle, Berkshire.

Retreat from Moscow (1812)

Napoleon's looted Russian dispatch case Source: Archives of the Earls of Pembroke, Wilton House, Wiltshire Location: Wilton House, Salisbury, Wiltshire.

War of 1812 (1812–1815)

Regimental Colour and National Colour of the 4th Regiment of Infantry Source: Captain John Ford, *Flag Book*, Royal Hospital Chelsea; Locations: Firing Line: Museum of The Queen's Dragoons and The Royal Welsh, Cardiff Castle; The Royal Hospital Chelsea, London (replicas). *Colour of a New York Regiment* Sources: Captain John Ford, *Flag Book*, Royal Hospital Chelsea, London; regimental histories of the Royal Berkshire Regiment; Locations: National Army Museum, London; Royal Hospital Chelsea, London (replica). *Colour of the Kentucky Regiment* Sources: Regimental histories; Captain John Ford, *Flag Book*, Royal Hospital Chelsea; Location: National Army Museum, London. *Colour of 68th Regiment James City Light Infantry and Standard of 1st Hartford Dragoons* Sources: Captain John Ford, *Flag Book*, Royal Hospital Chelsea; Captain C.G.T. Dean, *The Royal Hospital Chelsea*, (1950); Location: Shropshire Regimental Museum, Shrewsbury, Shropshire. *The Disgraced Colours of the 2nd Regiment of Infantry* Sources: Captain John Ford, *Flag Book*, Royal Hospital Chelsea; Rev. G.R. Gleig, *Chelsea Hospital and its Traditions*, (1839); Locations: Unknown.

The Hundred Days (1815)

Hougoumont a lock plate, part of a balustrade, and several bricks Sources: Army Rumour Service; various regimental histories; Locations: Guards Museum, Wellington Barracks, London; Royal Green Jackets (Rifles) Museum, Winchester; Regimental Collections of the Grenadier and Coldstream Guards. *The Eagle of the French 45th Regiment* Sources: Regimental history of the Royal Scots Greys; *www.waterlooassociation.org.uk* (accessed October 2019); Location: Royal Scots Dragoon Guards Museum, Edinburgh Castle. *The Eagle of the French 105th Regiment* Sources: *www.waterlooassociation.org.uk*; various regimental histories; Location: National Army Museum, London *Marengo* Source: Jill Hamilton, *Marengo: The Myth of Napoleon's Horse*, (2003); Locations: Household Cavalry Museum, Horse Guards, London; Officers Mess of The Queen's Guard, St James's Palace, London; National Army Museum, London. *Napoleon's carriage, burnous, travel desk-set, pocket book and cloak clasp* Sources: Royal Collection Trust (RCIN 61156); records of Newcastle Discovery Museum; *www.exhibitions.lib.cam.ac.uk/waterloo*; Levens Hall archives; Locations: Windsor Castle, Berkshire; Newcastle Discovery Museum, Newcastle-upon-Tyne; Levens Hall, Cumbria. *Marshal Ney's snuff box* Source: Regimental histories; Location: The Green Howards Museum, Richmond, Yorkshire. *The Wellington Monument and Canova's* Napoleon Source: Julius Bryant, *Apsley House: The Wellington Collection*, (2015); Locations: Park Lane, London; Apsley House, London. *18th Hussars' silver trumpet* Source: Regimental histories; Location: Newcastle Discovery Museum, Newcastle-upon-Tyne. *Tenth Hussars' silver trumpet* Source: Regimental histories; Location: The King's Royal Hussars, Tidworth, Wiltshire. *Chisholm's silver spoons* Source: Regimental histories; Location: National War Museum, Edinburgh. *Wellington's State Funeral Carriage* Source: Wellington archives; Location: Stratfield Saye House, Hampshire.

First Anglo-Ashanti War (1823–1831)

An elephant-horn trumpet Source: National Army Museum records Location: National Army Museum, London.

Sindh Campaign (1843)

The Amir of Sindh's alabaster chair Source: Regimental histories & museum records Location: Cheshire Military Museum, Chester.

Crimean War (1853–1856)

The Arundel Collection of Crimean War items Source: The Norfolk Family archives, Arundel Castle, West Sussex; Location: Arundel Castle, West Sussex. *The Sevastopol Chairs* Source: Regimental histories Locations: Cheshire Military Museum, Chester; National Army Museum, London. *Bath's missing canons* Source: Bath & North East Somerset Archives Location: Unknown *Newcastle-under-Lyme's canon* Source: Museum guide Location: Brampton Museum & Art Gallery, Newcastle-under-Lyme.

Indian Mutiny (1857–1858)

Hindu Rao's table Sources: Regimental histories & anecdotes Locations: Officers Mess, Royal Gurkha Rifles, Camberley; The Rifles, Peninsula Barracks, Winchester; The Guides Infantry, Pakistan. *A pearl earring* Source: Regimental histories Location: The Royal Green Jackets (Rifles) Museum, Winchester. *The Delhi Purple Sapphire* Source: *www.nhm.ac.uk/natureplus/blogs/behind-the-scenes/tags/delhi_purple_saphire* [sic] (accessed October 2019); Edward Heron-Allen, *The purple sapphire: and other posthumous papers; selected from the unofficial records of the University of Cosmopoli, by Christopher Blayre*, (1921); Location: Natural History Museum, London. *The skull of Havildar Alum Bheg* Source: *www.bbc.com/news/world-asia-india-43616597* (accessed October 2019); Kim Wagner, *The Skull of Alum Bheg*, (2018) Location: Unknown.

Second Opium War (1856–1860)

A gold-plated snuff box and other knick-knacks Source: Woolley & Wallis Auctioneers, Salisbury, Wiltshire; Location: Private collection. *The Empress Dowager's Pekingese dog Looty* Sources: Royal Collection Trust (RCIN 406974); General Sir John Hart Dunne, *From Calcutta to Pekin*, (reprinted, 2009) Location: Deceased.

Abyssinia Expedition (1867–1868)

Emperor Tewodros's Drum of Gold Source: *The Lion & the Rose* (regimental magazine of The King's Own Royal Regiment); Locations: Regimental collections of the Royal Scots Dragoon Guards, Duke of Lancaster's Regiment and Yorkshire Regiment. *The Glory of Kings and an Emperor's Crown* Sources: *www.vam.ac.uk/event/14gkkD4W/magdala-1868-updated*; *www.vam.ac.uk/blog.museum-life/magdala-1868* (both accessed October 2019); Locations: British Museum, London; Victoria & Albert Museum, London; Raguel Church, Addis Ababa, Ethiopia. *Emperor Tewodros's hair* Source: *www.bbc.co.uk/news/world-africa-47441042* (accessed October 2019); Location: National Army Museum, London; repatriated to Ethiopia, 2019.

Third Anglo-Ashanti War (1873–1874)

Items from King Kofi Karikari's palace Sources: Regimental histories; Wallace Collection website; Locations: Royal Green Jackets (Rifles) Museum, Winchester; Wallace Collection, London.

Anglo-Zulu War (1879)

Lieutenant Gonville Bromhead's Zulu weapons Source: Bromhead family; Location: Private collection. *Surgeon Reynolds's 'operating table' and the Rorke's Drift chair* Sources: Various regimental histories; Locations: Officers Mess, 160th (Welsh) Brigade, The Barracks, Brecon; South Wales Borderers Museum, Brecon. *The Victoria Cross* Source: Catriona Davies, 'Author [John Granville] explains myth of the gunmetal VC', *Daily Telegraph*, 28 December 2005.

Urabi Revolt (1879–1882)

The Kafr el Dawwar drum Source: Regimental histories; Location: The Rifles Berkshire and Wiltshire Museum, The Wardrobe, Salisbury. *The Duke of Connaught's coffee pot, Colonel Urabi's Koran, and Lord Wolseley's pistols* Sources: Various including regimental histories; Locations: Unknown. *The Duke of Connaught's Egyptian flag* Source: Royal Collection Trust; Location: Unknown; last recorded at Windsor Castle, Berkshire, c.1882–1900. *Grape shot* Source: Regimental history; Location: Shropshire Regimental Museum, Shrewsbury.

Mahdist War (1881–1899)

The Mahdi's head Source: Alan Moorehead, *The White Nile*, (1960) Location: Moslem cemetery at Wadi Halfa. *Panels from the Mahdi's tomb* Sources: Family recollections; records of The Highlanders' Museum, Fort George, Inverness-Shire; Locations: Private collection; The Highlanders' Museum, Fort George.

Third Anglo-Burmese War (1885)

Four carved and gilded wooden bees Sources: Family recollections; museum guide books; Locations: Private collection; Victoria & Albert Museum, London; Pitt Rivers Museum, Oxford. *A Buddhist shrine* Source: *www.collections.vam.ac.uk/item/057777/shrine-unknown* (accessed October 2019); Location: Victoria & Albert Museum, London *A Betel Box* Source: *www.collections.vam.ac.uk/item/010747/betel-box-and-unknown* (accessed October 2019); Location: Victoria & Albert Museum, London. *King Thibaw Min's head* Source: Regimental history; Location: The Royal Hampshire Regiment Museum, Winchester *The Nga Mauk ruby* Source: *www.bbc.co.uk/news/resources/idt-sh/who_stole-burmas_royal_ruby* (accessed October 2019) Location: Unknown.

Boxer Rebellion & Siege of Peking (1899–1901)

A cloisonné opium dish and a cloisonné incense burner, Lady MacDonald's tea pot, home decorations and the medics' clock Sources: Records of the Royal Welch Fusiliers Museum; family recollections; Robert Graves, *Good-Bye to All That*, (1929); Dr Paul Bevan, (2015); Richard Higgins; Locations: Royal Welch Fusiliers Museum, Caernarvon Castle; private collections; Royal Army Medical Corps; Anglesey Abbey, Cambridgeshire.

Second Boer War (1899–1902)

The Fighting General's table, General Cronje's revolver, a Boer flag and drum, President Kruger's pipe and a pennant of the Danish volunteers Sources: Various regimental histories; Locations: The Green Howards Museum, North Yorkshire; Royal Military Academy Sandhurst; Cheshire Military Museum, Chester; Shropshire Regimental Museum, Shrewsbury.

First World War (1914–1918)

Robert Graves's ball of chalk Source: Robert Graves, *Goodbye to All That*, (1929); Location: Royal Welch Fusiliers Museum, Caernarvon Castle Lawrence of Arabia and the Hejaz Railway station bell Sources: Bodleian Library, Oxford; The T. E. Lawrence Society; *www.nabataea.net* (accessed October 2019); T.E. Lawrence, *Seven Pillars of Wisdom*, (1926); Robert Graves, Goodbye to All That, (1929) Location: Unknown. *German trench wallpaper* Source: *www.iwm. org.uk/collections/item/object/30088026* (accessed 2019); Location: Imperial War Museum, London. *The Blue Boy* Source: RAF Club Secretary Location: Royal Air Force Club, Piccadilly, London. *Imperial German plaque from the Temple of Apollo at Baalbek and the Kaiser's bronze wreath* Sources: *www.iwm.org.uk/collections/item/object/18128* (accessed October 2019); *www.iwm.org.uk/collections/item/object/30083872* (accessed October 2019); The T.E. Lawrence Society Locations: Unknown; Imperial War Museum, London. *A Luger pistol butt* Source: The Keep Military Museum, Dorchester; Location: Officers Mess, 160th (Welsh) Brigade, The Barracks, Brecon.'

Second World War (1939–1945)

The Dry Roger Sources: The late Major Willie Lloyd LG and the author; Colonel Hon Humphrey Wyndham MC, *The Household Cavalry at War: First Household Cavalry Regiment*, (1952); Location: Officers House, Household Cavalry Regiment, Bulford Camp, Wiltshire. *Hitler's Table from Bad Godesberg* Source: Colonel Hugh Boddington, former Chief of Staff, HQ London District; Location: Headquarters London District, Horse Guards, London. *The Rafwaffe* Source: Sally Bennett, 'Brief History of the Rafwaffe (Flight 1426)', on *www.bbc.co.uk/history/ww2peopleswar* (accessed October 2019) Location: Royal Air Force Museum, London. Fritz *the Wehrmacht pet* Source: *www.royalhampshireregiment.org.uk* (accessed October 2019); Location: (photograph) Royal Hampshire Regiment Museum, Winchester. *Tirpitz the pig* Source: *www.iwm.org.uk/collections/item/object/30088283* (accessed October 2019); Location: Imperial War Museum, London. *The* Tirpitz *bulkhead* Source: IX (B) Squadron Association; Location: Royal Air Force Museum, London. *Himmler's compass* Source: Captain Martin Proudlock

MC Location: Currently in storage; hopefully to be displayed at new Salisbury Plain Heritage Centre in 2020. *Hitler's desk and cutlery* Sources: *Daily Mail*, 1 June 2014; Paul Fraser Collectibles; Richard Dimbleby, *Desert Island Discs*, (radio recording, 1958); Locations: The Keep Military Museum, Dorchester; unknown. *The spoils of Berchtesgaden* Source: Auction catalogue; Locations: Unknown. *Grand Admiral Donitz's Baton* Sources: Records of the Shropshire Regimental Museum; *www.wcstumpmilitaria.blogspot.co.uk* (accessed October 2019); Location: Shropshire Regimental Museum, Shrewsbury. *A Japanese regimental flag, an officer's sword, and an Imperial sword hilt* Sources: Family memories; Malcolm Page, *A history of the King's African Rifles and East African Forces*, (1998) Location: Private collection.

Malayan Emergency (1948–1960)

A Communist's cap Source: Family memories; archives of The Household Cavalry Museum, Combermere Barracks, Windsor; Location: Unknown.

Indonesia-Malaysia Confrontation (1963–1966)

The skull of a Chinaman Source: General Sir Jeremy Mackenzie GCB OBE DL; Location: The Highlanders' Museum, Fort George, Inverness.

The Troubles, Ulster (1968–1998)

A bottle of IRA poteen Source: The author; Location: Drunk!

Falklands War (1982)

An Argentinian Army Artillery Laser Rangefinder Source: The author; Lord Levene of Portsoken KBE; Location: Unknown.

ACKNOWLEDGEMENTS

There are a number of people without whom this book would never have been conceived, let alone written. Foremost amongst these are former Life Guard turned currency trader, Damien Lipman, and Philip Mould, the art dealer and star of the *Antiques Roadshow* and *Fake or Fortune*.

It was Damien Lipman, an accomplished part-time commentator with whom I have worked on a number of major military events, who proposed to a researcher for Radio 4's *Today Programme* that I would be able to contribute to a feature the programme proposed broadcasting, about the spoils of war in the Wellington Collection. In researching material for the radio show, on which I made only a fleeting appearance, I had a *eureka* moment: there were more than enough spoils of war in military museums, royal and private collections to fill several books on the subject – and no one had yet attempted the task.

Philip Mould's contribution came a month or two later. In the course of my Radio 4 research, I had stumbled over an item held in a military museum in Wales, which at first sight appeared to be a very valuable piece of Chinese Imperial cloisonné, lying unrecognised in a display case. I discussed my discovery with Philip, with a view to him including it in one of his television programmes. In the event, an expert appraisal revealed that the item was of relatively low value, but Philip nonetheless continued selflessly to encourage me by giving me a great many useful introductions in the worlds of publishing and broadcasting.

I am eternally grateful to both of them.

I would also like to thank Lyn Davies of Lyn Davies Design for designing the book and for help with the cover imagery, and Paul Cattermole for the photograph of Tipu's Tiger Mortar; my researcher, George Gray, who did much of the leg work; Tim Knox, Director of the Royal Collection Trust; General Sir Redmond Watt KCB KCVO, David Hellens and In-Pensioner Chris Melia of the Royal Hospital Chelsea for access to the Royal Hospital's archives; Field Marshal Lord Guthrie of Craigiebank GCB GCVO OBE, Alice Pearson and Pete Storer for access to the Household Cavalry's collection; Major General Nick Eeles CBE & the Trustees of the Royal Artillery Historical Trust; Lieutenant General Jonathan Riley CB DSO PhD MA & the Trustees of the Royal Welsh Fusiliers Museum; Chris Hall TD, Major General Peter Currie CB CBE, Major General Sir Evelyn Webb-Carter KCVO OBE, Captain Christopher Tarleton Fagan and Peter Ferris USMC for their assistance with my research; private owners including the Duke of Norfolk, the Duke of Wellington OBE, the Earl of Pembroke, Sir Anthony Weldon Bt (who is also my publisher), General Sir Jeremy Mackenzie GCB OBE, Caroline Watson, Dave and Celeste Shave-Smythies, Piers and Patrick German, the late Captain Martin Proudlock MC and Richard Bagot; Colonel Simon Doughty and Brigadier Robin Bacon for their unfailing support; Samantha Wyndham, who every day read and then ruthlessly edited the text as it rolled off my computer, checked and often corrected facts and provided me with valuable criticism, none of which I have dared to ignore; and Philip Evans, who gamely put up with my endless witterings about the delights, surprises and shocks I had encountered in the course of my research.

Finally, I would like to thank Her Majesty The Queen for her Gracious Permission to allow me to include items from the Royal Collection, all the many museum directors and collectors who assisted me with background data and access to their collections – and Mr Andrew Lloyd, Director of the Army Museums Ogilby Trust, whose opposition to this book, without having read a word of it, and his instruction to his beneficiary museums to boycott it (thankfully, an instruction that was largely ignored) made me absolutely determined to see it in print.

CAJ

INDEX